The Religious Body Imagined

The Religious Body Imagined

Edited by

Pamela D. Winfield,
Mina García
and Katherine C. Zubko

SHEFFIELD UK   BRISTOL CT

Published by Equinox Publishing Ltd.

UK Office 415, The Workstation, 15 Paternoster Row, Sheffield, South Yorkshire S1 2BX
USA ISD, 70 Enterprise Drive, Bristol, CT 06010

www.equinoxpub.com

All chapters first published in the journal *Body and Religion* volume 3, no. 2 and volume 5, no. 1.
© Equinox Publishing Ltd 2020–2022.
First published in book form 2024.

© Pamela D. Winfield, Mina García, Katherine C. Zubko and contributors 2024

All rights reserved. No part of this publication may be reproduced or transmitted in any form or by any means, electronic or mechanical, including photocopying, recording or any information storage or retrieval system, without prior permission in writing from the publishers.

British Library Cataloguing-in-Publication Data

A catalogue record for this book is available from the British Library.

ISBN-13 978 1 80050 971 0 (hardback)
         978 1 80050 972 7 (paperback)
         978 1 80050 973 4 (ePDF)
         978 1 80050 458 5 (ePub)

Library of Congress Cataloging-in-Publication Data

Names: Winfield, Pamela D, editor. | Garcia, Mina, editor. | Zubko, Katherine C, editor.
Title: The religious body imagined / edited by Pamela D Winfield, Mina Garcia, and Katherine C Zubko.
Description: Sheffield, South Yorkshire ; Bristol, CT : Equinox Publishing Ltd, 2024. | Includes bibliographical references and index. | Summary: "This edited volume examines the ways in which the human body has been imagined, imaged, and discursively produced in particular places, times, and religious traditions. It brings together representative papers from most of the world's major traditions and geo-historical locations, and explores the religious body's various functions, roles, and transformative effects through a range of disciplinary and theoretical lenses. It is organized according to novel, thought-provoking thematic foci that advance the field and that can be generative for classroom use"-- Provided by publisher.
Identifiers: LCCN 2023029821 (print) | LCCN 2023029822 (ebook) | ISBN 9781781799710 (hardback) | ISBN 9781781799727 (paperback) | ISBN 9781781799734 (pdf) | ISBN 9781800504585 (epub)
Subjects: LCSH: Human body in the Bible. | Human body (Islamic law) | Human body.
Classification: LCC BS680.B6 R45 2024 (print) | LCC BS680.B6 (ebook) | DDC 233/.5--dc23/eng/20231006
LC record available at https://lccn.loc.gov/2023029821
LC ebook record available at https://lccn.loc.gov/2023029822

Typeset by Sparks – www.sparkspublishing.com

Dedicated to Brian Pennington and his unconditional support through
the Center for the Study of Religion, Culture and Society at Elon University

Contents

Acknowledgments	ix
List of figures	x
Introduction *Pamela D. Winfield and Mina García*	1

Part I Gendered bodies

1	People of the book, women of the body: Ultra-orthodox Jewish women's reproductive literacy *Michal Raucher*	13
2	The male body and Catholic piety in early modern Spain *Elizabeth Rhodes*	35

Part II LGBTQ+ bodies

3	Harvey Milk's (sexual and sacred) body *William K. Gilders*	59
4	Non-binary sexual and gender identities in the community: The *khunthā* as an isolated being in the mosque *Saqer A. Almarri*	80

Part III Migrating bodies

5	Lope's *El Hamete de Toledo*: The infidel's body as conquered land *Mina García*	105
6	The embodied palimpsest: Dancing kinesthetic empathy in bharatanatyam *Katherine C. Zubko*	123

Part IV Microcosmic bodies

7	Religion and the imperial body politic of Japan *Pamela D. Winfield*	153

8   Surveilled, harmonized, purified: The body in Chinese religious
    culture   178
    Ori Tavor

Part V Sensational bodies

9   Seeing, imagined, and lived: Creating *darshan* in transnational
    Gaudiya Vaishnavism   201
    Anandi Silva Knuppel

10 'The body is a tool for remembrance': Healing, transformation, and
    the instrumentality of the body in a North American Sufi order   223
    Megan Adamson Sijapati

Index   245

Acknowledgments

The editors would like to thank the many institutions and individuals who helped to make *The Religious Body Imagined* a reality. Specifically, we wish to thank the Center for the Study of Religion, Culture and Society (CSRCS) at Elon University in North Carolina, which hosted the original 2019 symposium that served as the seed for the present volume and provided funding for indexing. We extend our gratitude to the original conference participants: Shuxi Yin, Clyde Ellis, Brent Plate, Saqer Almarri, William Gilders, Sarah Dove, Anandi Silva Knuppel, Megan Adamson Sijapati, Anca Sincan and Elizabeth Rhodes, as well as the additional contributors who could not attend, Michal Raucher and Ori Tavor.

This project would not have been possible without the foresight of Janet Joyce, Founder and Managing Director of Equinox Publishing, Cameron Barlow, Managing Assistant of *Body and Religion*, Tom Fryer at Sparks Publishing Services Ltd, and the patience of many authors and peer reviewers as we brought this manuscript project, started just before the pandemic, to final fruition.

We especially wish to thank all the supportive friends and families who have helped make this volume a reality. We couldn't have done it without them.

List of figures

Figure 3.1: Deacon Diana Wheeler holding an icon of Harvey Milk, November 27, 2019, San Francisco. Photograph by the author.　64

Figure 5.1: Photo courtesy of AlmaViva Teatro.　114

Figure 6.1: *Agathi* boat scene: dancers creating the structure of the boat. (Photo credit and permission: R. Prasana Photography. Courtesy of Apsaras Arts Dance Company.)　133

Figure 6.2: *Agathi* boat scene: performing *bhavas* expressing grief, fear, and shock after the child's body has been tossed overboard. (Photo credit and permission: R. Prasana Photography. Courtesy of Apsaras Arts Dance Company.)　138

Figure 7.1: Amaterasu emerging from her cave. Woodblock print, Utagawa Toyokuni III, 1857 (Creative Commons).　158

Figure 7.2: Shintō mirror; the material 'spirit body' of the *kami* (*goshintai*) and one of the three imperial regalia of Japan. Photograph by the author.　159

Figure 7.3: Birushana/Lochana Buddha, the monumental embodiment of the *dharmakāya*. Cast bronze with traces of gold, Tōdaiji temple, Nara, Japan. Eighteenth-century restoration of 752 statue by Emperor Shōmu (Creative Commons).　163

Figure 7.4: Four wrathful Wisdom Kings surrounding Fudō myōō (not pictured). Tōji temple, Kyoto, Japan. Commissioned by Kūkai in 826 (Creative Commons).　167

Figure 9.1: Meditating upon the Deity (Śrī Śrī Rādhā Gopīnātha Mandir 2000:4–5).　209

Introduction
Pamela D. Winfield and Mina García

Since antiquity, the relationship between the body and the soul has been full of friction. From Socrates and Plato onwards, the body has traditionally been portrayed as the prison of the soul, and has carried the burden of being perishable, imperfect, and inconsequential; in other words, a burden for the perfectionist desires of the soul, always in search of the transcendental union with the divine. However, the essays in this collection offer a new horizon in this intricate relationship, and propose new forms of collaboration and interdependence between the two, opening before our eyes a wide range of possibilities for the embodiment of the sacred.

This edited volume examines the ways in which the human body has been imagined, imaged, and discursively produced in particular places, times, and religious traditions. It brings together representative articles from most of the world's major traditions and geo-historical locations. It offers in-depth analyses of Hindu, Daoist, Buddhist, Jewish, Catholic, Muslim, and secular-but-sanctified queer bodies in places as diverse as ancient China, premodern Japan, medieval Egypt, early modern Spain, and contemporary America, Israel, and Sri Lanka. It explores the religious body's various functions, roles, and transformative effects through a range of disciplinary and theoretical lenses, namely visual culture, literary, performance and cultural studies, ethnography, space/place, ritual, postcolonial theory and social justice as it pertains to embodiment.

Most significantly, this volume presents thought-provoking thematic foci that contribute to and advance the field in new ways. We propose five sections, each including two chapters, that explore a particular type of body such as Gendered Bodies, LGBTQ+ Bodies, Migrating Bodies, Microcosmic Bodies, and Sensational Bodies. These two chapters can be considered individually, comparatively within their section, or across categories to spark fruitful conversations about institutional power, religious violence, ritual, art, healing, or embodied agency. As a result, this volume contributes new and original research as well as theoretical insights that can be generative for classroom use and that can substantially help to expand our understanding of the interdisciplinary field of sacred corporeality.

Background

The general idea for this volume on religious conceptions of the body first began as an international symposium on *The Religious Body Imagined* at Elon University in February 2019. It was co-convened by Pamela D. Winfield, Mina García, and Brian Pennington under the auspices of Elon's Center for the Study of Religion, Culture and Society (CSRCS). However, this resulting publication is not a simple conference volume, but rather a culled, curated, and reconfigured study that stands on its own as a thematically organized approach to the religious body in action. Given the disruptions of the global pandemic and the Russian invasion of Ukraine, the present configuration of chapters, topics, and contributors departs significantly from the contours of the 2019 symposium. Throughout the many challenges of the past several years, the steady editorial hand of Katherine Zubko has stewarded the peer review and publication process for each contributor's article in the journal *Body and Religion*, but the present interdisciplinary volume of global scope invites conversations and thought-provoking thematic foci that go beyond the boundaries of each individual chapter.

The case studies compiled in this volume help us to better discern how our own embodied experiences shape our conceptions of the sacred, however fluidly they may be defined. Conversely, it also examines how our bodies express, re-instantiate, and re-embody the invisible contours of our socially-constructed sacred idea(l)s in concrete physical forms. As St. Paul wrote in his letter to the Corinthians (1:12), 'Just as a body, though one, has many parts, but all its many parts form one body,' so it is with this edited volume, which literally in-corporates diverse perspectives into one publication that functions as a body of literature on sacred corporeality. It is a multifaceted meditation on the religious body, as it was imagined across time and space.

Rationale and existing literature

The Religious Body Imagined makes a significant contribution to previous literature in the field of religion and body studies. Specifically, it contributes to and advances the field ever since the humanities and sciences took the 'embodied turn.' Scholars generally agree that this trend began with linguistics in the late 1980s (Nevile 2015), but it did not come into its own in the field of Religious Studies until the mid-1990s. Jane Marie Law's *Religious Reflections on the Human Body* (Law 1995) was the self-proclaimed 'first cross-cultural and interdisciplinary survey on the relationship between religious practice and ideology and the human body.'

Sarah Coakley's *Religion and the Body* (Coakley 1997) then became the standard anthology for any Religion and the Body course for many years, but Coakley's explicitly bifurcated West vs. East structure and its old-fashioned World Religions model quickly became outdated. Ken Brintnall's *Embodied Religion* (Brintnall 2016) and Yudit Greenberg's *The Body and Religion: Cross-Cultural Perspectives* (Greenberg 2017) offered updated approaches to understanding bodies in relation to religious praxis. Brintnall's 22 chapters specifically emphasized gender, sexuality, and religious discipline, and Greenberg introduced students to various religious views on such topics as food, marriage, tattooing, and death. These led to the publication of several collected anthologies and special journal issues dedicated specifically to religion and food, or religion and health and wellness. Many were focused on a single religious tradition in the contemporary period, such as Christian connections to yoga and cross-fit, but not all.

The present thematically organized volume contributes to this conversation by proposing advanced scholarship that applies appropriately selected theoretical or methodological approaches to heretofore unexamined pre-modern and modern/contemporary content. In presenting a series of paired chapters on gendered bodies, LGBTQ+ bodies, migrating bodies, microcosmic bodies, and sensational bodies, this volume offers fascinating glimpses into how the religious body has been imagined and cultivated, as well as problematized and negotiated, through visual, literary, and lived realities around the world and throughout the ages.

Chapter summaries

Gendered bodies

This section on gendered bodies examines contemporary ultra-orthodox Jewish women whose bodies are literally pregnant with a kind of authority that they otherwise lack when not expecting. It also convincingly argues that the category of 'embodied religiosity,' which scholars typically only apply to female mystics in late medieval Catholic Spain, also extends to religious men of the period whose accounts of religious asceticism and ecstatic experience were erased from Church teachings. These two chapters using ethnographic and socio-literary theory raise important questions about embodied authority, authenticity, and the possibilities and pitfalls of institutional religion.

Michal Raucher's 'People of the book, women of the body: Ultra-orthodox jewish women's reproductive literacy' relies on two years of ethnographic research among Haredi mothers in Jerusalem. Her research reveals that the women's lived experience of repeated pregnancies cultivates a kind of embodied knowledge and self-reliant, self-validating authority that no longer consults the normative rabbinic and male-dominated authority systems that regulate all other sectors of Haredi life. In so doing, Raucher expands our understanding of embodied female agency in a tradition that has long been assumed to subjugate women.

In contrast to Raucher's explicit focus on the female-identified body, Elizabeth Rhodes investigates a handful of understudied texts related to 'The male body and Catholic piety in early modern Spain.' She observes that monks in monasteries also imagined themselves as conjugal brides of Christ and engaged in many of the same devotional practices as the better studied nuns in Spanish and colonial Hispanic convents. Because these men practiced 'ardent devotion to the Eucharist, strict food management and manipulation, as well as extreme asceticism justified by pious intentions,' just like the nuns did, Rhodes calls into question the presumed gendered nature of early modern Catholic piety.

LGBTQ+ bodies

The section on LGBTQ+ bodies considers the sacred and sexual body of the martyred 'queer saint' Harvey Milk, as well as Sharia law's legal prescriptions for locating the transgender (*kuntha*) adherent in the gendered space of the mosque. These two chapters queer our conceptions of institutional religion, and demonstrate that alternative conceptual and physical spaces can be created to negotiate non-heteronormative religiosity.

William Gilders' article on 'Harvey Milk's (sacred and sexual) body' focuses its gaze on a specific body: that of Harvey Milk, the first gay activist to be elected as a member of the San Francisco Board of Supervisors. Gilders addresses the overlapping of two apparently contradictory motifs, which have transformed the figure of Milk into an icon: explicit sexuality and the martyrological tradition, which come together in the representations of a 'queer saint,' in both senses of the word; that is, a political activist in the defense of LGBTQ+ rights, but also a non-conventional sacrificial lamb, assassinated for a greater cause. Gilders analyzes these parallels in the exhibits that remember the sexualized figure of Milk, and that are strongly influenced by the religious iconography around saints and relics.

Saqer A. Almarri takes up the theme of sexual identity in their illuminating study of 'Non-binary sexual and gender identities in the community: The *khunthā* as an isolated being in the mosque.' In this analysis, Almarri provides a historically, historiographically, and theoretically rich analysis of a fourteenth century legal manual by the Shāfi'ī jurist al-Isnawī (d. 772 AH/1370 CE), who details the exact legal and therefore logistical standing of an intersex person within the segregated prayer space of the Mamlūk mosque. The manual acknowledges and attempts to accommodate the *khunthā* within the mosque's strictly binary social space, but Almarri argues that dedicating a prayer row between the cisgendered men and women, and ordering each *khunthā* to exit the mosque one-by-one after the women and before the men, actually 'outs' them before the congregation and socially isolates them instead of integrating them into the community of worshippers.

Migrating bodies

The section on migrating bodies analyzes the recent critical staging of a once-popular seventeenth-century Spanish Catholic play that converts the soul body of a *converso* Moor through ritual dismemberment of his body. It also excavates the layers of meaning and moods (*rasas*) in contemporary Indian dance choreography about fleeing Sri Lankan refugees at sea. This pair of chapters using textual analysis and dance theory prompts one to consider the precarity of displaced Others, especially when threatened by hostile human and natural forces.

Mina García looks at the religious body in counter-reformation Spain in 'Lope's *El Hamete de Toledo*: The infidel's body as conquered land.' In this baroque tragedy with religio-political overtones, the celebrated playwright Lope de Vega (1562–1635) dramatizes the then-current anti-Muslim sentiments of King Philip II conveyed in the Morisco Expulsion Decree of 1609. Lope's drama specifically stages the *auto-da-fé* of a sympathetic yet enslaved Muslim nobleman who ultimately converts to Christianity upon physical torture and pain of death. A recent adaptation that re-stages Lope's play by AlmaViva Teatro (Living Soul Theater) highlights the inhuman injustice of Othering, especially in the Islamophobic context of contemporary Euro-American immigration policies and President Trump's Muslim ban.

Katherine C. Zubko likewise looks at the on-stage representation and performance of religious bodies in 'The embodied palimpsest: Dancing kinesthetic empathy in bharatanatyam.' Zubko turns her attention to the refugee crisis following the Sri Lankan civil war (1983–2009) as it was portrayed in Apsaras Arts' production of *Agathi: The Plight of the Refugee* (debuted in

Singapore, 2017). She demonstrates how its choreographic sequences - which are traditionally used to represent Hindu myths and *rasas* (aesthetic moods) such as compassion - can be reframed to explore issues related to social justice. Zubko's analysis exposes the porosity of the performative body, which extends beyond the dancers' bodies to emotionally touch the audience members with the immigrants' experience. Zubko's study thus lays bare the multitude of layers that constitute this novel dance production and creates a scholarly palimpsest that makes the invisible visible and contributes to aesthetic studies on kinesthetic empathy.

Microcosmic bodies

The section on microcosmic bodies outlines the concentric layers of corporeal, socio-political, and metaphysical bodies in premodern East Asia. It examines medieval Chinese Buddhist and Daoist templates for aligning one's interior world with exterior reality, so that one's own body harmonizes with the Way of the larger world body. Likewise in Japan, Buddhism promoted an elaborate visual and ritual culture that equated the emperor's physical body with the larger 'country-body' (*kokutai*) in the premodern period, thereby legitimating the emperor's person as the site of state authority and power.

Ori Tavor's article, 'Surveilled, harmonized, purified: The body in Chinese religious culture,' takes us to ancient China, where he explores the pervasiveness of the body as a central concept in medieval Chinese religious culture. Taking apocryphal medieval Buddhist scripture, *The Sūtra of Trapuṣa and Bhallika*, as his point of departure, he traces references to the body beyond its physicality, entering the symbolic realm that perceives the body as a microcosm of the social, political, and metaphysical worlds. Tavor argues that the importance of synchronizing this symbolic body with the natural cycles of the universe became central in the emerging doctrines of Buddhism and Daoism, two of China's main organized religions. This notion of the microcosmic body and its social and political correlations remains central in Chinese religious culture today.

Pamela D. Winfield invites us to join her on a journey throughout the history of Japan, in order to elucidate the treatment given to the emperor's body, not only physically, but also visually and ritually. In her article, 'Religion and the imperial body politic of Japan,' Winfield argues that, although this notion of body politic only emerged technically during the early modern period, it was already present in premodern Buddhist teachings and was reinforced by cultural enactments that identified the body of the emperor with his empire and sought out the health of the former to ensure the wellbeing of the latter.

Winfield provides a rich historical, historiographical, and theoretical analysis of the emperor's rhetorical, artistic, and ceremonial body-state, emphasizing the centrality of his human, physical body while framing his religious and political authority over Japan.

Sensational bodies

The section on sensational bodies expands the definition of *darshan* beyond just 'seeing and being seen by deities' to all the other senses that engage with deities such as Krishna. It also investigates the felt environment of a contemporary American Sufi enclave in Pennsylvania. This pair of chapters, which both engage ethnographic as well as textual materials, stress the importance that all five senses bring to the holistic process of self-cultivation and religious experience.

Anandi Silva Knuppel looks at the lived experiences of practitioners in the ritual setting of contemporary Hindu devotional expression. In her chapter on 'Seeing, imagined and lived: Creating *darshan* in transnational Gaudiya Vaishnavism' she first presents the traditional rules and protocols for taking *darshan* (to see and be seen by the deity), but then also presents contemporary firsthand accounts that expand and redefine *darshan* beyond the merely visual dimension. These include multisensory embodied performances of dancing, singing, eating, listening, chanting and dressing the image of Krishna. Relying on eight years of ethnographic work among the International Society of Krishna Consciousness (ISKON) community in the southeastern United States, Knuppel's essay reveals that these multisensory 'darshanic moments' help 'to purify the devotee from their 'material conditions' so that they *can* proceed to further their devotion and love.'

Finally, Megan Adamson Sijapati explores the instrumentality of the body through a focus on religious praxis. 'The body is a tool for remembrance: Healing, transformation, and the instrumentality of the body in a North American Sufi order' focuses on a Shadhiliyya Sufi Muslim community based in the foothills of the Appalachian Mountains in western Pennsylvania. The practices and beliefs of this *tariqah* (Sufi order) are derived from the guidance of its recently deceased Shaykh, Muhammad al-Jamal (d. 2015), from Jerusalem, who began teaching in the United States in the 1990s. Drawing upon two years of fieldwork, Sijapati discusses the centrality of the body to these Sufis' religious experiences and to their understandings of themselves and their relationship with the divine. The chapter elaborates on the ways in which the body is instrumentalized in the production of religious experience and self in the community's healing practices and posits the body as a site where religion *happens*.

Conclusion

Taken as a whole, these chapters offer disciplinary perspectives on some of the most vibrant cultures and historical periods of our world. The book introduces the gendered authority of present-day Israeli ultra-orthodox Jewish pregnant women as well as ultra-pious early modern Catholic Spanish male monastics. It examines the trans body in the medieval Egyptian mosque and the sanctified body of the American gay icon Harvey Milk. It highlightes the trauma of migrating bodies as depicted in contemporary Sri Lankan dance, and critically analyzes the representation of a Moor's torture in a counter-reformation Spanish drama. It explores the microcosms of classical Chinese Daoist subtle bodies and the Japanese Buddhist imperial body politic, and it examines the sensorium of American Hindu devotees and a contemporary American Sufi community.

The Religious Body Imagined is therefore an invitation to explore the human experience of embodiment as it pertains to religious thought and practice on the ground. Its geo-historically diverse case studies as well as its multi-disciplinary approaches offer a journey into the plasticity of religious expression, and implicitly suggest that cross-cultural conversations about human embodiment possess the potential to help bridge religious divides.

About the authors

Pamela D. Winfield is Professor of Buddhist Studies in the Department of Religious Studies at Elon University in NC. She is the author of *Icons and Iconoclasm in Japanese Buddhism: Kūkai and Dōgen on the Art of Enlightenment* (Oxford University Press, 2013) which won the AAS-SEC Book Prize in 2015. She is also the lead co-editor (with Steven Heine) of *Zen and Material Culture* (Oxford University Press, 2017), and has edited three special issues of the peer- reviewed interdisciplinary *CrossCurrents Journal* (2014, 2017, 2019). Her research has been supported by grants from the American Academy of Religion, the Association for Asian Studies, and the Asia Cultural Council among others, and her scholarship on the visual, material, and embodied dimensions of Japanese Buddhism has appeared in *The Japanese Journal of Religious Studies, Studies in Chinese Religions, Material Religion,* and other edited volumes with Oxford University Press, Columbia University Press, Brill, Routledge, Shambhala, Springer, and others.

Mina García is a Professor of Spanish in the Department of World Languages and Cultures at Elon University, where she teaches Spanish language and literature. Her research interests include the role of literature in the expansion of the Spanish empire, Early Modern Spanish literature, transatlantic studies and Latin American colonial culture and literature with special attention to the role of the *Other*: conversos, *moriscos*, and witches. She has authored multiple articles and book chapters as well as numerous conference papers. Her first book, entitled *Magia, Hechicería y Brujería: Entre La Celestina y Cervantes* was published by Editorial Renacimiento (Seville, Spain) in 2010. Her second book, *Idolatry and the Construction of the Spanish Empire* was published by University of Colorado Press in 2018. Her third book, *Social Justice in the Spanish Comedia*, is a co-edited volume in which she is both contributor and editor together with Erin Cowling, Tania de Miguel Magro and Glenda Nieto Cuebas. It was published by University of Toronto Press in 2021.

References

Brintnall, K. (ed.) (2016) *Embodied Religion*. Michigan: Macmillan.
Coakley, S. (ed.) (1997) *Religion and the Body*. Cambridge: Cambridge University Press.
Greenberg, Y. (2017) *The Body and Religion: Cross-Cultural Perspectives*. New York: Bloomsbury Publishing.
Law, J. M. (ed.) (1995) *Religious Reflections on the Human Body*. Cambridge: Cambridge University Press.
Nevile, M. (2015) The Embodied Turn in Research on Language and Social Interaction. *Research on Language and Social Interaction* 48(2): 121–51.

Part I
Gendered bodies

1 People of the book, women of the body: Ultra-orthodox Jewish women's reproductive literacy

Michal Raucher

Abstract

Jews have often been referred to as 'People of the book.' This is because books, specifically those that contain rabbinic legal discourse, are understood to be authoritative guides for Jewish life, and those who have achieved mastery in the content of the books are considered authorities. Although 'people of the book' is often used to refer to all Jews, book culture has been almost entirely constructed by men, particularly among ultra-Orthodox Jews. This article offers a different framework, one which sees women's religious authority growing out of embodied reproductive experiences. Haredi (ultra-Orthodox) women challenge the dominant paradigm for religious authority by insisting that their pregnant bodies replace books and rabbis. While a woman's body might be seen as an impediment to her religious authority, I argue that women become capable of exercising religious authority through their embodied experiences of bearing children. During my two years of ethnographic research with Haredi women in Jerusalem, I found that after giving birth to two or three children, Haredi women felt authorized to make decisions about their pregnancies without consulting a rabbi. After a woman has two or three children, she develops what I refer to as 'reproductive literacy,' meaning she knows how to use her embodied reproductive experiences as knowledge, expertise, and thus authority over reproduction. Through a close reading of pregnancy advice books and an analysis of how Haredi women use but later reject these books, I show that how Haredi women embody authority to make decisions about pregnancy and childbirth. In so doing, Haredi women challenge the paradigm of books as pathways toward authority

Keywords: reproduction; ultra-orthodox jews; Judaism; pregnancy; israel; women; literacy; embodiment; bodies; body

Introduction

Jews have often been referred to as 'people of the book' (Heilman 1983). This is largely due to the prominence of the Torah and rabbinic literature in the construction of religious tradition. For centuries, Jews have studied these books and turned to them as modernity offered new challenges for the tradition (Friedman 1987:235–56). This is especially true among ultra-Orthodox Jews in Israel, where 'communities of scholars' have been created as a result of their investment in studying these books. Yeshiva culture has blossomed since the 1950s, as more men continue their studies well into adulthood and have made careers out of remaining in the yeshiva, a school for religious education (Friedman 1987; Heilman 1983). Books, specifically those that contain rabbinic legal discourse, are understood to be authoritative guides for Jewish life, and those who have achieved mastery in the content of the books are considered authorities. Even young boys who attend a yeshiva and learn the stringent laws in the books are expected to return home and be authorities for their families (Friedman 1987). After years of studying the laws in the books, men are permitted to become rabbis. This, combined with a growing reliance on rabbinic authority, has resulted in ultra-Orthodox communities that rely on books and rabbis entirely (Stolow 2010). In these communities, the books and all their attendants (rabbis, scholars and yeshivas) are the source of authority in the Haredi world.

Although 'people of the book' is often used to refer to all Jews, book culture has been almost entirely constructed by men, particularly among ultra-Orthodox Jews.[1] The descriptor is one that prioritizes men's experiences and men's pathways toward religious authority. Furthermore, it is one that has depicted Jewish culture as entirely disembodied (Eilberg-Schwartz 1992). This article offers a different framework for seeing women's religious authority growing out of embodied experiences.

While women's lives are undoubtedly shaped by religious books and those who read the books, ultra-Orthodox women are not permitted entry into the yeshiva, and the access they have to rabbinic texts is limited and mediated by interpreters, namely fathers, sons, husbands or rabbis. Although women are educated in non-religious topics and serve as primary breadwinners for their families, they are not literate or skilled in the reading of these texts. This is largely due to the fact that women's bodies are needed for other valuable endeavors – working and raising children. Ultra-Orthodox women get married at around age 20 and have a total fertility rate of 6.5 children (Jeffay 2011). They spend a majority of their adult lives pregnant or caring for young children (Teman and Ivry 2011). They also become grandmothers in their forties, and will subsequently help to take care of their grandchildren as well. Haredi (ultra-Orthodox) women, therefore, support their husband's continued yeshiva studies, and the creation of more yeshiva students. In this way, although women are part of book culture, they are not directly the people of the book. Furthermore, because religious authority is granted through one's knowledge of the books, women are generally understood to lack religious authority in ultra-Orthodox Judaism.

Haredi women challenge this paradigm by insisting that their pregnant bodies replace books and rabbis. While a woman's body might be seen as an impediment to her religious authority, I argue that women become capable of exercising religious authority through their embodied experiences of bearing children. During my two years of ethnographic research with Haredi women in Jerusalem, I found that after giving birth to two or three children, Haredi women felt authorized to make decisions about their pregnancies without consulting a rabbi. After a woman has two or three children, she develops what I refer to as 'reproductive literacy,' meaning she knows how to use her embodied reproductive experiences as knowledge, expertise and thus authority over reproduction. Embodied reproductive experiences are sources of authoritative knowledge because of theological and cultural ideologies that draw a direct line between a woman's pregnant body and God. Written in pregnancy advice books and contained within Haredi teachings that were often repeated to me is the idea that when pregnant, a woman is acting in a God-like capacity of creation, and that the umbilical cord connects her not only to the fetus, but also to God. According to this theology, this direct line bypasses the rabbis and legal books that otherwise serve as interpreters of divine will. A Haredi woman uses her reproductive literacy in subsequent pregnancies as she selectively involves rabbis and doctors to the extent that they respect her authority. Haredi individuals are expected to consult their rabbis when making most decisions, especially those that are related to healthcare (Ivry 2010; Weingarten and Kitai 1995). Women are aware of that expectation, but they maintain that because of the responsibility they alone have to reproduce and raise children, and the fact that pregnancy happens in their bodies, they can make decisions outside the normative decision-making structure (Raucher 2020).

Reproductive literacy and the authority it engenders does not extend to other areas of Haredi life, but it represents a significant shift in the way Haredi life imagines authority to be granted through book literacy. Haredi women maintain that pregnancy is their responsibility and the area they know best. Haredi Jews understand pregnancy to be, as one of my informants described, 'what a Jewish woman does.' Put another way, pregnancy is a 'way of life' for

Haredi women (Teman and Ivry 2011). These statements point to the ownership and authority that Haredi women express while pregnant. They also indicate that Haredi women construct their identities through pregnancy because this is a significant piece of what distinguishes them from Haredi men. Reproduction, therefore, parallels the yeshiva. Just as men are responsible for the maintenance of Haredi life through its adherence to the laws in the books, women are responsible for the continuation of Haredi life through reproduction. Haredi women's reproductive activities are vitally important to the perpetuation of Haredi Judaism, and internal discourse about reproduction reinforces the role their bodies play in creating more Jews (Bilu 2012; Raucher 2016; Taragin-Zeller 2015). Therefore, as women exercise their authority over reproduction through reproductive literacy, they are challenging the structure wherein authority is granted through book-learning. Here, Haredi women demonstrate that bodies grant authority to make decisions about the maintenance and continuation of Haredi life.

This challenge to book-granted authority is found specifically in the way women performatively use pregnancy advice books. These books are displayed prominently on their home bookshelves, but when I asked women what they had learned from the books, they could not think of anything. Although they read these books during their first pregnancies, some did not remember what the books contained, and others provided me with broad summaries of the content without indicating what they had actually learned. As I read the pregnancy books, this surprised me because the themes in the books seemed to parallel themes from women's reproductive narratives. I argue that for Haredi women, having these books demonstrates their adherence to Haredi norms about the status of books in the community and the importance of reproduction. During their first pregnancies, they follow the instructions in the books, but during later pregnancies they reject ideas in the books that challenge their own authority. The knowledge they prioritize is not that which is gained in the yeshiva, but rather that which is gained through multiple pregnancies and the knowledge that pregnancy and childrearing will define their adult life. Reproductive literacy allows them to exercise authority over pregnancy-related decisions based on their embodied experiences of pregnancy. Haredi women do not prioritize books (pregnancy-related or otherwise) in their development of authority. Instead, they prioritize their embodied experience as a source of authority, demonstrating that they are cultivating a sense of authority as women of the body.

Literature review: Jewish studies and Jews with bodies

For decades, the field of Jewish studies had focused overwhelmingly on texts and textual analysis, reinforcing the idea of Jews as people of the book (Kirshenblatt-Gimblett 2005). In the mid 1990s, this idea of Jews as (solely) people of the book, began receiving significant critique. Notably, Howard Eilberg-Schwartz's *People of the Body* raises a number of counterpoints to this idea. The problem, he explains, is that thinking of Jews as people of the book means thinking about them as disembodied (Eilberg-Schwartz 1992). In the decades following the publication of *People of the Body*, Jewish studies scholars engaged in a corporeal turn. They embarked on a new approach in Jewish studies, termed 'Jewish cultural studies' by Jonathan and Daniel Boyarin (Boyarin and Boyarin 1997, cited in Kirshenblatt-Gimblett 2005:448). In 2005, Barbara Kirshenblatt-Gimblett commented on this corporeal turn in Jewish studies, noting that it included a focus on gender and sexuality, but pointing out that 'Text has not gone away. Rather, the corporeal turn has intensified interest in text and offered new ways to think about text as a social, corporeal, and material practice' (Kirshenblatt-Gimblett 2005:448). In other words, even when scholars claimed to have taken a corporeal turn in Jewish studies, their focus remained the text. As scholars perpetuated this definition of Jews and Judaism, they created a limited set of characteristics for what it means to be a Jew. Eilberg-Schwartz explains:

> It defines Jews as those people who participate in the activity of learning and interpreting Scripture. But, of course, not all Jews have engaged in such activities. Illiterate or non-learned Jewish men and Jewish women, who generally were not encouraged or allowed to study, do not qualify as 'People of the Book' and hence seemingly fall outside the category of 'Jews.' (Eilberg-Schwartz 1992:1)

In fact, there are many ways in which being Jewish is an embodied identity. Recent work on ultra-Orthodox Jews demonstrates this point (Aran 2006; Aran, Stadler and Ben-Ari 2008; Baumel 2006; Davidman 1991). For instance, Ayala Fader's ethnographic research with Hasidic girls in Brooklyn demonstrates that for young Hasidic women in America the constant tension between the body and the soul or the material and the spiritual is resolved by those who can embody the spiritual elements of Hasidism (Fader 2009). Orit Yafeh's work with Haredi kindergarten children demonstrates that even girls as young as five years old are taught that the clothes they wear, the style of their hair and the sound of their voice can arouse a man and thus must be controlled. As a result, young girls become overly aware of their body's presence and the role it plays in religious affairs (Yafeh 2007). Other research on Haredi women's bodies has considered their head coverings (Goldman Carrel 1999:163–80; Manolson 1997; Seigelshifer 2006; Weiss 2009; Zalcberg 2007), their modest clothing (Oryan 1994; Taragin-Zeller 2015, cited in Fishman Barack 2015:308–26; Yafeh 1999) and their pregnancies (Gantz 2003; Ivry, Teman and Bernhardt 2011; Taragin-Zeller 2017; Teman and Frumkin 2011). The body and the embodied experience are central components to a woman's identity and subjectivity as an Orthodox Jew.[2]

Men, by contrast, had been considered as almost entirely cerebral until recent scholarship looked at men's embodiment as part of the cultural construction of Orthodox Judaism (Stadler 2007). For instance, Yehuda Goodman's article on ultra-Orthodox men at a mental health rehabilitation center explores the connection between mental illness and bodily action in the Haredi world (Goodman 2009). Gideon Aran's ethnography of Haredi postures and movements also adds to the discussion around Haredi men's bodies (Aran 2006). Aran demonstrates that different parts of their bodies are ascribed different moral values. The penis, for instance, is understood to be 'the essence of physicality and the sources of impurity', according to Aran (Aran 2006:86). Feet also hold special significance as the lowest part of one's body and therefore susceptible to exposure from demons or impurities on the ground. Haredi men, therefore, will always cover their feet with shoes or socks, even at night or when outside in warm weather (Aran 2006:87–8). According to internal Haredi discourse, a man's ability to ignore or suppress his body is the reason he is able to attain the high level of intellectual skill needed to become a religious authority.

Despite women being unable to suppress their bodies and therefore unable to attain that level of book literacy, women attain another kind of literacy – reproductive literacy, or the expertise in reproduction. This expertise is gained not through books or studying, but through the embodied experience of pregnancy. This concept of reproductive literacy builds on Sallie Han's term 'prenatal literacy', or the ability to read, understand and apply all the pregnancy signs and symptoms, tests and ultrasounds (Han 2013). Han argues that as American women gain prenatal literacy, they can better understand and interpret both their experiences of pregnancy and the medical information they receive. Initially, Haredi women use pregnancy advice books to help them gain prenatal literacy. These books, which I describe in depth below, provide medical and religious answers for various prenatal questions. When pregnant for the first time, Haredi women use these books and gain the type of literacy the books want them to have – a literacy that still requires them to turn to their rabbi for his authority (Ivry 2010). 'Reproductive literacy', however, speaks to a woman's advanced experience with pregnancy (usually during her third pregnancy), wherein she learns how to rely on her own embodied experiences for authority. No longer willing to turn to rabbis who have never themselves been pregnant, or books, which represent the world of the rabbis, women with reproductive literacy make their own medical and religious decisions about contraception, prenatal testing, ultrasounds and birth. Reproductive literacy is the ability to read their own embodied experiences and consider those experiences as granting them religious authority.

Methodology

The findings I discuss here are based on a larger ethnographic study of Haredi women's reproductive experiences. From 2009 to 2011, I interviewed twenty-three Israeli Haredi women in Jerusalem. I visited each woman multiple times, getting to know them as their pregnancies progressed. I accompanied them to doctors' appointments and ultrasound examinations. Each woman I spoke to had at least three children, who often played at the park or slept in the other room while we spoke. I reached each woman through snowball sampling, relying on earlier contacts to help me to reach more women. Haredi women were happy to speak with me. Although not Haredi myself, I identified then as religiously observant, and I speak Hebrew fluently. This positionality meant that I was familiar enough with their world to understand the basic terms and premises. Women did not have to explain religious terms, so we could jump right in to talking about their pregnancies. Because I was married, they could share more intimate details of their life with me.

Women were happy to talk with me about their pregnancies. Despite the high fertility rates, women told me that they resisted talking to others about pregnancy. This is due to the fears and taboos that surround pregnancy in Haredi communities. Pregnancies are not acknowledged or discussed by strangers on the street, women do not receive presents for a new baby before it is born, and they do not name a fetus. Furthermore, because of the cultural and religious norms that require a woman to receive permission from her rabbi before getting an ultrasound, women feared telling a friend about an ultrasound because that friend might report a woman who acted without a rabbi's permission. I, on the other hand, had no contact with their rabbis, and women assumed that their community would not be reading my publications. Nonetheless, I have changed all identifying details about the women I spoke to in order to preserve their anonymity.

While in Israel, I also interviewed doctors, doulas and midwives who provide medical services to Haredi women. I observed ultrasound examinations at two prenatal clinics in Jerusalem that cater to Haredi women. These clinics display advertisements for modest clothing stores, stack women's prayer books on the tables in the waiting room and contain certifications from prominent rabbis in the community. The doctors who work at these clinics know that rabbis want to be included in major (and minor) medical decisions. I also observed a course of prenatal classes for Haredi women as well as several other religious classes.

In my conversations with women, and while observing in various settings, I heard about the pregnancy advice books I discuss in this article. The clinics had copies of these books in the waiting room, the books were sold at prenatal seminars in Meah Shearim, a large Haredi neighborhood of Jerusalem, and importantly, women I interviewed showed me their copies. I purchased these books during my two years in Jerusalem, but I did not read them thoroughly until I returned to the United States. Upon reading them, I discovered that they contained many of the same themes I had found in my interviews. In 2017, I turned to these books in earnest and analyzed their content alongside my interviews. The data for this article come primarily from the interaction between these pregnancy books and my conversations with Haredi women. The conversations and sections I feature are representative of the broader findings.

People of the book during first and second pregnancies

Discursively, Haredi life is predicated upon the idea that bodies and books are in constant tension, and in order to achieve intellectual success a person must control the influence of their body. Haredi society aims to elevate the spiritual and intellectual development of Jewish men, and it does this through the sustained study of rabbinic texts. Bodies – both male and female – are potential threats to a young man's spiritual and intellectual development. As pleasure-seeking sources of distraction, bodies prevent a man from full reflection. In order to control the influence of the body, Haredi discourse has redefined the self as disembodied. Although yeshiva students experience the self as embodied in their personal lives, the male student must remove himself from his body, in order to attain high levels of understanding and reflection. Only when the student limits the interference of his body can he study the books (Englander 2014). The books, therefore, are both meant to control and limit the influence of bodies. This section illustrates this point in the way women interact with books and rabbinic authority during their first and second pregnancies. During these pregnancies, before Haredi women gain and use their reproductive literacy, they see themselves as people of the book. Like the men in their lives, they understand that the role of books is to control their bodies and the fetuses inside them. In these early pregnancies, they follow the instructions in pregnancy advice books to turn to rabbis and doctors with any questions. As girls, the Haredi women I spoke to received little sexual education, and they did not engage in any physical sexual activity with men until they got married, usually around the age of twenty. They were shocked to get pregnant soon after their wedding, because they simply did not understand the biological process. Pregnancy books and rabbis offered them guidance about balancing religious obligations with medical concerns, birthing options, how to prepare for internal examinations and information about their changing bodies. These books helped women to navigate the many questions they had as they embarked upon their first pregnancies.

When I visited Haredi women in their homes, they showed me two pregnancy advice books that sat on their bookshelves: *B'Sha'ah Tovah: Madrich Refu'i Hilchati L'herayon v'Leida* (In a Good Time: A Medical and Halachic Guide for Pregnancy and Labor) (Finkelstein and Finkelstein 2002 [1996]) and *Hachana Ruchanit L'Leida* (Spiritual Preparation for Labor) (Hasdai and Hasdai n.d.). Some removed them from their shelves to show me. As I held these two books in my hands, I noticed the differences between these books and all the other books displayed on their shelves. The majority of books on their shelves have black or brown covers with gold writing indicating the contents. These other books belonged primarily to their husbands, who had spent hours poring over their content, sometimes learning them word for word. Among dozens, if not hundreds, of books on rabbinic literature and sacred texts, women kept these two pregnancy books. *B'Sha'ah Tovah* and *Hachanah Ruchanit* both have colorful covers; one even has a picture of a baby. Aside from some prayer books and perhaps a copy of the Hebrew Bible, these pregnancy and labor advice books were women's contribution to scholarship in their homes.

B'Sha'ah Tovah: A Medical and Halachic Guide for Pregnancy and Labor was co-written by a nurse-midwife, Michal Finkelstein, and her husband, Rabbi Baruch Finkelstein. The book was first written in English in 1993, as the Finkelsteins are American by origin, and then translated into Hebrew in 1996. The Finkelsteins released a revised and expanded version in English in 2001 and in Hebrew in 2002. The women I spoke to had the more recent Hebrew version, so I refer to that version here.[3] Feldheim Publishers, a large publishing house in Jerusalem and New York, published the book. *B'Sha'ah*

Tovah is a phrase congratulating someone upon hearing of their pregnancy. It means 'in a good time,' or 'in a good hour,' meaning that the birth should come at the right time. This pregnancy advice book structures itself as a medical book about pregnancy *and* a religious book about pregnancy. The second book, *Hachana Ruchanit L'Leida* (Spiritual Preparation for Labor), is an anthology of writings primarily by women about labor and delivery. Another married couple, Moshe and Dafna Hasdai, edited and published this anthology, and although there is no publication date in the book, Dafna Hasdai remembers publishing it in the late 1990s. The anthology contains a collection of short Hebrew essays from rabbis, rabbis' wives and doulas. It is a book of religious instructions and inspiration about pregnancy, birth and motherhood.[4]

One of the messages featured prominently in *B'Sha'ah Tovah* is that a woman has to incorporate – and learn how to balance – rabbinic and medical instructions during pregnancy. The book contains certifications from prominent Haredi rabbis, alongside certifications from doctors, illustrating their equal standing. This book also provides both medical and religious information about fetal development, telling women that information from rabbis and doctors can be consistent. Throughout the book, the Finkelsteins remind their readers that rabbis want them to visit doctors and utilize modern medicine to take care of themselves and their growing fetuses. This messaging intends to solidify a place for both doctors and rabbis in a woman's prenatal care. The Finkelsteins reject the exclusion of either one. They explain:

> We found that the two extreme attitudes towards medicine are not correct: the one who relies on a miracle to protect his health is considered a fool. Those who think that their health is entirely in the hands of modern medicine and not in heaven's hands are considered to be non-believers. We are required to find the golden path that merges one's faith [*bitachon*] with one's effort [*hishtadlut*]. (Finkelstein and Finkelstein 2002 [1996]:36)

When the Finkelsteins mention 'faith' and 'efforts,' what they mean is that a person should incorporate both religious and medical instructions. Women who walk this 'golden path' are those who consult doctors and rabbis and work in a triadic relationship with both for their reproductive care. In *Hachanah Ruchanit L'Leida*, Nurit Glazer shares a similar message:

> Many times when a woman arrives in the labor and delivery room and they give her a gown and they measure her blood pressure, everything they need to do, she enters into an entirely different world. She forgets that she also has her own considerations

and she has a role in the matter. Suddenly she is just a minor part of the play. She forgets that she has the right to say 'no' sometimes, or to bring her own opinion and request something. (Glazer n.d.:18)

When Glazer mentions a woman's opinions, or her 'own considerations,' she is speaking about religious obligations. Glazer continues, explaining that religious women often feel that the secular medical system is antagonistic toward their needs, but if a woman asks nicely she can get what she needs from the doctors. For example, a religious woman who enters the hospital will be concerned about covering herself modestly. Glazer wants religious women to learn how to ask for a blanket instead of being embarrassed in the hospital gown. Glazer, like the Finkelsteins, intends to teach women that their religious needs and their medical needs can be met simultaneously, and that doctors and rabbis can help produce healthy babies.

During their first pregnancies, women turn to these books a great deal, internalizing their messages about the need to adhere to religious and medical instruction. I met Dalia when she was pregnant with her fourth child. She showed me the pregnancy books on her bookshelves, but told me she hadn't looked at them since her first pregnancy. Dalia grew up Haredi and became a dancer, already an unusual career for a Haredi woman. Soon after getting married, she opened a dance studio for Haredi girls, and she feared getting pregnant would interrupt her ability to dance. Afraid to discuss birth control with her husband or rabbi because she knew they would oppose it, Dalia got pregnant in the first few months of marriage. During this first pregnancy, Dalia's husband and rabbi expressed their concerns about her dancing. Although they had no medical expertise, they were afraid that dancing would threaten the pregnancy. Obeying rabbinic authority, she decided that she should 'please him, please the baby, please everybody, just like all Haredi women.' Dalia stopped dancing during her first pregnancy because that is what the rabbi wanted her to do.

For Dalia and other Haredi women, conforming to religious and medical demands continued into their second pregnancies, despite some internal questioning. Because of some light bleeding at the beginning of her second pregnancy, the doctor instructed Dalia to go on bed rest for a few weeks. Dalia challenged this restriction: 'I did have thoughts of "what do I need this for?" It is not like I'm committed to babies. If not this one, another will come.' She admitted that she would not have had an abortion because that is not 'responsible,' but her thoughts and feelings indicate that Dalia was beginning to express her own desires in this pregnancy, as opposed to the first. Nevertheless, Dalia listened to the medical and religious instruction that she cease dancing during her pregnancies. The pregnancy advice books that Dalia read during her first pregnancy had taught her that these two epistemological realms work in tandem to produce healthy babies, so Dalia heeded this advice. As women like Dalia followed the instructions in these books for their first and second pregnancies, they were both respecting the reverence for books and the message that the books contained. They accepted the idea that rabbis (and doctors sanctioned by rabbis) should guide their pregnancies because this was consistent with the general respect for books and book knowledge as that which should control bodies.

Pregnancy rituals provide another illustration of the ideology that books control bodies, including pregnant bodies. In these rituals, what one does with a religious book will affect what happens with the fetus. Four weeks from her due date, Devorah invited me to accompany her to her fetal ultrasound appointment. While there, the doctor told her that her fetus was not head down, but rather in a breech position. Her doctor said there was a chance the fetus would flip again before labor, but that at this point there was a higher chance of a C-section because he would not deliver a baby who was in the breech position. Devorah wanted to avoid a C-section because if she delivered this way, it might limit how many subsequent pregnancies she could carry. As we talked about Devorah's desire to avoid a C-section, she remembered a *segula* (folk ritual, tradition or amulet) she had once heard about flipping a fetus in utero.[5] We briskly walked home and opened the front door of her apartment. The door opened into the living room where a dilapidated couch sat against the wall on the right-hand side of the room. Her living room was sparsely decorated, but immediately in front of us as we entered her apartment was an entire wall of bookshelves, filled with *seforim* (sacred books).[6] All of the Haredi homes that I entered looked like Devorah's. Decorations were sparse, furniture was worn, toys were strewn throughout the house, and bookshelves overflowing with books about rabbinic law were placed in the main room of the house. A house with a lot of books conveys to visitors that the men within the home have devoted considerable time to learning the contents of those books. This is a marker of status for a Haredi family (Benor 2012:63).[7] It demonstrates not only that a man has the intellectual ability to learn what is considered to be very difficult material, but also that the family has devoted itself to this ideal lifestyle of the *avrech* family where a husband stays in a learning community while his wife supports the family (Yaffe *et al.* 2018). Devorah started scanning the bookshelves. Gleefully, she pulled a few books off the shelves and turned them around so that they were standing up straight. With each flipped book, she whispered a prayer asking God to hear her request. According to the *segula*, if the *seforim* in one's house are upside down, flipping them could flip the fetus into the right position. This was the superstition she remembered, and she hoped that by turning the books in her house, she could turn the fetus in her uterus as well.

Women told me about other *segulot* (plural *segula*) that echo a similar relationship between books and fetuses. In these examples, we see again that books are tangible representations of fetuses. When a woman is in the ninth month of pregnancy, her husband is often given the honor of opening the Ark containing the Torah scrolls during morning prayers. This action is a *segula* meant to ensure a woman's womb begins to open for an easy delivery. Waiting until his wife is in the ninth month of pregnancy to ask him to open the Ark, the congregation makes it clear that they do not want the delivery to come earlier than the ninth month. In this *segula*, the Ark parallels the womb, and the Torah scrolls inside the Ark are like the fetus inside the womb. Judaism's most holy books, the Torah, are seen as being similar, at least in this *segula*, to a fetus. Here, a pregnant woman's husband is granted the ability to not only protect the fetus from an early delivery, but to actually begin the process of labor for his wife. Although the origin of these *segulot* is not clear, we can see that they establish a relationship between holy books and babies. Devorah believed that turning around books in her home would lead to the fetus turning around as well. Additionally, men open the Ark to reveal the Torah scrolls (considered to be the holiest of books) so that their wife's cervix might open to reveal a baby. In these *segulot*, the directionality flows from books to babies. What men do with the books, or what women do with their husbands' books, will affect the fetus in some way.

Initially, Haredi women believe that pregnancy books, or rabbis who know the laws in the books, should serve as guides for their pregnancies. During their first (and sometimes second) pregnancies, Haredi women turn to husbands, rabbis and books for guidance. They believe that books control bodies. This is what makes them people of the book. Pregnancy rituals reflect this as well. Even fetuses become people of the book because of the rituals wherein books control fetuses. The intention behind these rituals is to bolster the role of books in Haredi life, and to illustrate the way in which bodies can be controlled by books. Here, we see that books can influence life, even when not considering their content. Books as objects and what they symbolize have power over bodies.

In subsequent pregnancies, however, women come to see these rituals differently. As they gain reproductive literacy, they reject the idea that books can control their bodies or their fetuses. Instead, they see that books and bodies are interchangeable. Recall that the Ark symbolized a woman's body, and the Torah scroll symbolized a fetus. If books can symbolize bodies, then bodies can symbolize books. If books are meant to control bodies, then bodies have the potential to control books. This is precisely what Haredi women conclude after multiple pregnancies. They come to see their bodies – and the future Haredi Jews they carry – as more authoritative than the books and those with book knowledge.

Reproductive literacy: bodies over books

In later pregnancies, women express a relationship between doctors, rabbis and their own preferences that challenges the norm for religious authority in Haredi life. Instead of relying on books and those who are literate in rabbinic texts to determine the best course of action when it comes to decisions around contraception, ultrasounds, prenatal testing, abortion and labor, Haredi women draw on their reproductive literacy. As defined above, reproductive literacy refers to the knowledge and authority women have gained through the embodied experience of pregnancy. Haredi discourse understands that women's bodies connect them directly to God during pregnancy. This idea is contained with the pregnancy advice books that women read during their first pregnancies, and it is one of the few ideas they maintain in later pregnancies. Although they reject the books' insistence on consulting rabbis and doctors for pregnancy guidance, women continue to support the idea that pregnancy connects them to God. This is because this direct connection to God allows women to bypass the rabbis who otherwise serve as intermediaries between the Haredi public and divine will. The embodied experience of pregnancy distinguishes women from the rabbis who might otherwise guide their decisions. Haredi rabbis (all men) will never be pregnant. They, therefore, will never have reproductive literacy.

One can find these ideas about a pregnant woman's direct connection to God within the pregnancy advice book, *Spiritual Preparation for Labor*. In Nurit Glazer's essay, 'Spiritual preparation for labor,' she writes, 'Labor is woman's opportunity, in a rare and concentrated way, to connect to God, and this is a forbidden opportunity to waste' (Glazer n.d.:17). Sylvia Dahari and Tami Perlman suggest that praying during labor and delivery is a way to speak directly to God. They show that the letters of the word for birth in Hebrew, *Leidah* can be separated to write *L'yad Hashem*, or 'next to God.' The authors say that birth, therefore, is an opportunity to be next to God in prayer: 'This is the reality of the ability of very high prayers. Everything we pray will be received' (Dahari and Perlman n.d.:35). Ilana Berninson wants women to think of themselves as vessels for God during labor because women bring blessings to this world on behalf of God: 'We are partners in something holy. At this time, we have to partner in this activity with God and not let any barriers interfere with that' (Berninson n.d.:51). These authors emphasize that pregnant women have direct connections to God, which allow them to bypass rabbinic authority. Women's authority, they claim, resides in their embodiment of the divine ability to reproduce. Rabbis, authoritative because of the books they have mastered, are seemingly irrelevant here.

Many of the authors in this anthology also point to the Haredi understanding that pregnancy and labor for a woman parallel exile and redemption for the Jewish people. Clarifying a complex rabbinic teaching, Bracha Toverdovitch writes, 'Babies before pregnancy are like the nation of Israel in the time of the exile. The moment of labor symbolizes the moment of redemption' (Toverdovitch n.d.:36). Toverdovitch continues to explain that a woman's good deeds during pregnancy, like the Jewish people's good deeds during exile, will lead to the redemption: 'The stage of exile is the stage of preparation and growth for the arrival of the Messiah' (Toverdovitch n.d.:39). In other words, women – like the Jewish people in exile – are not just supposed to wait for someone else to bring about a healthy baby. Instead, 'Pregnancy is the critical stage in the future development of the baby. Every change in environment, diet, can influence [the fetus] for better for worse' (Toverdovitch n.d.:38). This language of exile and redemption and the parallels authors draw with pregnancy and birth not only elevate the physicality of a woman's experience by framing it in religious terms, but they also remind women that they play a significant role in fetal development and the healthy birth of a baby (Gribetz 2017:173–204).

Haredi women expressed these ideas in the way they rejected rabbinic and medical advice and simultaneously bolstered their own connection to God and thus authority over pregnancy. Hila, who was pregnant with her sixth child when we spoke about her rejecting medical advice, expressed the belief that pregnancy is the embodiment of divine authority. She explained, 'God gave me this body, and I have to provide for it, and I have to take care of it. I am raising a child in me that's not only a child but a Jewish child.' Hila and other Haredi women view their bodies as direct gifts from God, a gift endowed with great responsibility because of the religious identity of this future child. This responsibility is also what sanctions Hila's authority. Because God has trusted her with this responsibility, in other words, Hila has moral authority and does not need to trust anybody else to tell her what to do during the pregnancy. The embodiment of pregnancy allows Hila to work directly with God, without the need for rabbinic intermediaries. She can bypass both rabbis and doctors.

Moriah, a doula with five children of her own, emphasizes that it is through the physical act of pregnancy and childbirth that women can reach God. In fact, Moriah rejects the normalization of modesty concerns that Glazer writes about above. She thinks that women focus too much on remaining modest in the birthing room or saying the correct psalms during birth; she wants them to look at pregnancy and birth as a gift from God and thus imbued with an opportunity for building a relationship: 'You are so religious? You say blessings all the time? Start seeing God. God gave this to you. Know that. Trust that. Let him talk to you … it's a very physical experience, but it is a paradigm for life … we have a spiritual goal for it. We can rise above the physical and touch the other side.' She encourages women to feel as if their bodies are not problematic, but rather the pathway towards religious authority. For Moriah, modesty is a religious ideal that does not help women see that birth is already imbued with religious significance. Instead of remaining modest, Moriah requests that Haredi women remember that the ability to birth is a direct gift from God and as such it is a physical experience that transcends the material realities and requirements.[8] Here, Moriah is calling on Haredi women to use their reproductive literacy as a foil to rabbinic literacy.

Maya also understands pregnancy to be the performance of God's work and therefore as something that supersedes the law. This is because pregnancy allows women to connect with God in a way that men cannot. She was six months pregnant with her fourth child when she talked with me about pregnancy as an opportunity to connect with God. Maya's reflections on a woman's connection to God during pregnancy and labor bolstered her views on the irrelevance of rabbinic legal rulings for pregnant women. Not only is the Talmud outdated on issues related to pregnancy, Maya claimed, but the rabbis know nothing about pregnancy and birth. Maya did not mean that the rabbis do not possess basic information about reproduction, but rather that their bodies have not been imbued with significance by God as a woman's pregnant body has. This intimate relationship – expressed through a woman's body – gives women authority over pregnancy and birth, an authority that the rabbis do not possess simply because they are all men.

The fact that women connect with God through their bodies should, according to Maya, teach women that they should rely on their reproductive literacy. Maya explained that relying on one's body is closer to what God wants from us than what one may find in a book. Sarcastically she insisted, 'You trust doctors, you trust medicine, you trust everybody but you do not trust yourself. Trust anybody because they went to school and they learned. Don't trust yourself even though you've lived in your body for twenty years.'

Relying on one's body for knowledge during pregnancy is, for Maya, relying on God.

It is curious why women I spoke to, those who already had at least three children, claimed not to have learned anything from these books. If this is the case, why did their descriptions of embodying divine authority sound so much like the writings in *Hachana Ruchanit L'Leida?* And furthermore, if they have not learned anything from these books, why do they hold such a prominent place on their bookshelves, sitting among their husband's holy books? I maintain that there are a few competing commitments here. Women have, indeed, learned from these books to talk about pregnancy as an embodiment of divine authority. However, the books also contain a great deal of instruction about consulting with rabbis and doctors during pregnancy, two authorities who challenge women's embodiment of divine authority. These books, furthermore, make it seem like women did not learn this idea through the embodiment of pregnancy, but rather only through reading these books. Women, therefore, reject the idea that they learned anything from these books. If they said they had learned something from these books, they would be challenging their own reproductive literacy, while also acknowledging that they are ignoring the instructions within the books. The way women talk about pregnancy advice books in later pregnancies indicates that they are pushing back against the expectation that books should guide and instruct their reproductive lives. Instead, they prioritize their reproductive literacy, their embodied knowledge of pregnancy.

Keeping the books on their shelves presents us with another set of competing ideas. Despite the authority granted to them by multiple pregnancies, women display these books alongside their husbands' books as part of their adherence to Haredi norms. The presence of these pregnancy advice books makes it seem like women have followed rabbinic advice during those pregnancies. Displaying the books gives others the impression that that they are playing by the rules of Haredi life in following the instructions in the books. In another way, however, keeping the books on the shelf, next to her husband's books, is a woman's attempt to equate books with babies. Pregnancy books become markers of status, evidence of her contribution to the maintenance and continuation of Haredi life, just like her husband's books. Women are attempting to balance the scales of Haredi life, and demonstrate that bodies that create babies are on an equal footing with the instructions in the books.

Conclusion

Haredi communities are predicated on everyone remaining committed to the authority of the books and the rabbis who interpret them. This is what it means to be the people of the book. Challenging rabbinic law means removing oneself from the Haredi community and losing contact with family and friends (Fader 2017). Rabbis have worked tirelessly to use rabbinic law in order to control, limit and suppress Haredi bodies, both male and female. As a result, Haredi life has often been studied as 'book culture,' seemingly composed of disembodied Jews. Only recently have scholars taken up the task of considering how bodies have also been constructed in Haredi communities. And yet, most scholars have primarily engaged with the question of how laws are exercised to control Haredi bodies.

This article explored how Haredi women challenge this paradigm by insisting that their pregnant bodies replace books and rabbis. During their first and second pregnancies, Haredi women turn to pregnancy advice books, which teach them how to rely on both rabbinic and medical guidance during pregnancy. For later pregnancies, Haredi women rely on their reproductive literacy, or the knowledge and authority they have gained as a result of their repeated pregnancies. They understand this reproductive literacy to override the rabbinic reliance on books because they see reproduction as an experience that provides them with direct access to God. No longer needing rabbinic intermediaries, Haredi women rely on their embodied experiences to inform their reproductive decisions. Ultimately, as they keep these books on their shelves, alongside their husbands' books of rabbinic discourse, Haredi women are saying that their pregnancies provide as much stature in the Haredi world as their husbands' books. As producers of Haredi Jews, women's bodies are also cultivating authority.

About the author

Michal Raucher is assistant professor of Jewish Studies at Rutgers University.

Acknowledgments

This article is based on my book, Conceiving Agency: Reproductive Authority among Haredi Women (Indiana University Press, 2020). An early version was presented at the American Academy of Religion conference in 2015. I received a number of grants to support the research on which this article is based. I am appreciative of support from the Fulbright Foundation, the Wenner-Gren Foundation, the Memorial Foundation for Jewish Culture, the Crown Family Foundation at Northwestern University, and the Charles Phelps Taft Research Center at the University of Cincinnati. I was encouraged to write this article by Pamela Winfield, whose seminar on religious bodies inspired me think about bodies, books, and authorities more deeply. Kathryn Dugan, Justine Howe, and Amanda Baugh offered critical feedback. I am grateful for the anonymous readers and editors at Body and Religion for their helpful comments and questions. Any errors remain my own. Above all others, I express gratitude to the Haredi women who welcomed me into their homes and lives, and I hope I have respected their stories.

Notes

1. The author is aware of recent changes in Orthodoxy that have allowed women entry into the yeshivot and the study of certain rabbinic texts, but this article focuses on ultra-Orthodoxy, where this is not the case.
2. In *Becoming Un-Orthodox*, Lynn Davidman explains that embodied rituals are one of the things that distinguishes Orthodox Judaism from Christianity (Davidman 2015).
3. Translations from the Hebrew are the author's own.
4. Translations from the Hebrew are the author's own.
5. Although the word *segula* has a variety of definitions and applications across the Haredi world, one of my informants clarified it as: 'anything can be a *segula* if someone wants it be a way of connecting with God.' Indeed, these rituals help Haredi women connect their pregnant selves directly to God. This connection is central to their reproductive literacy. For more on *segulot* (plural), see Rock-Singer (2018).
6. *Seforim* literally just means 'books,' but when my Haredi informants use it, it refers to their sacred books.
7. Benor points out that most Orthodox families display these books prominently as a demonstration of their attachment to these texts.
8. In 'Like a snake in Paradise,' Stadler and Taragin-Zeller also found that young Haredi women in Israel are reinterpreting norms of modesty in order to carve for themselves a 'direct path to "the All Mighty" ' (2017:138).

References

Aran, G. (2006) Denial does not make the Haredi body go away. *Contemporary Jewry* 26: 75–113. https://doi.org/10.1007/BF02965508

Aran, G., Stadler, N. and Ben-Ari, E. (2008) Fundamentalism and the masculine body: the case of Jewish ultra-Orthodox men in Israel. *Religion* 38: 30. https://doi.org/10.1016/j.religion.2007.09.002

Arthur, L. (ed.) (1999) *Religion, Dress and the Body.* New York: Berg. https://doi.org/10.2752/9781847888839

Baumel, S. (2006) *Sacred Speakers: Language and Culture among the Haredim in Israel.* New York: Berghahn Books.

Benor, S. B. (2012) *Becoming Frum: How Newcomers Learn the Language of Orthodox Judaism.* New Brunswick: Rutgers University Press.

Berninson, I. (n.d.) Time of labor: time of cancellation. In M. Hasdai and D. Hasdai (eds) *Hachana Ruchanit L'Leida* (Spiritual Preparation for Labor) (in Hebrew).

Bilu, Y. (2012) 'To make many more Menachem Mendels': childlessness, procreation, and creation in Messianic Habad. *Contemporary Jewry* 32: 111–34. https://doi.org/10.1007/s12397-012-9084-0

Boyarin, J. and Boyarin, D. (eds) (1997) *Jews and Other Differences: The New Jewish Cultural Studies.* Minneapolis: University of Minnesota Press.

Dahari, S. and Perlman, T. (n.d.) Labor: next to God in prayer. In M. Hasdai and D. Hasdai (eds) *Hachana Ruchanit L'Leida* (Spiritual Preparation for Labor) (in Hebrew).

Davidman, L. (1991) *Tradition in a Rootless World: Women Turn to Orthodox Judaism.* Berkeley: University of California Press.

Davidman, L. (2015) *Becoming Un-Orthodox: Stories of Ex-Hasidic Jews.* Oxford: Oxford University Press.

Eilberg-Schwartz, H. (1992) *People of the Body: Jews and Judaism from an Embodied Perspective.* Albany: State University of New York Press.

Englander, Y. (2014) The image of the male body in Lithuanian ultra-Orthodox thought in Israel and corresponding strategies for forging an a-feminine public sphere. *Journal of Contemporary Religion* 29(3): 457–70. https://doi.org/10.1080/13537903.2014.945729

Fader, A. (2009) *Mitzvah Girls: Bringing up the Next Generation of Hassidic Jews in Brooklyn.* Princeton: Princeton University Press. https://doi.org/10.1515/9781400830992

Fader, A. (2017) Ultra-Orthodox Jewish interiority, the internet, and the crisis of faith. *HAU: Journal of Ethnographic Theory* 7(1): 185–206. https://doi.org/10.14318/hau7.1.016

Finkelstein, A. (1997) Preparing Haredi girls for their monthly cycle and sexual maturity (in Hebrew). MA dissertation, Hebrew University of Jerusalem, Israel.

Finkelstein, M. and Finkelstein, B. (2002 [1996]) *B'Sha'ah Tovah: A Medical and Halakhic Guide for Pregnancy and Labor* (in Hebrew). Feldheim: Jerusalem.

Fishman Barack (ed.) (2015) *Love, Marriage, and Jewish Families Today: Paradoxes of the Gender Revolution*. Waltham: Brandeis University Press.

Friedman, M. (1987) Life tradition and book tradition in the development of Ultraorthodox Judaism. In H. Goldberg (ed.) *Judaism Viewed from Within and Without* 235–56. Albany, NY: SUNY Press.

Gantz, M. (2003) Childbirth and women's strength in the Haredi community in Israel (in Hebrew). MA thesis, Hebrew University, Israel.

Glazer, N. (n.d.) Spiritual preparation for labor. In M. Hasdai and D. Hasdai (eds) *Hachana Ruchanit L'Leida* (Spiritual Preparation for Labor) (in Hebrew).

Goldman Carrel, B. (1999) Hasidic women's head-coverings: a feminized system of Hasidic distinction. In L. Arthur (ed.) *Religion, Dress and the Body* 163–80. New York: Berg.

Goodman, Y. (2009) 'You look, thank God, quite good on the outside': imitating the ideal self in a Jewish ultra-Orthodox rehabilitation site. *Medical Anthropological Quarterly* 23(2): 122–41. https://doi.org/10.1111/j.1548-1387.2009.01051.x

Gribetz, S. K. (2017) Pregnant with meaning: women's bodies as metaphors for time in biblical, second temple, and rabbinic literature. In J. Ben-Dov and L. Doering (eds) *The Construction of Time in Antiquity: Ritual, Art, and Identity* 173–204. Cambridge: Cambridge University Press. https://doi.org/10.1017/9781316266199.010

Han, S. (2013) *Pregnancy in Practice: Expectation and Experience in Contemporary US*. New York: Berghahn Books.

Hasdai, M. and Dafna (eds) (n.d.) *Hachana Ruchanit L'Leida* (in Hebrew).

Heilman, S. (1983) *The People of the Book: Drama, Fellowship and Religion*. Chicago: Chicago University Press.

Ivry, T. (2010) Kosher medicine and medicalized halacha: an exploration of triadic relations among Israeli rabbis, doctors, and infertility patients. *American Ethnologist* 37(4): 662–80. https://doi.org/10.1111/j.1548-1425.2010.01277.x

Ivry, T., Teman, E. and Bernhardt, B. A. (2011) Pregnancy as a proclamation of faith: ultra-Orthodox Jewish women navigating the uncertainty of pregnancy and prenatal diagnosis. *American Journal of Medical Genetics Part A* 155(1): 69–80. https://doi.org/10.1002/ajmg.a.33774

Jeffay, N. (2011) In Israel, Haredi and Muslim women are having fewer children. *The Jewish Daily Forward*, 15 July 2011. Retrieved on 8 August 2012 from http://forward.com/articles/139391/in-israel-haredi-and-muslim-women-are-having-fewer.

Kirshenblatt-Gimblett, B. (2005) The corporeal turn. *Jewish Quarterly Review* 95(3):447–61. https://doi.org/10.1353/jqr.2005.0058

Manolson, G. (1997) *Outside/Inside: A Fresh Look at Tzniut*. Jerusalem: Targum Press Inc.

Oryan, S. (1994) Nothing more beautiful than modesty: communication models in the socialization of Haredi girls (in Hebrew). MA dissertation, University of Haifa, Israel.

Raucher, M. (2016) Ethnography and Jewish ethics: lessons from a case study in reproductive ethics. *Journal of Religious Ethics* 44(4): 636–58. https://doi.org/10.1111/jore.12160

Raucher, M. (2020) *Conceiving Agency: Reproductive Authority Among Haredi Women in Jerusalem*. Indiana University Press.

Rock-Singer, C. (2018) *Prophetess of the Body: American Jewish Women and the Politics of Embodied Knowledge*. Submitted in partial fulfilment of the requirements for the degree of Doctor of Philosophy at the Graduate School of Arts and Sciences, Columbia University.

Seigelshifer, V. (2006) From tichels to hair bands: modern Orthodox women and the practice of head covering. MA thesis, Hebrew University of Jerusalem, Israel.

Stadler, N. and Taragin-Zeller, L. (2017) Like a snake in paradise: fundamentalism, gender and taboos in the Haredi community. *Archives de sciences sociales des religions* 177:133–56. https://doi.org/10.4000/assr.29300

Stolow, J. (2010) *Orthodox by Design: Judaism, Print Politics, and the ArtScroll Revolution*. Berkeley: University of California Press, 2010.

Taragin-Zeller, L. (2015) Between modesty and beauty: reinterpreting female piety in the Israeli Haredi community. In S. Fishman Barack (ed.) *Love, Marriage, and Jewish Families Today: Paradoxes of the Gender Revolution* 308–26. Waltham: Brandeis University Press.

Taragin-Zeller, L. (2017) Have six, have seven, have eight children: daily interactions between rabbinic authority and free will (in Hebrew). *Judaism, Sovereignty, and Human Rights* 3: 113–38.

Teman, E. and Frumkin, A. (2011) God sent ordeals and their discontents: ultra-Orthodox Jewish women negotiate prenatal testing. *Social Science and Medicine* 72(9): 1527–33. https://doi.org/10.1016/j.socscimed.2011.03.007

Teman, E. and Ivry, T. (2011) Pregnancy as a way of life among ultra-Orthodox Jewish women. Paper presented at the 81st Annual Meeting of the Eastern Sociological Society, 24–7 February 2011, Philadelphia, Pennsylvania.

Toverdovitch, B. (n.d.) Towards spiritual motherhood. In M. Hasdai and D. Hasdai (eds) *Hachana Ruchanit L'Leida* (Spiritual Preparation for Labor) (in Hebrew).

Weingarten, M. and Kitai, E. (1995) Consultations with rabbis. *Journal of Religion and Health* 34(2): 135–40. https://doi.org/10.1007/BF02248769

Weiss, S. (2009) Under cover: demystification of women's head covering in Jewish law. *Nashim* 17: 89–115. https://doi.org/10.2979/nas.2009.-.17.89

Yafeh, O. (2007) The time in the body: cultural construction of femininity in ultraorthodox kindergartens for girls. *Ethos* 35(4): 516–53. https://doi.org/10.1525/eth.2007.35.4.516

Yaffe, N. M., Solak, N., Halperin, E. and Saguy, S. (2018) 'Poor is pious': distinctiveness threat increases glorification of poverty among the poor. *European Journal of Social Psychology* 48: 460–71. https://doi.org/10.1002/ejsp.2342

Zalcberg, S. (2007) 'Grace is deceitful and beauty is vain': how Hasidic women cope with the requirement of shaving one's head and wearing a black kerchief. *Gender Issues* 24(3): 13–34. https://doi.org/10.1007/s12147-007-9043-3

2 The male body and Catholic piety in early modern Spain

Elizabeth Rhodes

Abstract

Features of embodied female piety adduced from late medieval texts are now established categories of interpretation for religious experience in the early modern period. These include intense Eucharistic devotion in relationship to food culture, extreme food manipulation and exaggerated violence against the physical self. However, evidence from documents by and about early modern religious men indicates that male and female ascetic piety had more in common than not during this period. Strategies of backgrounding or masking those practices when carried out by men made them less visible in comparison to those practised by women, due to gender inflections in religious politics.

Keywords: embodied piety; religious asceticism; food culture; food and religion

> Do not reveal your private experience of God to your spiritual children or to anyone else, because experience will show that doing so will reveal so little secret about it that you could not believe unless you were to try it yourself.
> (St Juan de Ávila, 'Letter to a young priest', 1544; from cited edition, Vol. V, p. 23)

It is now a truism that pre-modern Christian piety practised by women is distinctively grounded in affective and physical imitation of Christ's passion, intense devotion to the Eucharist and particularly severe asceticism. In her ground-breaking books *Holy Feast and Holy Fast* (1987) and *Fragmentation and Redemption* (1991), Caroline Bynum expanded on work by other medievalists such as Michael Goodich, in order to construct her thesis about the prominent role of embodied piety among religious women of western Europe. While rejecting facile binary conclusions about women and men, Bynum and those who endorse her conclusions nonetheless distinguish male from female piety based on what documents record members of each gender doing to and with their physical selves, and female piety thereafter has been designated as uniquely embodied (Bynum 1987, 1991; Goodich 1981). It would be difficult to overestimate the influence of these patterns which, having originated in the context of medieval studies, are now commonly applied to other periods. As historian Jodi Campbell notes when opening her chapter on Spanish food and religion from the fifteenth through seventeenth centuries, Bynum's work remains 'the model for understanding ties between food and holiness' (Campbell 2017:135, n. 1). The pervasiveness of the same model holds for related pious practices, such as Eucharistic devotion and food abstinence.

What follows provides evidence from early modern Spanish texts by and about religious men that describes those men deeply engaged in the behaviours prominently ascribed to women in pre-modern Christianity. These texts do not refer to said practices as effeminate or unmanly, nor do they mention female religious figures as models. On the contrary, they represent those behaviours as normal features of heroic male Catholicism. Men's engagement with embodied piety is no surprise in itself, since, as scholars often note, men were its first well-known practitioners: Bernard of Clairvaux (1090–1153), Francis of Assisi (1182–1226) and Henry Suso (1295?–1366). Beyond the realm of medievalism, however, a different dynamic has influenced how scholars understand who was practising their faith in that way.[1]

In the last forty years, feminist scholars of early modern Europe have focused on texts by and about religious women, bringing to light a large corpus of previously unrecognised documents that date from the fifteenth through seventeenth centuries. Convents and other archives have been scoured, up-ending masculinist contentions in the process ('There were no women writers ...'), and old books have been newly edited. Early modern hispanism has experienced a revival thanks to this initiative. Electa Arenal and Stacey Schlau's 1989 ground-breaking anthology of convent writing, *Untold Sisters: Hispanic Nuns in their Own Works*, was followed by Isabel Poutrin's 1995 *La voile et la plume*, which indexed 113 early modern religious women of Spain who wrote about their own lives or whose lives were documented by others. There was, and is, much work to be done.

Research on early modern religious men lags far behind. Male monastery archives remain unexamined, documents in other archives by and about spiritually exuberant religious males of the period await attention, and fundamental questions about men's religious life, such as their relationship to food and the Eucharist as food, have not been posed. While published theological treatises and guides to prayer and confession written by religious men abound, documents about their personal piety are scarce. Highly affective published works by early modern religious men are also abundant, but most are prescriptive texts designed to guide readers' emotions, not offer first-person accounts of their authors' devotional experiences. Even John of the Cross' first-person poetry, heady and sensual, ventriloquises a female voice rather than speak in first person.[2]

Such scarcity of evidence is understandable, since biographical information about most well-known male religious figures was motivated by the desire to provide posterity with data about their public versus private lives, lives devoted to helping others, saving souls and fortifying Catholic institutions, all while evidencing the exalted virtues of humility and obedience. Accessing their private devotions is also challenging because, as the epigraph above indicates, male religious individuals were acculturated to keep their private experience of God to themselves and, by and large, they did. Often busy with multiple professional responsibilities, those who were not members of contemplative orders were obliged to fit their private devotions and prayer practice into their active lives. In contrast, religious women were expected to devote many if not most of their waking hours to prayer, and those who wanted an active apostolate usually struggled to realize one. In writings by and about early modern religious men, the tendency to background or fade out the intimacies of their piety behind their institutional and community-based priorities renders men's pious practices hard to see, but not invisible.

Digging into documents from early modern Spain produces evidence that intensely embodied piety was a normalised path to God for both religious men and women.[3] The sample of texts that follows reveals those men practising ardent devotion to the Eucharist, strict food management and manipulation, as well as extreme asceticism justified by pious intentions. With this modest offering, my objective is to start a conversation, not to demonstrate that gender did not matter in early modern religious practice. I suggest that scrutiny of works by and about religious men and period-specific nuancing are necessary steps in determining to what extent the practice of early modern Catholicism can be rightly called gendered in the context of embodied piety.

Eucharistic devotion

Avid, affective devotion to the Host is now understood to be a hallmark of female piety. By 1500, however, the sacrament of the Eucharist was multivalent in ways it had not been before, and the expansion of its signifying power into fields of meaning beyond theology, combined with the religious sentimentality encouraged during the sixteenth-century Catholic reform, altered the meaning of this ritual and made it appealing to women and men alike. As the unity of Christian Europe cracked along the fault lines of the sacraments, the doctrine of transubstantiation became a feature of denominational as well as personal identity (see Wandel 2006). Attentiveness to the Host was a way to affirm one's belief in the Catholic God, the one who abided in the communion wafer in a way the Protestant God did not. For Spaniards, the politics of communion acquired a special valence because the Spanish Hapsburg dynasty cultivated Eucharistic veneration as a means to affiliate their family's status with that of the divinity. Charles V, who ruled Spain from 1516 to 1556 and was also the Holy Roman Emperor, was 'personally responsible for the increase of the Eucharistic cult among his subjects' (Tanner 1993:207, 214).

Visible Eucharistic piety, such as longing for frequent communion and fainting spells, tears or raptures triggered by consuming what Spanish Catholics believed was the blood and body of Christ, provided individuals with a means to affirm their membership in an increasingly nationalised community of belief. Worshippers who experienced intense emotions in proximity to the Host visibly bore witness to the presence of God in that community, thereby supporting not only the primacy of the Catholic faith, but also Catholic dynastic power and status. The uncontrollable tears shed by saints Ignatius of Loyola (1491–1556) and Juan de Ávila (1499–1569) when saying or attending Mass were not only symptoms of their individual piety, but also of devotion to and affiliation with the Spanish Catholic Church and its territories. Males from a wide swath of society, not only famous priests and preachers, participated in energetic Eucharistic devotion. Francisco de Yepes (1520–1607), a beggar, weaver, mystic and father of eight, was famous during his lifetime for his longing to commune daily, but was instructed during a communion locution to do so only on Thursdays.[4] At the other end of the social spectrum, Francis Borgia (1510–72) had the same desire throughout his career as a Jesuit, and one of Borgia's icons is the Eucharist.[5]

The holy man and hermit Gregorio López (1542–96) ran away from the Spanish imperial court at age 20 and sought a life of prayer and severe asceticism in Zacatecas, Mexico. In subsequent years, he was so detached from the Catholic ceremonial cult that he was repeatedly investigated for heresy, although the authorities exonerated him each time. Nonetheless, his first biographer Francisco Losa insisted that López had 'a burning desire to receive Christ our Lord sacramentally', although López himself never wrote of that burning desire.[6] One could reasonably suspect that Losa mentioned his companion's Eucharistic fervour in order to quell any lingering suspicions about the hermit's orthodoxy. Whether true or piously invented, the detail indicates that holy men were not only willing but perhaps expected to sustain intense desire to partake of God in the Eucharist.

The communion meditation of the renowned Dominican preacher, confessor and author Luis de Granada (1504–88) provides eloquent testimony of the pan-gender nature of early modern Eucharistic piety that characterised the Catholic reform. By far the most printed religious writer of his day and an author whose books travelled the globe in a multitude of languages, Luis de Granada is rarely studied now. His meditation offers a rare first-person exhortation to a highly emotional engagement with God through the Host, written by a man. Addressing Christ as 'my husband and my father', he enjoins himself to experience God directly, using a lexicon of food consumption: 'May I love you, Lord, covet you, eat you and drink you. My God, sweet honey, mildest milk, delightful repast and repast of the great, make me believe in you, that I might enjoy you in worthiness.' The spousal imagery of his meditation intensifies as he adds, 'In this sacrament, you [God] wished above all to reveal to my soul the love of husband to wife, and to treat me as such [a wife]. Give me, then, Lord, this same desire [of wife for husband] to relate to you … such that [my heart] cannot be parted from you in death or in life.' To the extent that Luis de Granada was in tune with the Catholicism of his day – and the popularity of his books indicates that he was – it is safe to say that Eucharistic fervour articulated in terms of eating was central to the devotional practices of men as well as women.[7]

Food management and manipulation

Luis de Granada's meditation reveals a clear association between the Eucharist and sustenance, referring to taking communion as eating and drinking God and exalting the food at the divine table as honey, milk and life-sustaining repast. Bynum describes the significance of eating in the Middle Ages as having particular meaning for women, who she says controlled food handling and used the Eucharist as alimentation to effect their own salvation and thereby participate in Christ's painful achievement of the same (Bynum 1987:250).

The question of whether religious women had a closer relationship to food than religious men might be productively put to the test in the early modern context, considering several factors that conditioned food practices, such as age, social class, religious order or affiliation, and ethnic identity. Documents by and about men reveal a surprising amount of food-related activity, including food handling as well as food asceticism. One of the first Iberian cookbooks, *El cocinero religioso* (The [male] religious cook), was written by an Augustinian friar. The first known manuscript of a convent cookbook, *El recetario de Marcilla*, was written (or copied) by a friar in Navarra, and the most famous cookbook of early modern Spain, *Los cuatro libros de la confitería* (1592), was by Miguel de Baeza of Toledo. In Serrano Larráyoz' study of convent kitchens, almost all cooking texts cited are by men (Campbell 2017:17; Serrano Larráyoz 2008). This is not to say that women were not as active as men in food production, preparation and consumption. But before conclusions about the gender of early modern food culture are made, some consideration should be given to the men in and around the kitchen, since they were active if not dominant in agricultural production, food gathering, selling, preparation and refinement.[8]

Early modern male religious communities in Spain did not allow women in them, at least officially. Inside those communities, men handled the food. According to his companion and first biographer Dionisio Vázquez (1527–89), Francis Borgia regularly sought out kitchen duty, as did many religious men. Vázquez records how Borgia not only did housework in Simancas alongside the novices he was directing, he also worked for the (male) cook in the kitchen, hauled water jugs and firewood for meal activities, lit the cook fires, did the dishes and served the brothers at table (Vázquez 2011:226–7, 294). While some men may have arrived to religious life with an understanding that food was women's business (an uncertain supposition), they soon met with another arrangement, and boys raised in those communities would have known no other way of life.

The Jesuit Aloysius Gonzaga (1568–91) voluntarily took on both kitchen labours and housework: 'Every munday and tuesday it was his custom every week to serve in the Kitchin. And he made it his chiefest work to wipe the dishes when they were brought from the table and to gather the scraps of meat to relieve the necessity of the poor.' Cristóbal López, secretary and companion to Pedro de Rivadeneira (1527–1611) for thirty-three years, recalls that when Rivadeneira was living with the first Jesuits in Rome, they assigned household chores by turn. Rivadeneira insisted on being assigned what López calls 'cosas de hombre' (men's business) and was sent to the kitchen to make an omelette. Although he burnt the omelette, the young man served it with self-satisfaction to Ignatius, who noted the boy's pride and chastised him, not for the bad cooking but the vainglory. In the beatification proceedings for John of the Cross, a Carmelite brother recalled that as a novice he spilled the entire pot of rice he had cooked for the community, to his immense distress. Arriving at that moment, John witnessed the young man's anguish and said, 'Son, don't worry about it! Serve up what else there is, since we have to eat, for Our Lord does not want us to eat rice today' (Ceparius 1627:273; Rivadeneira 2009:49).⁹

It is likely that who obtained, prepared, served and cleaned up for food events was less a function of gender than of diet community, and within diet communities, a function of social and age hierarchy inside those communities. Whereas studies of power structures in female convents of early modern Spain are readily available, who was assigned to cook and clean in male religious communities remains something of a mystery (see, e.g., Pérez Morera 2005). Francis Borja seems to have done kitchen duty voluntarily rather than by assignment. It may have provided him with the opportunity to exercise humility, since he had spent the forty years of his pre-Jesuit life in households of the highest nobility, in which cooking staff handled the food. A variety of motivations could have moved men to be in the kitchen, such as a talent or fondness for cooking, an effort to create an egalitarian community, to enhance the prestige of the monastery as a locale of fine dining for patrons, or the simple gratification of manual work in contrast to other types of responsibilities.

Some kitchen tasks were related to healing, since medicines were often concocted with heat, and cookbooks contained not only food recipes but also pharmacological formulas. The hermit Gregorio López compiled a manuscript collection of herbal cures, some of which he recalled from European sources and some of which he based on his extensive experimentation with native Mexican plants.¹⁰ López' collection is now esteemed in medicinal history. It is likely that efforts to find a remedy for his own enduring physical woes at least partially motivated his botanical research. According to Losa, López suffered from bouts of dysentery, ongoing recurrent high fevers and what was probably typhus. Combined with his immoderate penitential exercises, particularly his dietary mortification, this left him perpetually unwell: 'He was accustomed to eating but once a day, although it was a small repast of little sustenance; most of the time it was only roasted corn … . He never ate meat.' Losa also recalls that López never wanted anyone else to cook for him, and whenever someone from his large following gifted him with food they had prepared, it made him sick. (Losa 1613:7r–v, 96v).

In sum, the management of food was an important if not primary concern of anyone who didn't have or want someone else to manage it for them. An individual's relationship to their professional responsibilities may have conditioned to what extent food metaphors and miracles figured in accounts of their pious practices. Women had a more limited range of activities in which to signify their piety than men, because of their more restricted engagement in the larger world. With less activities to record, the ones in which they did engage were magnified in representations of their lives, particularly their consuming relationship with their physical bodies and inner worlds. In contrast, male food practices are one in a list of many endeavours, and thus may appear insignificant unless scrutinised.

Whether and how involvement in food culture influenced early modern male Eucharistic piety remains to be determined. Male writers dating at least from Augustine have resorted to food metaphors to express devotion to the Host, and, as the above quotation from Luis de Granada's communion meditation indicates, such ardour was a normative practice of early modern holy men who excelled in the direct knowledge of God. Since, as Campbell notes, bread and wine at that time were 'the foundation of diet groups who resided and dined together', the components of communion had a direct relationship with everyone's daily life.[11] It seems likely that male authors and biographers foregrounded accomplishments that conformed to heroic models of piety for men. Although evidence points to ardent Eucharistic devotion on their part, heroism for male religious figures was not to be proven by Eucharistic ecstasy or in-depth first-person descriptions of visions inspired by communion. But many did have such visions.

A related question is who made the Eucharistic Host, the central food on the Christian table. Originally, its fabrication was assigned to male religious figures, which would have influenced men's relationship with it. Leclercq states that medieval female religious figures also made it, citing Saint Radegund (520–87) as an example, noting that she did so in spite of regulations against it. Before the fourteenth century, laymen and laywomen participated in its production. The Council of Milan (1576) established that the Eucharistic wafer had to be baked and pressed in male monasteries (Leclerq 1910). Men's material and cultic relationship to the Host was obviously different from that of women, since women could only receive it, while men administered it as well as received it, and in some cases confected it as well. If and how this contoured each gender's Eucharistic fervour is a topic awaiting investigation.

Food asceticism

While both women and men participated in food-related activities in early modern Spanish religious communities, not everyone ate what was on the table. Taking one's body to extreme states with food denial was a traditional ascetic practice used by many holy individuals to test their self-control and display heroic virtue during this period. In the context of the late Middle Ages, Bynum analyses the self-starvation practised by some religious women as anorexia mirabilis, the voluntary suspension of food intake while being nourished by God, sometimes surviving solely on the Host. Food renunciation, she says, was also a means by which women gained some control over their lives in patriarchal society. She ascribes a Christological value to anorexia: 'Food meant flesh, flesh meant suffering, and suffering meant redemption.' In this paradigm, medieval women's food denial was not denigration of the female body, but rather 'an effort to plumb and realise all the possibilities of the flesh'. That effort led them into many types of penitential asceticism, including extreme fasting, practices that are, she maintains, 'significantly more common in female religiosity' (Bynum 1987:76, 220, 250).[12]

In the early modern context, this gender distinction is uncertain. In some cases, lack of awareness of religious men who refused to eat is due to early modern discretion, which is to say the covering up of that behaviour with a less problematic version of the story. Aloysius Gonzaga, mentioned above, died at age 23 while a Jesuit novice. He is famous today for having perished as a consequence of tending to plague victims. However, no victims of contagious disease were admitted to Our Lady of Consolation in Rome, the hospital where he presumably caught the plague. Early records of his brief life and Jesuit correspondence about him indicate that Aloysius had long starved himself to the point where his health was fatally compromised, and no doctors or superiors were able to compel him to eat.

According to Virgilius Ceparius, Aloysius' companion during his Jesuit years and his first biographer, the young man's eating habits began to deteriorate when he was eleven and he contracted strangury, a severe infection of the urinary tract, for which his doctors prescribed dietary abstinence. Aloysius followed this prescription so zealously that his health began to fail, to the alarm of his parents, and his father reportedly complained, 'This child seemeth to have a desire to make away himself.' Thereafter, Aloysius began to refuse food because '[not eating] began to be a pleasure to him', which 'did very much impair the whole state of his health otherwise, for with that slenderness of diet he did so far forth weaken his stomach, that afterward when he most could, he could not take meate and if against his appetite he took it, could he by any means retaine it … . [T]hat utterly corrupted the whole state of his body.' These steps follow the progression of anorexia nervosa, whose first phase is characterised by voluntary food denial. In the second phase, the body naturalises ongoing minimal nutrition to the point where the individual is physiologically unable to process food. Aloysius lost his sense of taste, which Ceparius attributes to his unworldliness but which is also a symptom of anorexia (Ceparius 1627:36–7, 64).[13]

The young man's Jesuit superiors were aware that Aloysius' extreme asceticism, particularly his refusal to eat, was pathological; doctors were called in, to no avail. There was no talk of anorexia mirabilis, although Aloysius had had a passionate devotion to the Eucharist that often left him 'with infinite force of piety dissolved into teares', a devotion he had from early adolescence. In November 1585, the Master of Novices wrote of the seventeen-year-old, 'he neither wanteth natural, nor celestial gifts, his health only excepted, which is so weake, that even his very aspect striketh fear unto us'. By the time Aloysius Gonzaga died, he had so severely damaged his own body that it is impossible to know what, or what combination of things, killed him. In his last letter, written to his mother ten days before his demise, he described his high fever and desire to die. High fever was a plague symptom, but he had suffered intermittent high fevers since the age of seven. He lingered in his final illness for over three months, whereas early modern plagues killed within three to five days after symptoms surfaced (Ceparius 1627:20–1, 49–50, 205; Gonzaga 1949:158).[14]

The story of Aloysius' brief life composed for the 1624 printing of Pedro de Rivadeneira's *Flos sanctorum* took the first steps in transforming the cause of the young Jesuit's death into the version of it that endures today. The medical efforts to prevent Aloysius' demise were erased, altering the cause of Aloysius' death from an incurable inner malady into radical piety. Describing the painful extremes of Aloysius' asceticism as productive and appropriate for the spiritual elect, the narrator concluded, 'he joined these asperities with continual and fervent mental prayer, and with other holy exercises and occupations characteristic of a man chosen and guided by God'.[15]

It seems that whereas self-starvation to the point of death, or to the point of abetting one's death, was acceptable in fourteenth-century Christendom for a holy person such as Catherine of Siena (1347–89), it was unsuitable for Aloysius Gonzaga as the Jesuits wanted posterity to know him. This discrepancy was not only a function of gender. The different versions of Aloysius' extreme asceticism, both of which are in texts of a more hagiographic than historic bent, point to a moment in time when thinking about embodied piety was shifting between Ceparius' original rendition documenting Aloysius' refusal to eat as excess that led to death, and the *Flos sanctorum*'s interpretation of it as laudable heroic piety. This inconsistency was characteristic of the period when definitions of curable emotional and physical maladies, versus divinely given opportunities for suffering, were in flux.[16] Other cases of severe food asceticism practised by early modern religious men, such as that of López cited above, indicate that Aloysius' self-starvation was not unique, although in neither case does that asceticism figure prominently in accounts of their lives.

Examples of other holy men whose dietary regiments took them to the brink of death are not hard to find, and as is the case with analogous female examples, they come wrapped in descriptions of extreme physical mortification, such as sleep deprivation and marathon hours of prayer. Recounting Aloysius' self-disciplinary regimen, the *Flos sanctorum* repeats Ceparius' report that Aloysius never protected himself in any way from cold, from which his frail body suffered constantly. He enumerates the young man's many penitential exercises that he carried out during his adolescence which included, among other things, three self-flagellation sessions per night as well as every day, using metal spurs when a spiked belt wasn't available, and fasting to such an extreme that, according to the *Flos* legend, it had to have been God that sustained him. Like many holy men of his day, and understandably given his severe renunciations, Aloysius reportedly had continual, severe headaches.[17]

Hyperbolic asceticism, including self-starvation, is a regular feature of heroic religious masculinity in early modern Spain. Two other Jesuit cases provide evidence of these extremes, and because they were both famous men, they likely served as models for others. The early mortification piety of Ignatius of Loyola (1491–1556) in Manresa, carried out during eleven months in 1522, took him to death's door. He reportedly stopped bathing and grooming, flagellated himself three times daily, spent seven hours a day at prayer on his knees, lived on bread and water when he ate at all, and slept on the ground when he slept at all. Had a female patron not found him there, he would have died. In his 1605 biography of Ignatius, Rivadeneira reports that the future saint compromised his health for the rest of his life with these excesses.[18]

This story is better known than that of Aloysius Gonzaga, in part because Ignatius later rejected his own immoderation. Such exaggerated asceticism typifies the initial exuberance of many holy individuals during their youth and often forms part of experimentations they later outgrow, or which ceases to be of interest as the male subject's other activities require greater narrative attention, as was the case with Bernard of Clairvaux.[19] Like Bernard, Ignatius eventually settled into a more moderate if consistent practice of harsh but controlled physical discipline, of the sort he prescribed in the *Spiritual Exercises*: to give the body what it needs but no more, and to use self-harming behaviours as penance for sin, but never to the point of doing long-lasting physical damage. As Gentilcore summarises, Ignatian mandates about food emphasised moderation, to become 'master of oneself, both in the manner of eating and in the quantity of food eaten'. The rationale for this decision was practical: for men, as Ignatius learned the hard way, it was impossible to do the work of God in the world with a compromised body, or, as he himself wrote, 'when a healthy mind is in a healthy body, all becomes healthy and fitted to a better service of God' (Gentilcore 2015:110; Ignatius of Loyola 1951).[20]

Religious women who did not work in the world, especially those who spent many hours of the day in prayer, did not have or need this justification. As Christopher Wilson explains, 'While early modern religious men were praised for the lives of external activity – preaching, missionary work, spiritual direction, martyrdom at the hands of those perceived as infidels – female routes to sanctity typically focused on heroic retreat from the world, mystical experience, and exemplary obedience to superiors' (Wilson 2009:190). Male as well as female religious individuals, however, did practise the extremes of physical mortification that Ignatius eventually eschewed, and while the Jesuits are on record advising against such excesses, other male religious orders had different practices of asceticism that await study.

His own advisements notwithstanding, Ignatius had to forcefully rein in a Jesuit brother who was killing himself with his embodied piety. Francis Borgia became a Jesuit at age 41, and thereafter practised ongoing habits of asceticism that rivalled those of his superior, practices he had begun a decade before. Overweight when he initiated his religious life at age 33, he started a regimen of very long hours at prayer, extreme fasting and harsh physical mortification which, as his first biographer Dionisio Vázquez says, 'wasted his strength away and ruined his health'. His molars fell out, he suffered from continual stomach and joint pain, and his skin hung in long, empty flaps around his waist. Doctors concluded that his excessive penances had destroyed the strongest physical constitution they had ever seen. In 1548, Ignatius intervened and ordered Borgia to cease those behaviours, eat what he was given, greatly reduce his prayer time and do no further harm to his body.[21]

That directive was somewhat effective. Like many male religious figures of his day whose life stories have survived, Borgia suffered from constant health problems but never abandoned his mortifications. In him one sees the problematic creativity also characteristic of women who seem to have been determined to do away with themselves in the name of God. In his later years, when he travelled a lot for his endless administrative assignments, Borgia was unable to 'take his discipline' without anyone else observing. This inspired him to carry along tools to hurt himself in a way no one else would see, probably cutting: 'he used to painfully make himself bleed, secretly carrying along some means to do so'.[22] Religious women were not the only ones who used their bodies as vehicles of transport to the divine along a trajectory of pain.

Male physical austerities were a required norm for spiritual virtuosity, but equally normative was the need to hide those austerities, as Borgia's secret penances indicate. In his life of Gonzaga, Ceparius describes the Master of Novices who instructed Aloysius, saying, 'This divinely happy man was in the habit of mortifying of his body with daily abstinences, frequent fasts, sharpe hairecloth, and disciplines, together with continual watchings very rigorous. Which although he did endeavour to do as privately as he might, notwithstanding it would not all together pass concealed from so many of his children … . He appeared a notable spectacle of modesty.' Ceparius records that in response to his religious superiors' attempts to restrain his physical mortifications, Aloysius wrote that he decided to imitate what those men actually did in private, which was to practise the same extremes, rather than what they told him to do, which was to moderate them (Ceparius 1627:165, 167, 234–5, 288–9, 290, 292).

Intensely embodied male piety could lead to real and textual censorship, further evidence of the practice of shrouding it. By 1549, the Jesuit Francisco Onfroy had openly prophesied that Francis Borgia would become Pope and use Jesuits to reform the Catholic Church, provided the Society transformed itself into a contemplative order. In the letter Ignatius wrote to Borgia enumerating reasons why Onfroy's presumed revelations were not to be credited, he noted the indiscretion with which Onfroy practised his asceticism, physical mortifications so violent that they produced haemorrhages and 'other disorders'. Ignatius continued, 'it seems fairly clear that he has upset his own imagination and done some harm to those powers of the soul wherein resides the judgement of particular things', adding that it was 'from the derangement of the senses that delirium comes' and attributing Onfory's ill-advised prophesies to the unfortunate man's excesses in meditation, which Ignatius called self-love.

Ignatius concluded by specifying what Onfroy failed to do: 'Persons who have received such extraordinary favours from God usually take the words of Isaiah as applying to themselves, "My secret for myself, my secret for myself" ' (Ignatius of Loyola 1959:202, 203–4). Men were not only encouraged to practise such secrecy, but required to do so in order to maintain their credibility, for to write or speak about their spiritual gifts signified the very imprudence that revealed them to be unworthy of such gifts in the first place. In one of his spiritual counsels, Francis Borgia instructed priests not to do public penances out of the decency owed their office, but insisted that they do them in secret. Early documents written by companions of the holy man Simón de Rojas (1552–1624) record his severe asceticism, and the anonymous introduction to the 1939 edition of Rojas' book about prayer claims that from the age of eight, he flagellated himself until the blood ran. Yet the saint's own many published writings and most biographies of him do not mention those practices at all (Aliaga Asensio 2009; anonymous 1983 [1939]; Borgia 1964:421; García Maestro 2009; Simón de Rojas 1983 [1939]).

Silence has long been a virtue celebrated in religious women. The same virtue, however, was also lauded in religious men, if somewhat differently. In accordance with formulaic features of holiness designed to protect the theology and the institution of the Catholic Church, silence about one's personal communion with God was enjoined for all, unless one's superior asked for descriptions of those events. When Juan de Ávila returned Teresa of Ávila's manuscript account of her spiritual life story to her, he reminded her not to share it, 'because the individual things by which God carries some along are not for others', advice he gave to his brothers in religion as well (Juan de Ávila 1970:573). Whereas early modern religious women were often allowed or required to recount their spiritual intimacies in first-person writing, men were socialised not to. Male servants of God were expected to preach, teach, confess, administer sacraments, attend to the poor, the needy, the infirm and the wealthy, as well as meet administrative and political responsibilities, all in places where religious women generally were not permitted to be, much less work. They were also instructed not to talk about the very experiences that mattered most to them and to their female counterparts, which were their personal activities performed for and with God.

Nonetheless, evidence of those intimacies can be deduced from trails of erasures as well as words that have survived. Simón de Rojas, known for his extreme Eucharistic fervour and the 'cruel' iron cilice he wore, self-identified as a slave of the Virgin Mary from the age of 20. Rojas' piety was apparently too exuberant for comfort, for the first biography of him, published in 1653 in only one edition, exudes the ecstatic nature of his embodied piety: *Sparks of the Love of God and His Mother which, Being Unable to Contain Them, the Ignited and Enflamed Heart of the Very Venerable and Most Reverend Master Fray Simon de Rojas Emitted*. The subsequent account of his life did away with that title, replacing it with one that steered masculinity away from such excesses: *First part of the Life of the Reverend Father Master F. Simón de Rojas* (Arcos 1670).[23] Other, more direct evidence has also disappeared. Rivadeneira's biography of Ignatius reports that after Ignatius' death, papers were found recounting

> his visions and revelations that he had from the Lord, which were so remarkable, and of that extraordinary and odd eight-day ecstasy that so amazes. And in the papers ... it is clear that those gifts were very ordinary and quotidian for him ... and in spite of

all this, it was a miracle if we ever heard him speak about it, or take into his mouth either revelation or vision.

Vázquez states that Francis Borgia 'trusted few with his secrets, and even fewer the spiritual ones', while Losa remarks that even he, Gregorio López' close companion for years, was unable to convince his friend to speak about his experience of God, for 'he never dealt with anybody about that'.[24]

Early modern embodied male piety has been disconnected from male spirituality, as if it were simply athleticism. In some cases, as in some cases with women, it may have been. But in all instances examined here, there is an enduring relationship between belief, body and painful discipline, as well as intense longing for God. There were certainly differences in the ways women and men practised embodied early modern Catholicism, since throughout the period everyone was living under the long shadow of gender stereotypes, and the lives they lived were in many ways different. It is clear, however, that religious men in general did not elaborate, in writing or in person, on their intimacies with God in the first person, and if they did, they guarded those writings closely. Women could write of little else with authority. Many people had those experiences irrespective of their gender identity, for they were the springboard to God as God was then understood. Gendered expectations might skew what records of both remain today, but those records are replete with surprises.

About the author

Elizabeth Rhodes is a professor of Hispanic studies at Boston College. A specialist in early modern Hispanic studies, she has had three Fulbright research grants, an NEH Faculty Fellowship, and has been a visiting fellow in the Women's Studies Program at the Harvard Divinity School. She is the author of *Dressed to Kill: Death and Meaning in Zayas's Desengaños* (2011; Toronto: University of Toronto Press), and her most recent publication (2020) is Indecent Theology: Sex and Female Heresy in Counter-Reformation Spain. *Renaissance Quarterly* 73(3): 866–896.

Acknowledgements

Special thanks to Alison Weber. Research for this study was made possible by the generous support of Boston College.

Notes

1. As Michael Aers (1994) notes, referring to 'men' and 'women' in classless, regionless, universalising terms is so reductive as to be inaccurate (3). Age and education are other important variables. The men studied in this essay were all white Catholics of orthodox intentions, although their ages, social classes and levels of education varied. The extent to which the individuals under consideration here can be considered constitutive remains to be seen.
2. On the place of Saint John of the Cross' poetic voice in mystical history, see Elizabeth Rhodes (2009).
3. Some of the texts that follow suggest a fluidity in gender that the male/female dichotomy does not accommodate and would be better categorised as spectrum sexual identity. See Ritch C. Savin-Williams (2016). I use the words 'man' and 'woman' to represent individuals whose own culture would have them identified as such. All cases that follow are from Spain except for that of Aloysius Gonzaga, who was born in Italy and spent years at the Spanish imperial court.
4. Francisco de Yepes was the older brother of Saint John of the Cross (Velasco 1992:335).
5. Ignatius was beatified in 1609 and canonised in 1622. Borgia was beatified in 1624 and canonised in 1670. Uncontrollable weeping in response to intense spiritual feeling, called the gift of tears, is a feature of many religions and considered desirable by believers. It was regularly attributed to early modern holy individuals (see Ezmar 2015). Rady Roldán Figueroa provides a thorough review of the history of frequent communion through the seventeenth century (2010:117–56).
6. '[U]n ardiente deseo de recibir a Cristo N[uestro] S[eñor] sacramentalmente' (Losa 1613:122r). Taking sacramental communion means receiving it seeking forgiveness of sin. All translations are mine and I have modernised Spanish quotations.
7. On the popularity of Luis de Granada, see Elizabeth Rhodes (1990). '[E]res mi esposo y mi padre. Ámete pues yo, Señor, codíciete yo, cómate yo y bébate yo. Dios mío, miel dulce, leche muy suave, manjar deleitable y manjar de grandes, hazme crecer en ti, para que te pueda gozar dignamente. Quisiste sobre todo esto descubrir a mi ánima en este sacramento amor de esposo a esposa, y tratarme como a tal. Dame pues, Señor, ese mismo corazón para contigo, de tal manera contigo que ni en vida ni en muerte se puede [mi corazón] apartar de ti.' (Granada 1988:114, 117.)
8. Campbell (2017) provides ample documentation of men's roles in all areas of food handling.

9   The quote is from John of the Cross: '¡Hijo!, no se le dé nada, reparta lo demás, que hay que comer, que no quiere Nuestro Señor que comamos hoy arroz.' (Arco Moya and Arco Moya 2006:101–2.) I thank Jodi Bilinkoff for generously sharing this reference.
10 Only portions of what is now known as *Medicinal Treasures of Gregorio López* ('El Tesoro de medicinas de Gregorio López') were written by López. Francisco Guerrero's introduction clarifies this (1982:8–29). Carolyn Nadeau (2018) describes manuscript miscellanea containing recipes for food, medicines and cosmetics.
11 Campbell cites Augustine (2017:15); for a reference to bread and wine, see p. 16.
12 The debate over the relationship between anorexia mirabilis and anorexia nervosa is ongoing. J. Griffin and E. Berry (2003) find that in both, the determining causation is guilt, induced by religious doctrine in the former and familial, religious or media pressure in the latter.
13 Taste aversion, in turn, inhibits the brain's ability to engage the 'start eating' hormones (see Frank *et al.* 2013).
14 For details on the plague, see Sheila Barker (2005) and Franco Mormando's introduction to the same volume (2005). On Gonzaga's superiors prohibiting his excessive physical mortifications and ordering him to eat, as well as his non-compliance, see Ceparius (1627:171–200).
15 '[J]untaba estas asperezas con una continua y fervorosa oración mental y con los otros ejercicios y ocupaciones santas y propias de hombre escogido y guiado de Dios.' (Rivadeneira 1624:601.)
16 Andrew Keitt (2005) elaborates on the transition from religious interpretation of behaviours associated with religious fervour and medical interpretations of the same.
17 Holy headaches, such as those suffered by Bernard of Clairvaux, follow in the wake of other intense practices of mortification or a life-threatening illness. By the early modern period, it is impossible to know whether a holy person's headaches are a trope of holiness or a real malady. Bernard's first biographers describe him suffering from this problem from childhood (Webb and Walker 1960:17).
18 'Y así, aunque era hombre robusto y de grandes fuerzas, a pocos días se enflaqueció y marchitó la fuerza de su antiguo vigor y valentía, y quedó muy debilitado con el rigor de tan áspera penitencia.' (Rivadeneira (1945:56).)
19 See Geoffrey Webb and Adrian Walker's (1960) edition of Bernard's first biography, written by three of Bernard's contemporaries.
20 The Ignatius quote is from his 1547 letter to Francis Borgia, cited in William W. Meissner (1992:304).

21 '[G]astarle la fuerzas y arruinarle la salud.' (Vázquez 2011:169, 170; Ignatius of Loyola 1966.)
22 '[U]saba sacarse sangre con dolor, trayendo para ello algunas artificios secretamente.' (Vázquez 2011:391.) On the hyperbolic austerities of the famous preacher and holy man Juan de Avila, which likewise provoked ongoing health problems, see Luis Muñoz (1964 [1635]:8).
23 The first biography, by Francisco Manzano (1653), was titled *Centellas de amor de Dios y su madre que sin poderse contener despidió el encendido y abrasado corazón del muy venerable padre y reverendísimo maestro Fr. Simón de Rojas*. On Simón de Rojas' influence on the Spanish royal family, see Martha K. Hoffman (2011:98–102).
24 Rivadeneira on Ignatius: 'las visiones e ilustraciones tan notables que tuvo del Señor, y de aquel éxtasis de ocho días tan admirable, extraordinario y extraño. Y en los papeles … se ve que estos regalos le eran muy ordinarios y cotidianos … y con todo esto por maravilla le oímos hablar, ni aun tomar en la boca revelación ni visión.' (1945:328.) Vásquez on Borgia: 'fiaba de pocos sus secretos y de menos los espirituales' (2011:374). Losa on López: 'nunca trataba de eso con otros' (1613:31v).

References

Aers, D. (1994) Figuring forth the Body of Christ: devotion and politics. *Essays in Medieval Studies* 11: 1–14.

Aliaga Asensio, P. (2009) *San Simón de Rojas, un santo en la Corte de Felipe III y Felipe IV*. Madrid: Biblioteca de autores cristianos.

Anonymous (1983 [1939]) Síntesis de su vida. In Simón de Rojas *La oración y sus grandezas*. Madrid: Postulación del Beato Simón de Rojas.

Arco Moya, J. del and Arco Moya, J. del (eds) (2006) *Proceso de beatificación de San Juan de la Cruz: Proceso de Jaen, años 1627–1628*. Córdoba: Publicaciones Obra social y cultura cajasur.

Arcos, F. de (1670) *Primera parte de la vida del V. y Rmo. P. M. Fr. Simon de Roxas … del Orden de la Santissima Trinidad de Redemptores*. Madrid: Julián de Paredes.

Arenal, E. and Schlau. S. (1989) *Untold Sisters. Hispanic Nuns in their Own Works* (trans. A. Powell). Albuquerque, NM: University of New Mexico Press.

Barker, S. (2005) Plague art in early modern Rome: divine directives and temporal remedies. In G. A. Bailey, P. M. Jones, F. Mormando and T. W. Worcester (eds) *Hope and Healing. Painting in Italy in a Time of Plague, 1500–1800* 45–64. Chicago: University of Chicago Press.

Borgia, F. (1964) In C. de Dalmases (ed.) *Tratados espirituales*. Barcelona: Juan Flors.

Bynum, C. W. (1987) *Holy Feast and Holy Fast. The Religious Significance of Food to Medieval Women.* Berkeley, CA: University of California Press.

Bynum, C. W. (1991) *Fragmentation and Redemption. Essays on Gender and the Human Body in Medieval Religion.* New York: Zone Books.

Campbell, J. (2017) *At the First Table: Food and Social Identity in Early Modern Spain.* Lincoln: University of Nebraska Press. https://doi.org/10.2307/j.ctt1hhfnq1

Ceparius, V. (1627) *The Life of B. Aloysius Gonzaga of the Society of Jesus … Written in Latin by the R. Fa. Virgilius Ceparius of the same Society and translated into English by R. S.* Paris: n. a.

Ezmar, C. (2015) Lágrimas de Santa Teresa. *Revista de espiritualidad* 74: 513–54.

Frank, G. K., Shott, M. E., Hagman, J. O. and Mittal, V. A. (2013) Alterations in brain structures related to taste reward circuitry in ill and recovered anorexia nervosa and in bulimia nervosa. *American Journal of Psychiatry* 170(10): 1152–60. https://doi.org/10.1176/appi.ajp.2013.12101294

García Maestro, J. P. (2009) San Simón de Rojas (1552–1624). Un místico de ojos abiertos para los pobres de ayer y de hoy. *Corintios* 13(131): 264–80.

Gentilcore, D. (2015) *Food and Health in Early Modern Europe: Diet, Medicine and Society, 1450–1800.* London: Bloomsbury Publishing. https://doi.org/10.5040/9781474219563

Goodich, M. (1981) The contours of female piety in later medieval hagiography. *Church History* 50(1): 20–32. https://doi.org/10.2307/3166477

Gonzaga, L. (1949) In P. B. Boz (ed.) *Lettere e opere spirituali di San Luigi Gonzaga.* Rome: Editrice A. V. E.

Granada, L. de. (1988) Escritos devocionales. In M. P. A. Ansa (ed.) *Confesión de un pecador delante de Jesucristo … compuesta por el Doctor Constantino. Añádese aquí dos meditaciones para antes y después de la sagrada comunión, compuestas por el padre Fray Luis de Granada* 109–24. Madrid: Universidad Pontificia de Salamanca, Fundación Universitaria Española.

Griffin, J. and Berry, E. M. (2003) A modern day holy anorexia? Religious language in advertising and anorexia nervosa in the West. *European Journal of Clinical Nutrition* 57: 43–51. https://doi.org/10.1038/sj.ejcn.1601511

Guerrero, F. (1982) Introducción. In F. Guerrero (ed.) *El Tesoro de medicinas de Gregorio López, 1542–1596* 141–66. Madrid: Cultura Hispánica del Instituto de Cooperación Iberoamericana.

Hoffman, M. K. (2011) *Raised to Rule: Educating Royalty at the Court of the Spanish Hapsburgs.* Baton Rouge: Louisiana State University Press.

Ignatius of Loyola (1951) Penance. In *The Spiritual Exercises* (trans. L. J. Puhl). Chicago: Newman Press. http://spex.ignatianspirituality.com/SpiritualExercises/Puhl#c05-1234

Ignatius of Loyola (1959) Letter to Francis Borgia. In W. J. Young (ed.) *Letters of St Ignatius of Loyola.* Chicago: Loyola University Press.

Ignatius of Loyola (2006) To Francis Borgia, by commission, Rome, September 20, 1548. In J. W. Padberg and J. L. McCarthy (eds) *Ignatius of Loyola, Letters and Instructions* 253–6. St Louis, MO: Institute of Jesuit Sources.

Juan de Ávila (1970). In L. S. Balust and F. M. Hernández (eds) *Obras completas, Volume 5, Epistolario*. Madrid: BAC.

Keitt, A. (2005) The miraculous body of evidence: visionary experience, medical discourse, and the Inquisition in seventeenth-century Spain. *Sixteenth Century Journal* 36(1): 77–96.

Leclercq, H. (1910) Host. In *The Catholic Encyclopedia, Volume 7*. New York: Robert Appleton Company. http//www.newadvent.org/cathen/07489d.htm

López, G. (1982) In F. Guerrero (ed.) *El Tesoro de medicinas de Gregorio López, 1542–1596*. Madrid: Cultura Hispánica del Instituto de Cooperación Iberoamericana.

Losa, F. (1613) *Vida que el siervo de Dios Gregorio López hizo en algunos lugares de la Nueva España … por el licenciado Francisco Losa, presbérito*. Mexico: Imprenta de Juan Ruiz.

Luis de Granada. (1988) Escritos devocionales. In M. P. A. Ansa (ed.) *Confesión de un pecador delante de Jesucristo, redentor y juez de los hombres compuesta por el Doctor Constantino. Añádese aquí dos meditaciones para antes y después de la sagrada comunión, compuestas por el padre Fray Luis de Granada* 109–24. Madrid: Universidad Pontificia de Salamanca, Fundación Universitaria Española.

Manzano, F. (1653) *Centellas de amor de Dios y su madre que sin poderse contener despidió el encendido y abrasado corazón del muy venerable padre y reverendísimo maestro Fr. Simón de Rojas*. Madrid: Domingo García y Morràs.

Meissner, W. W. (1992) *Ignatius of Loyola. The Psychology of a Saint*. New Haven: Yale University Press.

Mormando, F. (2005) Introduction. Response to the plague in early modern Italy: what the primary sources, printed and painted, reveal. In G. A. Bailey, P. M. Jones, F. Mormando and T. W. Worcester (eds) *Hope and Healing. Painting in Italy in a Time of Plague, 1500–1800* 1–44. Chicago: University of Chicago Press.

Muñoz, L. (1964 [1635]) *Vida y virtudes del venerable varón … Juan de Ávila*. Barcelona: Juan Flors.

Nadeau, C. A. (2018) Treating sensory ailments in early modern domestic literature. In R. D. Giles and S. Wagschal (eds) *Beyond Sight: Engaging the Senses in Iberian Literatures and Cultures, 1200–1750* 141–66. Toronto: University of Toronto Press. https://doi.org/10.3138/9781487510039-010

Pérez Morera, J. (2005) La república del claustro. Jerarquía y estratos sociales en los conventos femeninos. *Anuario de estudios atlánticos* 51: 327–89.

Poutrin, I. (1995) *La voile et la plume. Autobiographie et sainteté féminine dans l'Espagne moderne*. Madrid: Casa de Velázquez.

Rhodes, E. (1990) Spain's misfired canon: the case of Fray Luis de Granada's Libro de la oración. *Journal of Hispanic Philology* 15: 3–28.

Rhodes, E. (2009) Mysticism in history: the case of Spain's Golden Age. In A. Weber (ed.) *Approaches to Teaching Teresa of Ávila and the Spanish Mystics* 47–56. New York: Modern Language Association of America.

Rivadeneira, P. de (1624) *Vida del bienaventurado Luis Gonzaga, de la Compañía de Jesús. Segunda parte del Flos Sanctorum … 586–613*. Madrid: Luis Sánchez.

Rivadeneira, P. de (1945) Vida del bienaventurado padre San Ignacio de Loyola. In E. Rey (ed.) *Historias de la contrarreforma* 1–429. Madrid: Editorial Católica Sáez.

Rivadeneira, P. de (2009) In M. L. Sebastià (ed.) *Confesiones. Autobiografía documentada*. Bilbao: Ed Mensajero; Sal Terrae.

Roldán-Figueroa, R. (2010) *The Ascetic Spirituality of Juan de Ávila (1499–1569)*. Leiden: Brill. https://doi.org/10.1163/ej.9789004192041.i-266

Savin-Williams, R. C. (2016) Sexual orientation: categories or continuum? Commentary on Bailey *et al.* (2016). *Psychological Science in the Public Interest* 17(2): 37–44. https://doi.org/10.1177/1529100616637618

Serrano Larráyoz, F. (2008) Confitería y cocino conventual navarra del siglo XVIII. Notas y precisiones sobre el 'Recetario de Marcilla' y el Cocinero religioso de Antonio Salsete. *Príncipe de Viana* 69(243): 141–86.

Simón de Rojas (1983 [1939]) *Tratado de la oración y sus grandezas*. Madrid: Postulación del Beato Simón de Rojas.

Tanner, M. (1993) The Hapsburg cult of the Eucharist. In *The Last Descendent of Aeneas. The Hapsburgs and the Mythic Image of the Emperor* 207–22. New Haven: Yale University Press.

Vázquez, D. (2011) In S. la Parra López (ed.) *Historia de la vida del P. Francisco de Borja*. Gandía: CEIC Alfons el Vell de Gandía.

Velasco, Fr. J. de (1992) *Vida, virtudes y muerte del venerable varón Francisco de Yepes*. Valladolid: Junta de Castilla y León.

Wandel, L. P. (2006) The Catholic Eucharist. In *The Eucharist in the Reformation: Incarnation and Liturgy* 208–60. Cambridge: Cambridge University Press.

Webb, G. and Walker, A. (1960) *St Bernard of Clairvaux: The Story of His Life as Recorded in the Vita Prima Bernardi*. Westminster MD: Newman Press.

Wilson, C. (2009) Where's Teresa? The construction of Teresa of Ávila in the visual arts. In A. Weber (ed.) *Approaches to Teaching Teresa of Ávila and the Spanish Mystics* 190–201. New York: Modern Language Association of America.

Part II
LGBTQ+ bodies

3 Harvey Milk's (sexual and sacred) body

William K. Gilders

Abstract

Harvey Milk has been constituted as a queer saint. This article, in the self-identifying voice of a gay man, explores the significance of Harvey Milk's queer cultural sanctity in relation to his sexual embodiment, emphasizing that 'Saint Harvey' was a leading figure in a movement of sexual liberation and was himself a strongly sexual being, facts sometimes downplayed in his representation as a sacred figure in contrast with his vitally sexual pre-assassination body. Examining the phenomenon of the 'canonization' of a sexually embodied gay Jewish agnostic, the article asks what happens when Milk's sacralization is explicitly tied to his sexuality, focusing on a central question: can a saint be a sexual being, not peripherally or incidentally, but centrally and essentially?

Keywords: queer; sexuality; martyr; saint; sanctity; icon

Introduction

Harvey Bernard Milk was assassinated in San Francisco City Hall on Monday, November 27, 1978. A member of the Board of Supervisors (San Francisco's combined county and city council), Milk was the first openly gay man to win public office in San Francisco and in the entire state of California. Along with Mayor George Moscone, he was shot by Daniel White, a former member of the Board of Supervisors, for reasons that remain a matter of controversy (Eyerman 2012:402–3, 405). On Tuesday, November 27, 2018, I participated in a rally and march in San Francisco held in recognition of the fortieth anniversary of the assassinations of Moscone and Milk, within which the commemoration of Milk was given primary emphasis.[1] At the rally prior to the march, I met and spoke with an Episcopal Church deacon, who was carrying a Byzantine-style icon created by Robert Lentz in 1987, which represents Milk as a saint.[2] I was familiar with this image, having a copy printed on a card a friend sent me from San Francisco in 1990. This icon was utilized in the brochure for a 2003 exhibition about Milk organized by the San Francisco Gay, Lesbian, Bisexual, and Transgender (GLBT) Historical Society: 'Saint Harvey: The Life and Afterlife of a Modern Gay Martyr.' Lentz's icon is one of at least four images of which I am aware that explicitly represent Milk as a saint by deploying such traditional iconographic elements as the halo or nimbus.[3]

Harvey Milk is a queer saint – in two senses of the word 'queer.' First, he is a gay ('queer') man venerated by queer people within queer cultural contexts.[4] Second, he is an individual identified as a 'saint,' whose identity stands in various ways outside the traditional and conventional norms of religious cultural sanctity, as a dictionary definition of 'queer' has it: 'differing in some odd way from what is usual or normal' (Merriam-Webster n. d.). Milk was a gay Jewish agnostic, an activist in a movement for the rights and freedom of sexual minority communities that were in his lifetime, and have remained, under intense pressure from conservative religious activists. Nevertheless, Milk has been named, represented, and ritualized as a sacred figure through the creative deployment of conventionally religious cultural forms (almost entirely Christian in origin) in a variety of queer cultural contexts.[5] Taking this queer canonization as a starting point, this article explores the complex relationship between Saint Harvey Milk's queer sanctity and his queer sexuality, focusing on his embodied identity.

This study is presented in the self-identifying voice of a gay man and makes no pretense of being purely descriptive. In agreement with many other queer scholars, I take a queerly normative, but critically disciplined, stance in relation to the subject matter treated here.[6] This approach emerged from reflection on my own multivalently queer relationship to Harvey Milk, stimulated by an encounter with images of Milk while I was working in the archives of the San Francisco GLBT Historical Society on research for the larger project to which the present article is related. In May 2018, I was examining the contents of a box of miscellaneous items, with a particular interest in publicity posters from past November 27 commemorations.[7] Along with these posters, the box contained a large-size copy of the Lentz icon, which I briefly examined and set aside, noting that it must have been in the possession of Milk's former lover, Scott Smith, who had preserved the materials now in this archival collection. Then, as I dug deeper into the box, I came upon a small collection of old photographs of Harvey Milk from his time as a young naval officer (c. 1951–5). Several of these pictures showed Milk posing in a swimsuit, displaying a lean, muscular body. The Harvey Milk in these pictures was, I knew, a sexually active gay man. He had been sexually active, in fact, since the age of fourteen (Faderman 2018:21; Shilts 1982:6–7). Looking at the pictures, I took note of their evident erotic invitation; this was a man who wanted to be looked at with desire by other men, and I gave him the gaze he had invited. 'Not bad at all,' I thought. Then, disciplined scholar that I am, I recorded my own gaze as part of my data-gathering and reflected on the archival juxtaposition of beefcake images of Harvey Milk with his representation according to the conventions of Byzantine Christian iconography, in which he appeared like any other chaste holy figure. Saint Harvey had been sexy. From this raw initial observation has developed my inquiry into the relationship between sexuality and sanctity, between Harvey Milk's sexual body and his sacred body.

The body of a martyr

A martyr bears witness to the great value of an ideal or a cause by giving up their bodily life for it. But their bodily death is not the end of their life; the martyr lives on. The phenomenon of martyrdom is, of course, broader than categories of conventional religion. Indeed, it could be argued that martyrs for 'secular' causes are more self-sacrificial than 'religious' martyrs, because they may well die without any conviction of a metaphysical reward for their suffering, without clear hope for a conscious life-after-death. Such a martyr was the non-religious, culturally Jewish Harvey Milk, who nevertheless strongly anticipated his own death and prepared for it. In each of three versions of a political testament Milk recorded onto cassette tapes on November 18, 1977, shortly after his election, he referred to the possibility of his assassination, but only in the recording left with his friend and speech-writer, Frank Robinson, did he speak the now widely quoted words, 'If a bullet should enter my brain, let that bullet destroy every closet door' (Shilts 1982:372). With this declaration, Milk assigned significance to his anticipated death and invited others to do the same. In addition to the recorded wills, Milk left behind a poem, which Anne Kronenberg, his campaign manager and aide (and potential successor), read at his memorial service on November 30, 1978 (Shilts 1982:287):

> I can be killed with ease
> I can be cut right down
> But I cannot fall back into my closet
> I have grown
> I am not by myself

I am too many
I am all of us.

On November 27, 1978, Milk was in his office in San Francisco City Hall when Dan White arrived and asked to speak with him in the office that he, White, had vacated upon his resignation from the Board of Supervisors. Once they were in the office, White, a former police officer, produced his service revolver, loaded with hollow point bullets, five of which he fired into Harvey Milk's body. The last of those five explosive bullets was delivered at close range to the back of Milk's head, into his brain – making Milk's memorable words seem like a prophecy, with the violent fulfillment of its protasis requiring the realization of its apodosis. Harvey's nephew, Stuart Milk, a teenager at the time of his uncle's death and now the president of the Harvey Milk Foundation, has in fact applied the word 'prophecy' to his revered uncle's words in Facebook posts on the anniversary of his death (Milk, 2016).

Cleve Jones, who was twenty-four at the time and serving as one of Milk's City Hall aides, described arriving at City Hall while Milk's body was still in Dan White's office and catching sight of his mentor's feet through the open doorway. Jones recalled the thoughts that filled his mind in the hours that followed that encounter with Milk's dead body: 'The only thing I can think is that it is over. It is all over. He was my mentor and friend and he is gone. He was our leader and he is gone. It is over.' During the candlelight march and the vigil at City Hall, Jones continued to think, 'And now it was all over.' But Jones corrected his original thoughts, from his present vantage point: 'I was wrong. It wasn't over. It was just beginning' (Jones 2016:162–3).

In the hours, days, weeks, and months that followed Milk's death – leading up to the jury verdict in White's trial of mere voluntary manslaughter for his assassination of both Harvey Milk and George Moscone – the conviction solidified among Milk's friends and supporters that he could be rendered immortal through their work of memory, a conviction that found expression in a slogan: 'Harvey Milk Lives!' That slogan was shouted during the rioting at City Hall that followed the verdict in White's trial, although it was met with derision by some in the seething mob (Shilts 1982:330).[8] The morning after that so-called White Night Riot, it was found spray painted on a wall in Milk's Castro Street neighborhood, the graffito preserved in a photograph taken by Daniel Nicoletta, another of Milk's young disciples (Nourmand 2017:74–5). A year after Milk's death, a march from the Castro neighborhood to City Hall took place in re-enactment of the march on the night of November 27, 1978. In this march, a banner was carried, which Cleve Jones had painted, bearing the words, 'GAY LOVE IS GAY POWER – HARVEY MILK LIVES' (Cleve

Jones, interview with author, November 28, 2018).⁹ In a speech delivered at City Hall at the end of the march, Jones declared, 'We are here tonight to dedicate ourselves to the legend of Harvey Milk, that word of his dream and his struggle may spread across this and all nations … We are here to spread the word, so that our sisters and brothers everywhere may know of the life and death of Harvey Milk.' Jones then affirmed that Milk was a martyr, but 'not our first martyr, nor our last' (Jones 2016:184).

The body of a saint?

Harvey Milk indeed became a 'nationally known martyr for the gay rights movement,' who survived his bodily death through the agency of those who performed the work of generating, sustaining, and propagating his memory, 'agents of memory' (Krutzsch 2019:17; Vinitzky-Seroussi 2009:7–8). Many of those agents of memory, who knew and worked with Milk, firmly asserted that Milk's identity as a martyr did not make him a 'saint.' In the speech he delivered at the march on the first anniversary of Milk's death, Jones referred to him as 'the man who was neither genius nor saint,' and he repeated this judgment to me when I interviewed him (Jones 2016:184; interview with author, October 8, 2018). Likewise, Harry Britt, who was appointed to replace Milk on the Board of Supervisors, stated, 'He was no saint' (Harry Britt, interview with author, May 22, 2018).¹⁰ Whereas these agents of memory have vigorously rejected the identification of Milk as a saint, insisting quite correctly that 'martyr' and 'saint' are not identical identity categories, many LGBTQ+ Christians have followed their tradition's norms of equating the categories, have warmly embraced the iconic signification of Lentz's image of Milk, and have treated him as a saint of the Christian canon. For example, the Episcopalian deacon's mode of carrying the icon during both the 2018 and the 2019 assassination memorials, cradled in her arms and illuminated with a candle, corresponded closely with the standard ritualization of icons in Byzantine Christianity (Figure 3.1). There have even been instances of Milk's intercessions being invoked using the common Catholic formula of prayer to a saint, such as in Facebook and Twitter posts on November 27, 2018 by 'Out at St Paul,' the Lesbian, Gay, Bisexual and Transgender ministry at New York City's Roman Catholic Church of St Paul the Apostle: 'Harvey Milk, pray for us' (Facebook, Out at St Paul, November 27, 2018; @outatstpaul, November 27, 2018). Similarly, Kittredge Cherry, a minister in the Metropolitan Community Church, composed a 'Litany of Queer Saints,' which included the following petition:

Figure 3.1: Deacon Diana Wheeler holding an icon of Harvey Milk, November 27, 2019, San Francisco. Photograph by the author.

> Saint Harvey Milk, martyred gay rights pioneer, pray for us. We have a long way yet to go. Thank you, Holy Harvey, for having stood with the wounded and oppressed in the LBGTQI communities and now inspire all to work for justice as you did. Harvey Milk, such a beautiful soul, shine on always (Cherry 2021a).

This petition linked to Cherry's frequently updated essay about Milk in her *QSpirit* website, a rich source for information on the various ways in which Milk has been described, represented, and ritualized as a saint, as well as on contestations of that identification (Cherry 2021b).

Representing a perspective outside of Christianity, but linked to it in complex ways, Grand Mother Vish-Knew (formerly, Sister Vicious Power Hungry Bitch; Kenneth Bunch), co-founder of the Sisters of Perpetual Indulgence, enthusiastically affirmed to me that Milk is a saint in the same way that the Sisters of Perpetual Indulgence are nuns: 'We're twenty-first century nuns … Yeah, we're nuns. We're just *different nuns* … So, you can be a *different* saint. Different cardinal, different pope' (Grand Mother Vish-Knew, interview with author, October 6, 2018).[11] As Melissa M. Wilcox emphasized, the Sisters of Perpetual Indulgence do genuinely see themselves as nuns, quoting Sister Saviour Applause of the Russian River Sisters, who referred to the Sisters as 'fuckin' modern-day badass drag queen superhero nuns!' (Wilcox 2018:1). Likewise, for many LGBTQ people, Harvey Milk really is a saint – a fuckin' modern-day badass superhero saint, for the simple reason that he has been made one through the cultural production of some of his agents of memory. Without ignoring the denials of Milk's sainthood voiced by some of his most influential agents of memory, I take seriously his cultural canonization and seek to understand its relationship to his sexual embodiment, and to that of many of his admirers and devotees. Milk has been given a sacred body through the deployment of religious cultural forms in his memorialization.

Milk is a saint whose sexuality is not incidental to his identity, but rather essential and integral. His significance for LGBTQ people lies precisely in his having been an assertively 'out' gay man, who won a political office that he used to advance the wellbeing of other 'gay' people.[12] Milk would otherwise have no significance except as an assassinated city politician, whose memory would then probably be less significant than George Moscone's (Eyerman 2012:400). The case of Father Mychal Judge, the New York City Fire Department chaplain, who died on September 11, 2001, affords an illuminating comparison. While Judge's identity as a gay man is important for LGBTQ people, who find in him a heroic gay 9/11 martyr, Judge's sexuality can be treated as incidental to the context in which he served and gave his life (Cherry 2021b; Daly 2008). Judge could very well achieve official canonization by the Catholic Church, in spite rather than because of his homosexuality. Harvey Milk, in contrast, has achieved queer canonization precisely because of his queer identity.

The relics of a saint

The 2003 GLBT Historical Society 'Saint Harvey' exhibit had as its central element a display of the clothing Milk was wearing on the day of his death. Jordy Jones offered a sophisticated meditation on the ways in which Milk's displayed suit evoked both presence and absence. The suit was empty of Milk's substantial body. Yet it was displayed in a form that reflected how it appeared when worn on the body. Furthermore, the evident traces of Milk's blood on the clothing bore witness to the brutal fact that he had been wearing them when his body was penetrated by hollow point shells (Jones 2011). Lillian Faderman characterized the 2003 identification of Milk as 'Saint Harvey' as 'tongue in cheek' (Faderman 2018:229). However, the transgender historian Susan Stryker, who curated the exhibit, insisted that her intention was quite earnest – to make use of religious cultural forms to express the status accorded to Milk by LGBTQ people. Most strikingly, she displayed Milk's clothing in a cruciform arrangement, identifying Milk with Christianity's suffering savior and paradigmatic martyr. In her curatorial statement, Stryker was candid about the fact that her initial intention had been to honor Milk through parodic, 'camp' deployment of religious forms, something she believed he would have appreciated, given his known proclivities for self-deprecating humor and clowning. However, she insisted that working with Milk's personal effects profoundly changed her sense of what she was doing. I quote from the statement (a copy of which she shared with me):

> When it fell to me to curate the opening exhibit for our new gallery ... I knew the time had come to build my campy tribute to 'Saint Harvey.' But an unexpected thing happened on my way to camp. Working alone in the office late one night, unpacking box after box in search of suitable Milk memorabilia for this show, I came across the bag of Milk's personal effects sent back from the coroner's office to his survivors. There were the clothes, bullet-riddled and blood-stained, that he wore at the time of his death. I laid out upon the floor the shoes and socks, the pants and shirt and jacket, and was struck by the palpable absence of Milk's body. I was struck by the violent power of the homophobic act that had taken that body away. I sat with those clothes for a long time that night. They possess a gravitas that makes campiness difficult.

Stryker further emphasized in her curatorial statement – and in an interview I conducted with her – that she did not impose the language and imagery of sainthood upon Milk. Rather, these elements expressed an existing cultural phenomenon, the ways in which Milk was already being represented by his admirers (Susan Stryker, interview with author, November 8, 2018). The brochure for the exhibit emphasized this fact by stating that 'his personal possessions were treated like relics of a saint, lovingly tended and occasionally displayed by a band of friends' (GLBT Historical Society 2003). With Milk's death, mementos and keepsakes became the equivalent of 'relics,' as Stryker astutely observed.

The current (as of 2021) mode of displaying Milk's clothing in the GLBT Historical Society Museum on 18th Street in San Francisco is notably different from that of the 'Saint Harvey' exhibit of 2003, and thereby effects a different experience of presence and absence. The clothing is displayed flat, only partially unfolded, as if just removed from its storage box. It is behind a mesh screen, obscured to view, except when a button is pushed that turns on a light – as well as a holographic image of Milk's face, projected onto the museum floor, and the sound of Milk's voice from his recorded political testament. Milk's disembodied voice comes to the ears, while the eyes can take in the clothing. This mode of display reminded me of what is typically encountered in museum displays devoted to the Holocaust (Shoah), where personal effects of the murdered are displayed in ways that emphasize their absence; all that remains of a little girl, for example, are her shoes, piled up with many others. The difference, of course, in the case of the Milk display, is the speaking voice, which renders the gay martyr present, addressing the listener across time, inviting them to respond by coming out and giving others hope: 'You've gotta give them hope,' Harvey says.

Icons of his body

In his art historical study of Byzantine images of the saints, Henry Maguire emphasized the Byzantine Christian conviction that the bodies of their saints 'were made visible' through artistic images (Maguire 1996:3). While the belief systems that surround the cultural uses of images of Harvey Milk are obviously different from those of Byzantine Christianity, it is nevertheless the case, on a basic level, that such images have made Harvey Milk's body visible to those who engage with them. In this section of the article, I will explore some aspects of this engagement in relation to different types of images. My concern is with images of Harvey Milk that are *iconic*, that exercise an evocative power for the viewer (Morgan 2005:130). An iconic image invites engagement, most immediately and obviously, through visual contact, the gaze, understood as a transactional experience (Morgan 2005:2–5). Some cultural contexts may permit, encourage, or even mandate physical contact, the touch of fingers or the lips to the image, for example. All such modes of engagement enact a relationship between the individual actor and the subject of the iconic image. How this relationship is understood varies across cultural contexts and from individual to individual. Individual actors may or may not consciously embrace a culturally prescribed mode of engagement. A critic of their disposition might, for example, suggest that someone is simply going through the motions without the proper mental, emotional, or spiritual disposition. Not every image of a significant or respected individual is necessarily iconic in the sense in which I am using that term. Rather, images are iconized, made to function as icons, in order to have an evocative power for the viewer, through the ways in which they are treated, as signifying or evoking consciousness of cultural meanings or generating emotional responses. 'A body becomes iconic once something is done to it' (Stapleton and Viselli 2019:36). The same, I assert, holds true for the image of a body.

The construction of Milk as an iconic martyr-saint involved the interpretation of his assassination as anti-gay (homophobic) violence. It was vital for Milk's devotees that White be understood as acting out of such an animus. An early and striking example of the canonical interpretation of Milk's death can be found in the January 1979 issue of the feminist journal, *Off Our Backs*, in which a lesbian/feminist wrote about encountering teenagers in a car in San Francisco shouting anti-gay slurs just two days after Milk's death and thinking, 'How could anybody possibly doubt that Harvey Milk was murdered because he was gay?' She concluded her short reflection as follows:

> In her heart, every woman know (*sic*) why Dan White murdered Harvey Milk and that any man could have done it. It was male normality whose finger was on that trigger; it was woman hatred that was in those bullets. And underneath that controlled, emotionless demeanor, Dan White was probably shouting, 'You fuckin' queer, you fuckin' faggot—you woman!!' (Kornegger 1979:10)

In this interpretation of Milk's assassination, he was already an icon – an evocative, signifying image – before his death. The destruction of his body was, therefore, an act of iconoclasm, the destruction of that image, precisely because of what it evoked and signified. With Milk's death, the destruction of his body, the material things that have remained as foci for devotion (beyond his physical relics, such as his clothing) are various images, which have functioned, therefore, as icons of the icon.

Iconic images of Milk appear in different forms. Lentz's creation is unambiguously 'religious' (in the conventional sense of that term), especially when the image is interpreted through the explanatory text Lentz composed, which made it clear how he wanted the image to be received:

> In this icon he holds a candle, keeping vigil himself for the oppressed of the world. He wears a black armband with a pink triangle. This was a Nazi symbol for homosexuals and represents all those who have been tortured or killed because of cultural fears regarding human sexuality. Their number continues to grow with each passing year, and the compassionate Christ continues to say, 'As long as you did it to one of the least of these, you did it to Me.' (Lentz n. d.)

For Lentz, who quoted Matthew 25:40, Milk was a religious figure, because his life and death for gay dignity served Christ, whom Lentz understood to exist in solidarity with sexual minorities rather than in condemnation and rejection.

In contrast to Lentz's unambiguously religious Byzantine Christian icon, there are iconic images of Milk that are entirely 'secular,' strictly in the sense that they lack any embellishments that reflect religious cultural forms. The best known such image is a photograph taken by Daniel Nicoletta, which was reproduced on the postage stamp issued in Milk's memory, and which served as the basis for a memorial sculpture installed in San Francisco City Hall. In this image, Milk smiles warmly at the viewer, his face suffused with confidence and a hint of mischief. His tie is askew, caught by a breeze. Milk appears as a likable and accessible figure, who invites the kind of emulation that agents of memory such as Cleve Jones and Harry Britt have encouraged.

Nicoletta, like many photographers, has been zealous in guarding his rights as the creator of the image, and expressed distress when it has been reproduced without his permission, especially in altered forms (Daniel Nicoletta, interview with author, November 24, 2018). But, given the popularity of the photograph, it is not surprising that it has been used in a variety of ways to express particular interpretations of Milk's status. For example, in a 'St. Harvey Milk' image based on Nicoletta's photograph, which was carried by a member of New York City's Judson Memorial Church in the June 30, 2019 Queer Liberation March, Milk's nimbus was creatively and non-traditionally represented with flowers, a queering, perhaps, of the old motif of the martyr's victory wreath, modeled in turn upon the laurel wreaths awarded to Greek athletes. Milk's queer sainthood was rendered unambiguous by the text accompanying the image, 'St. Harvey Milk.' Nevertheless, this icon was less overtly Christian than Lentz's creation and carried no additional guiding interpretive text.

Another photograph by Nicoletta appeared in yet another icon, this one produced by a member of the House of All Sinners and Saints congregation in Denver, Colorado, at the request of then-pastor Nadia Bolz-Weber. The artist (who preferred to be named only as 'Bill') deployed various elements of traditional Christian iconography to enhance and re-contextualize the photographic image, so that the living Milk of the photograph becomes an after-living saint. As in many traditional Orthodox and Catholic images of martyr-saints, the mode of death was evoked, in this case with the representation of five jagged bullet holes. Behind Milk, San Francisco appeared as the place of his martyrdom, but it may also have represented a place of afterlife repose – the City by the Bay as instantiation of a heavenly city? (Bolz-Weber 2015:7–8; Bill, interview with author, November 20, 2018).

Of the iconic images of Milk I have treated here, representative of the substantial body of such images that exists, only Lentz's overtly Christian icon strongly signified Milk's homosexuality. This was accomplished through two elements. Milk's identity as a gay man was symbolized by his lavender shirt and the pink triangle armband (the latter an authentic element in the representation, since Milk wore such an armband when he took part in the 1978 San Francisco Gay Freedom Day Parade). His sexuality was also specified in Lentz's commentary text. In the case of the other images, it might be conceivable that a person unfamiliar with Milk could encounter one of them and fail to grasp that it represented a gay man. In this, the constant reality of queer invisibility asserts itself. The Lentz icon, of course, avoided this to a degree by the inclusion of the symbolic pink triangle armband. But, like any symbol, this one is only effective if the viewer knows the conventional meaning of the sign. Still, even this symbolically mediated indication of Milk's homosexuality does not automatically invite a viewer to think, in any particular way, if at all, of its behavioral expressions. Viewers of the icon are left to draw their own conclusions about the particular significance of the sexual identification based on their knowledge of Milk's life derived from other sources. It is to those sources that I now briefly turn.

Harvey Milk's sexual body

In *The Mayor of Castro Street,* Randy Shilts left the reader in no doubt that Milk had a powerful sex drive, upon which he frequently acted. However, investigating Shilts' archived research materials, I found that he still somewhat softened the image of Milk's sexual vigor, leaving out, for example, the blunt declaration by one of Milk's closest friends that he 'tricked a lot.'[13] As the novelist Armistead Maupin put it, Harvey Milk was 'a bawdy and unembarrassed guy – "sex positive," as we now so tiresomely call it,' who was 'part satyr, part Catskill comic' (Maupin 2009:7). Milk's rejection of sexual exclusivity and his embrace of the 'promiscuity' that was typical of gay male life in centers such as San Francisco in the 1970s was highlighted by Brett Krutzsch in his aggressively iconoclastic treatment of Milk's commemoration as a martyr. Although Krutzsch unfortunately misconstrued some of the archival data, his overall argument about Milk's beliefs about sexuality and how he acted upon them was basically valid. Milk was not a forceful advocate of married monogamy (Krutzsch 2019:20, 32–4).[14] Krutzsch's insistence on the illegitimacy of Milk's invocation by marriage equality activists (including Milk's protégé, Cleve Jones) because of the attitudes Milk expressed in the 1970s is much less convincing. It ignored the statements and actions by which Milk affirmed deeply committed same-sex relationships and the transformative effects of the AIDS crisis, the latter especially noted by Cleve Jones (Jones 2016:247–8).[15]

Certainly reflecting the impact of the growing marriage equality movement, the 2008 feature film, *Milk* (written by Dustin Lance Black and directed by Gus Van Sant), presented a somewhat sanitized image of Milk's sexuality, but without erasing its existence.[16] Indeed, the opening scenes of the film, which introduced Milk and his great love, Scott Smith, portrayed Milk cruising the younger man at the Christopher Street subway station in New York City and ending up in bed with him. This scene, therefore, clearly established Milk's sexual identity. Later in the film, its most sexually explicit scene showed the beginning of Milk's relationship with Jack Lira, the lover he took after a bitter break-up with Smith. In this scene, Milk and Lira grappled passionately, naked on Milk's bed. The film also contextualized Milk's sexuality within the world of 1970s gay male San Francisco by portraying his young supporters engaging in casual encounters with one another, in particular in a scene showing Cleve Jones engaging in oral-genital sex with Milk's campaign advisor Dick Pabich in a back room of Milk's camera store.

Harvey Milk was a sexually active gay man who became a leading activist in the gay rights movement, one of its iconic figures. However, most iconic images of Milk invite little or no reflection on the relationship between his sexuality and his sacralized iconicity as a gay martyr. There is, however, one notable exception to this general phenomenon.

The sex part

On September 17, 1987, as part of an event titled 'A Mass-in-Protest of Papal Bigotry,' the San Francisco Sisters of Perpetual Indulgence manifested the ritualized integration of Harvey Milk's sexual and sacred body through their canonization of the gay martyr as 'Saint Harvey Milk.' The challenge of performing an intentionally 'camp' veneration of Saint Harvey was exemplified in the canonization ceremony conducted by the Sisters of Perpetual Indulgence as the centerpiece of their Mass, which they performed on the day Pope John Paul II visited San Francisco. I would evaluate the rite as a triumph of liturgical camp – precisely because it teetered, like the roller skating drag nun who took part in the ceremony, on the edge of failure. The effectiveness of the rite as queer liturgy is that it simultaneously honored Harvey Milk as a martyr and as a sexually embodied gay man.

I can discuss this fascinating ceremony only in brief, barely doing justice to it.[17] The ceremonial event (textually identified as 'liturgy') consisted of three textually marked parts. Part I centered on 'the Pope's confession,' in which Pope Impious I (played by a lover of one of the Sisters) functioned as a stand-in for Pope John Paul II and admitted his various errors in confession to the presiding Sisters. This first part culminated with the 'Presentation of Papal Gifts: Cardinal Sanctified Sin's Exotic Dance Number.' This was a strip-tease performance, in which a male dancer went from wearing a miter and red robes to a leopard print G-string – a bluntly joyful celebration of gay male gaze of desire and the erotic body in contrast to traditional Catholic teaching about sexuality as upheld by John Paul II and Cardinal Ratzinger. When I discussed the event with Grand Mother Vish-Knew, I commented that I regarded the strip-tease as 'an important part of the whole ceremony,' to which he immediately responded affirmatively: 'the sex part … adding sex!' (Grand Mother Vish-Knew, interview with the author, October 6, 2018)

Part II of the ceremony, titled 'Harvey Milk's Last Election,' the central element in the ceremony, tightly framed as it was by Parts I and III, began with the 'Unveiling of His Holy Image,' the unfurling of a large black and white image of Milk (another of Daniel Nicoletta's photographs). The image covered over the cross, inscribed with the words, '2000 Years of Oppression,' which had previously been the central visual focus of the ritual. The next element in the liturgy was announced as a 'Lesson … from the Gospel of St. Randy read by Sr. Marquessa deSade.' The reading from Randy Shilts' *The Mayor of Castro Street* consisted of two contiguous sections from the chapter about the beginning of Milk's political career. The first section ended, 'Harvey was now a politician.' In this section, Milk was quoted as explaining his decision to become a political activist: 'I've got to fight not just for me but for my lover and his next lover eventually. It's got to be better for them than it was for me.' The next section focused on a visit by Milk's old lover, Joe Campbell, who had retreated to Marin County, describing Campbell's skepticism about Milk's new political identity and sense of mission. The segment (and the reading) ended with the following:

> The only thing Harvey said that made sense to Joe was when Campbell asked Milk why he had established his store at a run-down place like Castro Street. 'I like to sit in the window and watch the cute boys walk by,' Harvey said. That sounded like the old Harvey (Shilts 1982:72–3).

Unfortunately, there is no video recording of the end of the reading, which would have preserved the congregation's reaction. However, to judge by the preserved video footage from the ceremony, there would likely have been knowing laughter. The essential point is that the reading referred to two key facts about Milk: his zeal to make things better through his political activism and his robust sexuality. This punchline to the reading indicated that, in the canonization by the Sisters of Perpetual Indulgence, Saint Harvey would not, could not, replace the sexual Harvey. Gay sexuality was not incompatible with sainthood within the culture served by the Sisters.

After the reading, the 'Pontifical Proclaimer' introduced Sr Species of Crow (also known as Fag Nun Assunta Femia) to deliver a 'Canonization Oration.' Unfortunately, this oration was 'not available at time of printing' (according to the preserved script) and is only partially preserved in video footage. However, the final words of the oration in this video footage provide a good idea of its form and content:

> We ask your blessing and the blessings of your son, our holy horned one, on these holy rituals whereby we solemnize what is in our hearts. A Jewish faggot was murdered and his memory lives on in us. We ask your blessings on the ritualization of this sainthood of one of our many, many martyrs, named and unnamed.

The video footage provides an unambiguous indication of the gathered community's response to this recitation. A group that had been playfully raucous fell absolutely silent. The only sound in addition to the drag nun's voice was the ringing of the bells on the San Francisco cable cars on Powell Street, a sound that enhanced the ritual quality of the moment, in my judgment.

Following the oration, the congregation voted affirmatively on Milk's canonization, responding to the question: 'Is or isn't he worthy of our prayers of petition and veneration?' Pope Impious I then declared Milk to be a saint. Following this proclamation, the Pontifical Proclaimer announced the 'Litany for Justice for All,' which had first been used at the commemoration of 'the First Anniversary of the Martyrdom of Harvey Milk' (in 1979) as the 'closing benediction' for that event. In this context, it was recited 'in memory of Harvey and as a prayer of empowerment and healing in these violent and troubled times.'

Part III was a 'Communion Service' in which condoms were elevated, consecrated, and distributed as 'Our Holy Savior.' Thus, Milk's canonization as a gay saint was bracketed within affirmations of male homoerotic desire and its condom-protected, health-preserving fulfillment, ritually marking him as a saint for a community defined by a vigorously affirmed sexuality in the midst of the AIDS crisis.

Conclusions

I do not regard this study as representing the conclusion of a process of research and reflection, but only as a beginning. Therefore, I will conclude it in an open-ended manner. Brett Krutzsch was correct that much of the hagiography of Milk tended to downplay and domesticate his sexuality, frequently in the service of activism for marriage equality. This tendency is not, however, an inevitability. There is another potential direction in which Milk veneration can be taken and sustained. The ritual performed by the Sisters of Perpetual Indulgence suggested a different option for the way in which Milk can be affirmed as a queer saint, emphasizing cultural agency on the part (especially, but not exclusively) of gay men. Milk, in this cultural performance, was not a saint in spite of his robustly non-monogamous sexuality and his hostility to organized religion (especially Christianity). Rather, his sainthood integrally included those elements.

The exemplarity of sainthood invites Harvey Milk's devotees to follow his example. Many agents of memory have focused on Harvey as a role model for activism. But a fuller embrace of Milk's example could involve placing activism into an integral relationship with an unapologetically joyful embrace of sexual pleasure, in line with the core principles of the Sisters of Perpetual Indulgence, which affirm 'universal joy' and reject 'stigmatic guilt.' Cleve Jones, in fact, portrayed himself as having lived according to this structure of Milk discipleship in his memoir, which deftly combined accounts of his activism with anecdotes about his romantic and sexual relationships, making it evident that *both* aspects of his experience constitute his 'life in the movement.'

No iconic image of Harvey Milk himself is explicitly sexual, inviting an erotic gaze as do the originally private and not-yet-iconized (or, perhaps just barely iconized) images of the youthful naval officer.[18] To conclude this article, as a matter for further reflection, I ask what would happen if such images were fully iconized, deployed, and displayed in ways that encouraged meaningful engagement? Could the gaze of erotic desire and the gaze of reverent admiration coexist and comingle in a hypostatic union, as they have in the cases of other iconic images in gay male culture, such as those of Hadrian's beloved Antinous and of St Sebastian?[19] My own act of making these images of Harvey Milk's body (and others like them) the focus of reflection participates in the beginning of a process of iconization. The images now signify and evoke, if nothing else, questions about their significance.

About the author

William K. Gilders is an associate professor in the Department of Religion and the Tam Institute for Jewish Studies at Emory University, Atlanta, Georgia. He works in cultural history, especially its religious dimensions, ranging geographically and chronologically from the ancient Mediterranean world to twenty-first-century North America, with special attention to collective memory and the deployment of images and constructions of the past. His research presently focuses on cultural agency and creativity in North American LGBTQ communities.

Notes

1. The very first rally and march in honor of Moscone and Milk took place during the evening of the day of their assassinations. Hastily organized, the rally and subsequent march from Harvey Milk's Castro Street neighborhood to San Francisco City Hall drew thousands of participants. This event is well documented in two biographical books about Harvey Milk (Faderman 2018:218–19; Shilts 1982:279–81) and a documentary film (Epstein and Schmiechen 1984). The march is also effectively and affectingly represented in the feature film *Milk* (2008), written by Dustin Lance Black and directed by Gus Van Sant.
2. Brother Robert Lentz currently lives as a vowed Franciscan friar in a community in Maryland: https://www.trinitystores.com/artist/br-robert-lentz-ofm. Raised in a Byzantine Catholic family and formally trained in the Byzantine iconographic tradition, he was living as a layperson in San Francisco at the time when he created the Milk icon. The icon can be found on the website of Trinity Stores, which is the sole authorized distributor of Lentz's large body of iconographic work: https://www.trinitystores.com/artwork/harvey-milk-san-francisco
3. In addition to Milk's representation as a saint primarily on the basis of Christian iconography, he has also been portrayed as a sacred figure, drawing on elements of Asian (Hindu and Buddhist) iconography, by the American gay artist Carl Grauer, in his series, 'The Lavender Temple of Their Most Fabulous': https://www.carlgrauer.com/the-lavender-temple-test
4. I employ 'queer' in a common but not uncontested sense as encompassing 'all sexualities that are not hetero-normative' (Cregan 2012:152–3). I am sensitive

to the fact that many gay, lesbian, and bisexual people eschew the designation because of its violently pejorative origins and continued deployment as a term of abuse, rejecting the possibility of its reclamation and rehabilitation. I also recognize that many transgender individuals understand 'queer' to refer to sexuality rather than to gender identity and, therefore, not to include them.

5   It is vital to acknowledge the fraught nature of the Christian claiming and framing of Harvey Milk, a Jew. However, I believe that any critique of this cultural process and the agency of those taking part in it should build upon a clear understanding of the contextual situations and motivations of those cultural actors. Contributing to that understanding is the purpose of this article. It will, therefore, not engage with Jewish critiques of the modes of cultural canonization it explores. That will be the focus of a future study. Faderman (2018) is the essential starting point for reflection on Milk's Jewish identity and its significance.

6   For a clear and accessible basic statement on this approach, see Wilcox 2021:13–14.

7   Harvey Milk and Scott Smith Collection of Artifacts and Ephemera, 1973–1993 (#2002-43), Series 5, Posters and Ephemera, 1977–1993, Oversize Box 8.

8   Shilts refers simply to a 'well-known lesbian university professor' shouting the slogan without specifying her name. It was almost certainly the activist Sally Miller Gearhart, who had developed a close bond with Milk while working with him against 'Proposition 6' (also called the 'Briggs Initiative'), which would have led to the dismissal of openly gay and lesbian public school teachers as well as their vocal allies. I was unable to interview Gearhart to confirm this fact due to her frail health; she died on July 14, 2021 at the age of 90.

9   A photograph of the banner taken by the photographer Eli Reed can be seen in an online collection of his work: https://www.famsf.org/artworks/untitled-standing-figure-with-gay-love-is-gay-power-harvey-milk-lives-harvey-milk-candlelight-vigil-san-francisco. The photograph is misdated to 1978; Jones insisted to me that he did not create the banner until 1979.

10 Britt, an atheist who was once a Methodist minister, went on to insist that the label 'prophet' was, however, fully appropriate for Milk, likening him to Moses and other Old Testament prophets!

11 On the Sisters of Perpetual Indulgence and their relationship to Christianity (as well as other traditions), see Wilcox (2018).

12 In the 1970s, the term 'gay' was widely used as an umbrella term for both homosexual men and homosexual women, and even for those who are now referred to as transgender. I employ it here in that sense, in accordance with the usage of Milk and his contemporaries.

13 Wayne Friday, interview with Randy Shilts, August 13, 1980 (James C. Hormel LGBTQIA Center, San Francisco Public Library, Randy Shilts Collection,

Box 29, unnumbered folder, The Mayor of Castro Street. Interview Transcripts, 1974–1980).

14   Krutzsch (2019:182, n. 75) misidentified a letter from Milk to his lover, Scott Smith, as having been written by Smith to Milk, which led him to significantly misinterpret the dynamics of their relationship and Milk's role in its demise (James C. Hormel LGBTQIA Center, San Francisco Public Library, Harvey Milk–Scott Smith Collection, Box 2, Folder 18).

15   On the day he was sworn in, Milk walked from the Castro neighborhood arm in arm with his lover, Jack Lira, and when other new supervisors were introducing spouses and families, Milk said, 'It is well known that I'm a gay person, and in this state there is a law that says gay people cannot be married, but there is no law that says two human beings cannot love one another. I have a loved one.' Footage of Milk's walk with Lira and his statement inside City Hall can be found in an NBC News archival video: *Flashback: Meet San Francisco Supervisor Harvey Milk*, YouTube, November 27, 2018. https://www.youtube.com/watch?v=O9iYasWREzE

16   Concern with marriage equality was evident in Black's acceptance speech for the Best Original Screenplay award at the 2009 Oscars, which Cleve Jones quoted in full (Jones 2016:269–70). A video of the speech can be found on YouTube, posted April 18, 2014. https://www.youtube.com/watch?v=vfPXcCroPJc

17   Primary materials from the Mass-in-Protest consist of a congregational program, a full script of the ceremony, and a DVD copy of video recordings of substantial portions of the ceremony in the GLBT Historical Society Archives, San Francisco, Carol Jean Wisnieski collection of Pope John II (sic) protest materials (#2014-27). For a brief discussion of the event, see Wilcox (2018:71–3).

18   I suggest 'just barely iconized' because Lillian Faderman (2018) opted to include two of those navy photographs in her biography of Milk, and often deployed one in her public talks about her book, using them to represent Milk in his youth and making them available to a wide audience.

19   On Antinous, see, e.g., Lear (2015); on St Sebastian, see, e.g., Kaye (1996).

References

Black, D. L., and Van Sant, G. (2008) *Milk*. Focus Features.

Bolz-Weber, N. (2015) *Accidental Saints: Finding God in All the Wrong People*. New York: Convergent.

Cherry, K. (2020) Litany of queer saints. *QSpirit*. https://qspirit.net/litany-queer-saints

Cherry, K. (2021a) Harvey Milk: LGBTQ rights pioneer stood for equality. *QSpirit*. https://qspirit.net/harvey-milk-lgbtq-rights-pioneer-martyr

Cherry, K. (2021b) Mychal Judge, gay saint of 9/11 and chaplain to New York firefighters. *QSpirit*. https://qspirit.net/mychal-judge-gay-saint-of-911

Cregan, K. (2012) *Key Concepts in Body and Society*. Los Angeles: SAGE. https://doi.org/10.4135/9781473914650

Daly, M. (2008) *The Book of Mychal: The Surprising Life and Heroic Death of Mychal Judge*. New York: St Martin's Press.

Epstein, R., and Schmiechen, R. (1984) *The Times of Harvey Milk*. TC Films International.

Eyerman, R. (2012) Harvey Milk and the trauma of assassination. *Cultural Sociology* 6(4): 399–421. https://doi.org/10.1177/1749975512445429

Faderman, L. (2018) *Harvey Milk: His Lives and Death*. New Haven: Yale University Press.

Jones, C. (2016) *When We Rise: My Life in the Movement*. New York: Hachette.

Jones, J. (2011) A martyr in the archive: the life and afterlife of Harvey Milk's suit. *Somatechnics* 1(2): 372–87. https://doi.org/10.3366/soma.2011.0025

Kaye, R. A. (1996) Losing his religion: Saint Sebastian as contemporary gay martyr. In P. Horne and R. Lewis (eds) *Outlooks: Lesbian and Gay Sexualities and Visual Cultures* 86–105. New York: Routledge.

Kornegger, P. (1979) The meaning of Milk's murder for women. *Off Our Backs* 9(1): 10. https://www.jstor.org/stable/25792873

Krutzsch, B. (2019) *Dying to Be Normal: Gay Martyrs and the Transformation of American Sexual Politics*. New York: Oxford University Press. https://doi.org/10.1093/oso/9780190685218.001.0001

Lear, A. (2015) Antinous, the gay god. *The Gay & Lesbian Review Worldwide*, October 15. https://glreview.org/antinous-the-gay-god

Lentz, R. (n. d.) *Harvey Milk of San Francisco: Artwork Narrative*. Trinity Stores. https://www.trinitystores.com/artwork/harvey-milk-san-francisco

Maguire, H. (1996) *The Icons of Their Bodies: Saints and their Images in Byzantium*. Princeton: Princeton University Press.

Maupin, A. (2009) Forward. In D. L. Black (ed.) *Milk: A Pictorial History of Harvey Milk* 7–9. New York: Newmarket Press.

Merriam-Webster (n. d.) Queer. *Online Dictionary*. Accessed September 15, 2021. https://www.merriam-webster.com/dictionary/queer

Milk, S. (2016) Facebook post, November 27. https://www.facebook.com/stuart.milk/posts/10211205158873156.

Morgan, D. (2005) *The Sacred Gaze: Religious Visual Culture in Theory and Practice*. Berkeley: University of California Press. https://doi.org/10.1525/9780520938304

Nourmand, T. (ed.) (2017) *LGBT San Francisco: The Daniel Nicoletta Photographs*. London: Reel Art Press.

Out at St Paul (2018a) Facebook post, November 27. https://www.facebook.com/OutatStPaul/posts/2201544626547169

Out at St Paul (@outatstpaul) (2018b) Twitter post, November 27. https://twitter.com/outatstpaul/status/1067466464800710656

Shilts, R. (1982) *The Mayor of Castro Street: The Life and Times of Harvey Milk*. New York: St. Martin's Press.

Stapleton, R. F., and Viselli, A. (2019) Keyword: religion. In R. F. Stapleton and A. Viselli (eds) *Iconoclasm: The Breaking and Making of Images* 33–7. Montreal, Canada and Kingston, Ontario: McGill-Queens University Press. https://doi.org/10.2307/j.ctvnb7s6p

Vinitzky-Seroussi, V. (2009) *Yitzhak Rabin's Assassination and the Dilemmas of Commemoration*. Albany: SUNY Press.

Wilcox, M. M. (2018) *Queer Nuns: Religion, Activism, and Serious Parody*. New York: New York University Press.

Wilcox, M. M. (2021) *Queer Religiosities: An Introduction to Queer and Transgender Studies in Religion*. Lanham: Rowman & Littlefield.

4 Non-binary sexual and gender identities in the community: The *khunthā* as an isolated being in the mosque

Saqer A. Almarri

Abstract

The Mamlūk jurist ʿAbd al-Raḥīm al-Isnawī's legal manual on the cases involving a *khunthā* (an intersex person) was comprehensive on matters of religious practice. It allows us to understand the underlying doctrinal strategies that the jurists used in regulating the *khunthā*'s access to public life. This article attempts to examine specific strategies that al-Isnawī used in his legal manual's chapter on *ṣalāh* (ritual prayer). Through an exploration of the doctrines in the chapter affecting a *khunthā*'s comportment and location, I assess the possible consequences of such doctrines on the life of a *khunthā*. The major consequence is the *khunthā*'s social isolation in the name of accommodating them in a community's mosque by providing a specific row for them. The accommodation requires outing a *khunthā* as such within the community space, leading to further isolation, even when the *khunthā* is not a singular subject within the community.

Keywords: intersexuality; khunthā; gender variance

Introduction

In *Īḍāḥ al-Mushkil fī Aḥkām al-Khunthā al-Mushkil*, a legal manual written for judges of the Shāfiʿī school of Sunnī Islamic law, the Mamlūk jurist ʿAbd al-Raḥīm al-Isnawī (died 772 AH ~ 1370 CE) compiled a comprehensive work on what the legal expectations are for a religiously observant *khunthā* (plural *khunāthā*), who has yet to be assigned a sex. The *khunthā* is one of the many identities within a broader spectrum of sexual and gender diversity within Muslim societies. However, the *khunthā* is unique within that spectrum in being an identity described in the juridical literature of Islam, often in the context of complex problems of gendered inheritance rules. The *khunthā* may be understood (and translated) as an intersex person, with the caveat that the Islamic juridical literature often treats the *khunthā* as a complex hypothetical body for defining the boundaries between men and women within a sexual binary. The juridical literature can be read differently: it offers us an insight into how the jurists and judges of Islam and Muslim societies understood non-normative bodies, and other bodies that cannot be fitted into a sexual binary, and what effect that understanding had upon the world and the lives of people connected to those identified as *khunthā*.[1]

The manual was written during the Baḥrī Mamlūk Sultanate (1259–1382). The Mamlūks sparked fundamental changes in social and legal norms in Sunnī Islamic societies. Cairo, under the Mamlūk sultanates, became an important center for Sunnī Islam and replaced Baghdad, which had been recently sacked by the Mongols. The military caste of the Mamlūks reinstalled the Abbasid caliphate in Cairo, in order to legitimize the newly formed state, and established an alliance with the religious authorities to assist them in governing society (Hamzić 2016:109–11, 139).

These legal doctrines cover all aspects of life, both in ritual practice and social transactions, in a compilation of 208 hypothetical cases, showing how a religiously observant life is possible without knowing a *khunthā*'s sex. A majority of the solutions hedge around the simultaneous possibility of a *khunthā* being possibly male *and* possibly female. The manual, following the structure of most legal manuals of the Shāfiʿī school, contains a chapter on *ṣalāh* (ritual prayer), describing doctrines associated with the practices of *ṣalāh*, in both its solitary forms and its congregational forms, in a total of twenty-two cases. This work, like many other works of Islamic law, is an attempt to create a formal and sophisticated articulation of law, but as we will see, it fails to consider the complexities of everyday Muslim life (Hamzić 2016:122, 149). The chapter on *ṣalāh* is an excellent resource for understanding how jurists interpreted, and regulated, the relationship between the *khunthā* and the community by organizing the spaces of religious worship, which in themselves represented a microcosm of the community's wider social spaces.

The doctrines of the *Īḍāḥ* place the community's public spaces in a state of flux upon the *khunthā*'s arrival. This flux is resolved through a reorganization of the space to accommodate the *khunthā* in the community's midst, by using precautionary strategies presented by the jurists (Sanders 1991:89).[2] The chapter on *ṣalāh* addresses many different aspects of ritual prayer, while focusing on a *khunthā*'s participation in prayer congregations. In a series of hypothetical cases, the manual articulates legal doctrines that affect not only the *khunthā*, but also the entire community that a *khunthā* is a member of. The doctrines differ in form according to a person's sex within a sexual binary, and a *khunthā*, within this jurisprudence must be placed into the binary system.[3] These cases and doctrines can be read with an eye for lived and social practices; we can see how the bodies of men and women find their spaces in the social world. The *Īḍāḥ* describes the same for the body of a *khunthā*, and through it we can see how a *khunthā*'s body is placed in specified spaces, as they deal with various mundane issues of life such as the question of joining a congregation for a certain prayer, what to wear for that congregation, whether they will be accommodated in the mosque's spaces, and so on. The *Īḍāḥ* explores matters that range from the mundane (such as at what age a *khunthā* must observe prayer) and more serious matters (such as where a *khunthā* must stand for prayer).

The practices of worship in Islam

Worship in Islam is conducted in a number of forms; however, the most common institutionalized form held in mosques is *ṣalāh*, or ritual prayer. This form of worship, reiterated from Prophetic practice, is an obligatory ritual to be performed five times each day by all Muslims who have attained the age of legal responsibility. The ritual prayer is considered to be better for a Muslim when conducted communally, rather than in isolation. The communal form can be a domestic congregation; however, the main venue for communal ritual prayers is at a community's mosque. However, the mosque is not only the venue of worship, but is also a public community center, which provides a site for the gathering of a local community, along with a location for the education of local students. As an important site of public gatherings in a community, as well as the site of a prayer congregation, questions of access to the mosque become important, as this regulates access to the community at large and its affairs. These questions have been addressed primarily by scholars who have studied the status of women in Islam. The juridical debates on women's access to the mosque provide an important entry point for understanding how the *khunthā*'s access to the mosque is articulated within juridical literature. Indeed, discourses on women's access to the mosque frame and inform how the jurists deal with the *khunthā*'s access. The debate itself, at times controversial, continues into modern manifestations of Islam, particularly within diasporic Muslim communities, who are in a better position to examine the collective Muslim heritage of tradition and practice without the interference of state-appointed religious authorities.[4]

Women's access to the mosque alerts us to the question of the territoriality of Muslim sexuality, which Fatima Mernissi describes in *Beyond the Veil* (1987). She writes that Muslim sexuality is territorial, with each sex being allocated a specific space, and transgression of these boundaries endangering the social order. This leads to jurists engaging in extensive legal argumentation, in order to resolve problems that arise from organizing social spaces in such a way. Mernissi sees spatial boundaries within Islamic societies as a way to 'express the recognition of power in one part [of society] at the expense of the other.' These spatial boundaries divide the society into two 'sub-universes,' the public space of men and the domestic space of women, where men and women are in a conflictual relationship. The public/domestic divide in the *Īḍāḥ* and the conflictual relationship that arises from it places a burden of restrictions and precautions on a person against crossing such divides. An example of this is the access given to elderly women to public religious practices, and participation in public religious practices is comparable to access to participation in public social practices. We can see from the *Īḍāḥ* the attempt by a jurist to resolve the problems that arise from such spatial organization: problems including where a *khunthā* can find the space to engage in communal religious practices (Mernissi 1987:137–9).[5]

This problem of segregated spaces seems to be a later development in Islamic legal history, since the Prophet lived together with his wife in immediate proximity to the mosque in Medina. Mernissi, in a later book translated by Mary Jo Lakeland, writes that the mosque and the Prophet's dwelling were so close that they could be described as having 'spatial intimacy.' So close was his dwelling that he could simply lean in from the mosque into his wife 'Ā'ishah's doorway. This arrangement made the mosque and the Prophet's home a single unit, one where he could lead prayers from within 'Ā'ishah's apartment, as he was bedridden before his death (Mernissi 1991:111–12).

Leila Ahmed, on the other hand, offers us a substantially long history of women's participation in the affairs of Islam. She argues that this participation is not a subdued or subtle matter either; women are 'active interlocutors' in Islamic affairs just like they are in any other communal affairs. The normality of this active participation was unsuccessfully interrupted during the Caliph 'Umar's reign between 634 and 644 CE, when he attempted to restrict women from mosque attendance in Mecca (Ahmed 1992:60–1, 72).

For an understanding of the specifics of women's access to the mosque, I move on to explore three surveys of the legal doctrines affecting women and their access to communal prayers. I begin with Marion Holmes Katz's study of the debates among jurists on women's access to the mosque, then go on to examine Christopher Melchert's and Simonetta Calderini's studies of legal doctrines on prayers led by women. I then return to Paula Sanders' study of al-Sarakhsī's work on the *khunthā*, in order to see how she addressed questions of spatial organization.

Marion Katz, in *Women in the Mosque*, surveys the debates among Sunnī Muslim jurists on the extent to which women are allowed to use the mosque, along with a reconstructive history of that use across different regions, including a study of the debate on women's access to the Sacred Mosque in Mecca that was triggered by an incident in 1530 CE, when the authorities excluded women during the night and Ibn ʿAbd al-Ghaffār's unique treatise on the matter titled *Izālat al-Ghishāʾ*. The women's use of the mosque was significantly different from men's use. For example, while men gathered at the mosque for the Friday Congregations, the women of the Ḥijāz region of the Arabian Peninsula often gathered on Thursday evenings instead, and engaged in post-childbirth rituals in which men played no part (Katz 2014:7).

A significant portion of *Women in the Mosque* is dedicated to a comprehensive survey of legal manuals written by jurists from five schools of law in Sunnī Islam on access to the mosque. Katz notes that they tend to be quite repetitive in articulating doctrines over time, and indeed jurists often tend to cite previous juridical opinions within the same school of law. However, the legal doctrines do change, but in very subtle ways through terminologies and argumentation. The Shāfiʿī school is surveyed in detail, and Katz observes that there were three separate tendencies within the Shāfiʿī school. The first was the classical doctrine that could be traced to the founder of the school, which was consistently restated by many Shāfiʿī jurists, including al-Isnawī. This doctrine restricted mosque attendance by ruling that it was objectionable for young women (*al-shābbah*), but permissible for elderly women (*al-ʿajūz*). The second tendency was developed by jurists interested in Prophetic Tradition (hadith) reports, which shifted from an emphasis on age to questions of garment and comportment. The third tendency disapproved of women's attendance entirely and attempted to forbid it in various ways, including idealistic exhortations and appeals to the authority of jurists from outside of the Shāfiʿī school, including some who predated al-Shāfiʿī (Katz 2014:17, 41–71).

Christopher Melchert reflects on Sunnī and Shīʿī jurisprudence in relation to women's access to the mosque and focuses on doctrines about women's leadership of prayer congregations. He points out that some jurists of the Ḥanbalī school allowed women to lead prayer, even when leading a congregation of both men and women, although the leading occurs from the women's row (behind the rows of men). He charts how the levels of permissiveness across the schools shifted over a period of time: the Ḥanbalī school was initially the most permissive, followed by the Shāfiʿī school, but over time they all became much more restrictive. Melchert observes, most importantly, that the jurists' arguments in relation to women-led prayer were not a result of practical problems of religious observance, but rather to demonstrate their abilities to think through technicalities of law (Melchert 2006:64–8).

Simonetta Calderini surveys the early jurists whose legal opinions were not against prayers led by women. Some of these jurists were related in different ways to the early stages of the Shāfiʿī school or were themselves disciples of al-Shāfiʿī, and their opinions were based on readings of a Prophetic Tradition report describing Umm Waraqah leading a prayer congregation. The tradition report in question is subject to debate and accusations of narrative manipulation with regard to whether she led a truly mixed congregation or merely a domestic congregation with male kin, and whether that congregation was for one of the five obligatory prayers or merely a supererogatory prayer; each of these factors affect the scope of use of the tradition report. Calderini observes that this minoritarian legal position was a matter of legal methodology, rather than a matter of religious practice. Each of the jurists whose positions she examines were rejecting important elements of legal methodologies on developing doctrines, or prioritizing certain elements of them over others. Effectively, what was at stake were the specific legal hermeneutic tools used by the jurists: Abū Thawr al-Kalbī and Abū Sulaymān Dāwūd al-Ẓāhirī both rejected *raʾy* (the production of new legal doctrine by opinion) and *qiyās* (extrapolation of legal doctrines by analogy) to varying extents, while Abū Ismāʿīl al-Muzanī practiced al-Shāfiʿī's rejection of *taqlīd* (judicial conformism) (Calderini 2011:18–22).[6]

The observation of both Calderini and Melchert on the jurists' use of women's issues to demonstrate or stake out legal methodology is important for us in understanding al-Isnawī's reasons for writing the *Īḍāḥ*: it is written not as an expression of practical law, but rather as an expression of theoretical law. Katz, Calderini and Melchert each remind us that no one authority within a school of jurisprudence, including the 'founder,' is representative of the whole school. Al-Isnawī is no different in this case, in that his work is one expression of Islamic jurisprudence among many; an expression not of practice, but rather of the span of al-Isnawī's knowledge on this specific topic of jurisprudence compiled into a single volume.

Indira Falk Gesink reviews a large range of literature written by Sunnī, Shīʿī and Ibāḍī jurists. Through this comprehensive survey, Gesink outlines the dominant juridical trends where the *khunthā* can be understood as a third 'medial sex,' even when assigned a legal sex. The notion is underlined by the typical allocation of a medial spatial positioning, and unique rulings in legal matters that are not similar to either rulings for men or women. The ambiguity of the *khunthā*'s sex was productive enough for jurists to create unique rules on a wide range of legal matters (Gesink 2018).

Paula Sanders, in her foundational 1991 chapter, describes the legal doctrines regarding the *khunthā* in al-Sarakhsī's *al-Mabsūṭ* and the 'gendering' strategies that the jurists develop in order to place the *khunthā* as a social person in the world, while guarding the social order of that world. Sanders views the Islamic social world as having boundaries, where different spaces can be occupied by different categories of people depending on their location in the sexual hierarchy, where men have access to most spaces and women have their behaviors prescribed, in order to avoid creating social (if not cosmological) disorder. Sanders sees the hierarchy and boundaries preserved by the location of the *khunthā* in the Friday Congregation, where there is a middle space reserved for the *khunthā*, such that they can be the last row of men if a man, or the first row of women if a woman (Sanders 1991:75, 79–81).

The location of the *khunthā*'s body

To locate the *khunthā*'s space in the mosque and in the rest of the community, I turn to the work of two thinkers: Michel de Certeau's theoretical schema describing power in spatial organization and Kim Knott's thorough spatial approach to the study of religion.

Michel de Certeau understands *how* spaces are used rather than considering *what* spaces are being used. He does this by developing a schema of strategies and tactics to analyze the uses of space by incorporating power relationships that affects its use. Therefore, a powerful subject can be seen as engaging in strategies, whereby a place can be managed and organized, in order to prevent its misuse by others. A powerless and othered subject is forced to seek tactics and engage in them to use a space. This space, under the power of the strategists, was not made for them, and the law that governs it does not accommodate their presence (Certeau 1984:35–7). If we think of the distinction between the jurists and the *khunthā*, we can see how this distinction functions. A jurist has power to make laws, whereas a *khunthā* does not. It can be reasonably assumed that the jurists are almost always men, whose sex or social status is not subject to any doubt. This is unlike a *khunthā*, whose sex and social status is doubted constantly throughout their lives, and most especially when they move in public spaces. Upon their entrance into public spaces, the *khunthā* becomes a subject in active negotiation with the demands and expectations of their neighbors and strangers who move across the public social spheres. The jurists' legal doctrines are a part of these demands and expectations, and often find their way to enforcement, most especially in the mosque, through the other religious practitioners at the mosque. The purpose of this article is to understand the jurists' spatial strategies with respect to a *khunthā*'s place and its effects before we can venture to think of what resistance against them could possibly look like.

Kim Knott developed an analytical approach to examine how religion is expressed, constituted and experienced within space. Knott builds on Henri Lefebvre's, Doreen Massey's and Michel de Certeau's theories of space, in order to develop a method for studying religions and religious practices. The body is foundational to this approach – developed further in *The Location of Religion* – since it is through the body that space can be perceived as incorporating physical, mental and social dimensions. The body *is* the location of religion and a society's religious practices (Knott 2012:158; 2014:127–9).[7] This understanding allows us to see how different bodies are allowed into or prevented from accessing different types of spaces, and what effect that has. Knott's approach to studying religion through space considers it as having multiple properties. Among those properties are the extensibility of space, where we can examine a space in a moment in time while also being able to examine its long history. Further, a space simultaneously co-exists alongside and interconnects with other spaces. And importantly, space is filled with power, not only with the power of those wielding it actively, but also with the power of those who wield it at times passively and at times subversively.

In this sense, a mosque is not simply an isolated place in an isolated point of time and space. The mosque has behind it a long history of how Muslims came together to practice a part of their religion within a larger geography of the Muslim community. The mosque also has behind it the history of different regimes that imposed different rules and norms across history on to the people, and how they may approach such a space. Knott's approach is helpful for us to investigate how this functioned, and I use it here to examine how the jurists imagined the *khunthā*'s relationship with their immediate community. The jurists' powers are expressed across the space of the community, but most clearly in the mosque. One can then begin to speculate about the opportunities for resistance that a significantly less powerful *khunthā* can use to push back against this power (Knott 2014:26–7, 39, 127).[8] The jurists' doctrines regarding a *khunthā* give them access to the mosque while restricting their location inside the mosque. They create norms for religious practice and impose demands on the *khunthā* in return for access to the mosque's space.

These norms include restrictions on behavior, comportment and proximity to others present in the mosque, so that other worshippers' prayers are not invalidated. Compliance with these norms upon access to the mosque could, presumably, reassure the community's elite and allow the *khunthā* access to the community's affairs when conducted in the mosque and its geographical vicinity.

The restrictions on a *khunthā*'s behavior and comportment

Before a person may join the community's prayer congregation, they are expected to learn and understand the norms of behavior and comportment in such a public space. These norms are concerned with a person's age of obligation for prayer; their modesty zones and garments; and – upon entering a mosque – their use of voices.

The chapter in the *Īḍāḥ* begins with a discussion of a person reaching their age of obligation for prayer. The *Īḍāḥ* argues that the *khunthā* is probably similar to boys in their age of obligation for prayer. The underlying argument is based on the precautionary hedge against enforcing prayer on a child, or delaying disciplining the child for not observing their prayers (Almarri 2019:139–40, case 22).[9]

The age and sex hierarchy is built in such a way that the access of a *khunthā* to the mosque matches a woman's access. They are both encouraged to join domestic congregations, while being discouraged from joining a mosque congregation. A woman and a *khunthā* must be of sufficient age to join a mosque's congregation, in order to avoid 'the possibility of prohibited intermixing in isolated space' (Almarri 2019:149–50, case 34). The hierarchy of sex and age is combined in defining *which* women can attend the mosque's congregation: older women (*ʿajūz*), without detailing a specific age, are allowed to attend the mosque's congregation, if they desire it. However, younger women's (*shābbah*) attendance of the mosque's congregation is considered undesirable (*makrūh*), a legal qualification just short of complete prohibition.[10] The age distinction functions similarly for the *khunthā* as it does for women. In rendering the *khunthā*'s access to the mosque's space as undesirable, in order to protect against prohibited social intermixing, the *Īḍāḥ* inevitably leads to a form of legal isolation of the *khunthā*. This isolation leads to the gendering of social spaces: some spaces are for men, and other spaces are for women. And the jurists place a burden on a *khunthā* to move in these spaces with utmost caution due to their uncertain state, in isolation, to avoid any possibly prohibited socializing. These hierarchies are not exclusive to the *khunātha* and the women; they manifest for the men in the mosque as well, as we shall see in the section on 'The *khunthā* inside the mosque.'

Often, at the age of obligation for prayer, a person is taught about the acceptable behavior and dress for prayer. This involves learning about the modesty zone (*ʿawrah*) on a person's body. The modesty zone is a sex-specific zone on the body of a person, which must be covered for public modesty and decency. Given that the modesty zone is considered to be the minimum for public modesty decency, it is dealt with at home prior to leaving. The modesty zone during ritual prayer is the same as the modesty zone in ordinary public settings. However, the modesty zone during prayer affects the validity of one's own prayer. This allows the jurists to hold sway on defining the modesty zone. There are common agreements among jurists across the different Sunnī schools, such as the exclusion of the face of a free woman from the zone, and common disagreements, such as whether the free woman's backs of hands and soles of feet, or a man's navel and knees, constitute part of the modesty zone (Hsu 2003:403–5; 1994:19–28; Katz 2003:548–9; Tucker 2008:178–80).

The *Īḍāḥ*, in genre-typical fashion, surveys the different doctrines regarding the modesty zone. It describes how men's modesty zones differ from a free woman's, but are the same as an unfree woman's (Almarri 2019:141–2, case 25; Hsu 1994:25–6).[11] It follows by describing the *khunthā*'s modesty zone as that of the woman, including a similar distinction between free and unfree: a free *khunthā*'s modesty zone is their entire body except for their face and two hands. The case itself explores the possibility of a *khunthā* praying while covering only the area between the navel and the knees, following men's modesty zones. The jurist renders the prayer invalid, on the basis that covering the modesty zone is a condition for validity, and the *khunthā* may be a woman.[12]

The issue of garments comprises an extension of the modesty zone (Almarri 2019:142–5, 154–5, cases 26, 28, 29, 42). If a person understands the range of their modesty zone, then they understand what garments may be considered acceptable for participation in communal worship and for maintaining the validity of one's prayer. While the possibilities for garments are wide-ranging, it is possible to limit problems associated with dress as being 'underdressed,' or almost in a state of nudity, or being 'overdressed,' or wearing adornment, such as jewelery and silk. The *Īḍāḥ* does explore how a *khunthā* may possibly maintain modesty when almost nude, and it does this by prioritizing different critical parts of the modesty zone, depending on who is present in the space. While the case assumes that the *khunthā* will pray in a domestic or otherwise private space, it does not assume that the *khunthā* will be alone. The solution to the problem involves considering which of the *khunthā*'s pudenda is visible to those present in the same space. This creates motion in the body: if men are in the space, then the modesty zone covers the *khunthā*'s vulva; and if women are in the space, it covers the *khunthā*'s penis; and in the presence of other *khunāthā*, the *khunthā* is obliged to choose what must be covered. The case described is a rare, if not impossible, situation in everyday life; however, the technicalities underlying the case highlight the basic doctrine: it is essential for a *khunthā* to cover the non-common genital organ within a space. The unlikeliness of this case functions to illuminate how the jurists interpreted the potential erotic desirability of a *khunthā*'s body through the viewpoint of others present (Almarri 2019:143–5, case 29). At the other end of the garment spectrum is adornment with luxurious items such as silk and jewelery. Such adornment is understood in the *Īḍāḥ* and among jurists to be an erotic tool for a woman to wear for initiating a husband's lust, and therefore prohibited from being used by men as a form of vanity and effeminacy (*khunūthah*) (Almarri 2019:154–5, case 42).[13] Yet, despite the tendency for jurists to apply to the *khunthā* legal solutions extrapolated from the legal doctrines for women, the jurists prohibited the *khunthā* from adorning themselves with silk; however, the jurists allowed them to wear jewelery if they had worn it as a child.

While the *Īḍāḥ* matches the *khunthā*'s expected garments to be the same as women, an issue arises as to whether this could be interpreted as mimicking women by wearing garments understood to be womanly. The *Īḍāḥ* bypasses this problem by stating that the *khunthā* should not mimic women in their choice of garments. However, the *Īḍāḥ* refrains from explicitly prohibiting the *khunthā* from mimicking men. Yet, what garments can a *khunthā* be expected to wear if they are discouraged from mimicking women? The *Īḍāḥ* offers two possible solutions: first, that a *khunthā* should wear what they wish, with the requirement of sufficiently covering their modesty zone, thus allowing them the option of varying regularly between men's garments and women's garments. The second solution, preferred by the *Īḍāḥ*, is that they should choose once which garments to wear, and maintain that choice permanently (Almarri 2019:142–3, case 26). In the case of both these solutions, a form of social isolation manifests itself, through the potential suspicion and charge of mimicry of either men or women. The public's suspicion can be raised if they see a person's garment which does not necessarily match the normative gendering of garments, even if it has legal permissibility.

The *Īḍāḥ* is also concerned with regulating how the production and provision of garments for the *khunthā* is conducted. The typical hierarchy of sex is inverted from the hierarchy in the mosque's space, such that women are prioritized to produce and provide garments for the *khunthā*, followed by another *khunthā* (Almarri 2019:143, case 28). Here, again, the legal solution creates the possibility of social isolation, even from other *khunāthā* within their own community. The sociality of a *khunthā* is most at stake when others who are in similar social and legal circumstances are discouraged from socializing and providing for one another. The *Īḍāḥ* envisions a life for the *khunthā* as unshareable with others for the purpose of maintaining a religiously observant life. The jurists' vision is completely lacking in imagination regarding the possibility of a *khunthā*'s life that is not isolating. Here, one might speculate as to how a *khunthā* can resist and reject such an imposed social isolation, and one can also speculate as to how others in the community can resist the power of the jurists and religious authorities, in order to share a life with the *khunthā*.

The use of one's voice is a matter of concern in the space of the mosque (Almarri 2019:140–1, 143, 145–8, cases 23, 24, 27, 30, 32, 45). Vocalizing is an important element for prayer: the voice is used for reciting the *adhān* and *iqāmah* prior to starting the prayer, for the *takbīr* at the start and for each change of ritual posture, for reciting the Qurʾān, including a *tajwīd*-style recitation, and raising one's voice to notify the congregants of a matter of urgency or for special occasions. In most of these cases, the rules for women and *khunāthā* are largely indistinguishable; the use of their voice risks the validity of men's prayers. The doctrines allow for a woman or a *khunthā* to recite the *adhān* and *iqāmah* (the two calls for prayer) for themselves, but not for men. Even in the lengthiest case on the use of the *khunthā*'s voice, the *Īḍāḥ* argues that the doctrine should be similar to that for women: whisper the recitation in prayer in the presence of men who are not kin, but recite audibly when alone, with women or with male kin. Here, al-Isnawī differs from other jurists' opinions, each of which are listed and dismissed (Almarri 2019:145–6, case 30). However, the problem posed by the *khunthā*'s voice for the jurists points to the effect of social isolation from the community. This clearly arises not in the sharing of Qurʾānic recitation skills, but rather in the more mundane problem of alerting other worshippers of a matter of urgency in a way that does not invalidate their own or another's prayer. Here, the *Īḍāḥ* cites jurists who distinguish between men and women, where men can chant the *tasbīḥ*, a ritual statement glorifying God, and women clap, and it takes issue with this by considering clapping as unsuitable for the act of prayer, and seems to prefer that the women and *khunthā* have the choice to chant the *tasbīḥ*; however, the solution itself also risks the prayer, according to certain jurists' doctrines (Almarri 2019:147–8, case 32).

Each of the four elements described above (age, modesty, garments and voice) are related in varying degrees to acceptable behavior and comportment within a public space. Yet, for each element, the doctrines regarding the *khunthā*'s comportment lead inevitably to varying levels of social isolation.

A *khunthā*'s presence at a mosque could only be reasonably acceptable at a certain age of maturity, and before that age a *khunthā* is isolated from the mosque's community. A *khunthā*'s modesty demanded an expansive layer of garments, so that if they were in the presence of men, their isolation was marked by the garments' stark difference from those of men. Even during a *khunthā*'s presence in a religious space, the jurists of the *Īḍāḥ* did not deem it acceptable behavior for them to use their voice in worship because it would invalidate other worshippers' prayers.

The *khunthā* inside the mosque: isolated in a row

The *khunthā*'s arrival at the mosque puts the mosque's spatial organization into a state of flux. The *khunthā*'s arrival allows us to distinguish between the mosque's space and its organization before that moment and after that moment. The mosque's spatial organization is fixed and conventional before their arrival. The requirement of accommodating a *khunthā* worshipper, while maintaining the restrictions on social mixing, requires an active reorganization, in order to avoid the possibility of a woman standing next to men and a man standing next to women. This limitation and reorganization of the mosque's space, required by the jurists, enforces a certain isolation on the *khunthā* within an important communal activity. The mosque is the place in a community which primarily serves the purpose of hosting regular congregational prayer. It may at times serve other purposes, including hosting community schools, courts and other public functions. A *khunthā* who can go to the mosque to pray with the congregation is a *khunthā* who can be in public for other purposes. The obligation to participate in a congregation varies by sex: men are obliged to participate in a congregation (either through a collective duty to institute it, or as an individual duty for each man), whereas it is merely recommended for women to participate, and the *khunthā* follows the women's rule in the *Īḍāḥ*.

The *Īḍāḥ* divides congregations into three types: domestic congregations, mosque congregations and the Friday (*Jumʿah*) Congregation. The domestic congregation is reserved primarily for women, who are subject to restrictions on attending the mosque congregation. The mosque congregation, on the other hand, is an obligation for men to participate in during all five prayers throughout the day. The *khunthā* is similarly restricted under the same rule as for women, whereby they are expected to attend the domestic congregation, but are not obliged to do it (Almarri 2019:148–50, cases 33, 34). The discouraging of women from attending the mosque is due to the *Īḍāḥ*'s view that women's attendance at the mosque is a source of corruption stemming from intermixing in isolated spaces. This shows us the jurists' strategy for instituting the mosque as a space reserved only for men, by passively discouraging the presence of women in the mosque.

Another congregation usually meets at the mosque every Friday to replace the regular noon prayer. The Friday Congregation serves a special purpose and is the most crowded congregation of the week. It is a shortened version of the regular noon prayer, with two sermons given by a *khaṭīb* (the preacher), who is sometimes the same as the *imām* (the prayer leader), often requiring a quorum of forty men to validate it. The Friday Congregation, by being a special and crowded congregation, risks the intermixing of men and women if women choose to attend it, and therefore the *Īḍāḥ* recommends it only for older women. However, for the *khunthā* the problem posed by the risk of intermixing is set aside, in order to allow them to clear their conscience. This solution for the *khunthā* builds on the possibility that they may be a man and therefore have an obligation to attend the Friday Congregation (Almarri 2019:155–6, cases 33, 34). Yet, if the obligation is placed on the *khunthā* to attend the Friday Congregation, then it follows that their presence counts for the quorum of forty men. Each Friday Congregation needs a male preacher for the sermon, which must be heard by a quorum of forty men, and a male *imām* for the prayer, which comprises at least forty men. This does not seem to be the case for the *Īḍāḥ*. It argues that a quorum of forty *khunāthā* and no men for a Friday Congregation renders it not valid for the community at large. This is another example of social isolation, whereby a quorum of *khunāthā* gathered for an important regular social and religious function (to institute a Friday Congregation) is rendered irrelevant to the society they are a part of. The mosque's space does not exist without a community that gathers in it, and it co-exists with other spaces within it such as study groups, or neighboring it within a Muslim community, such as the markets, residences and other communal spaces, including the streets. A Friday Congregation instituted by *khunāthā* in a community and deemed irrelevant by the jurists suggests their power in denying communal agency to members of a community: both the power of the jurists in judging the value of spaces they are not a part of, but also the power of the seemingly powerless *khunāthā* in subverting the norms of the jurists by seceding, in order to institute their own counter-public space in the form of a quorum of *khunāthā* in a Friday Congregation.[14]

Mixed prayer congregations, in the world of the *Īḍāḥ*, are led by an *imām*, and women's congregations may be led by an *imāmah*. However, the *Īḍāḥ* also recommends that a *khunthā* should lead women in prayer and deems it better (Almarri 2019:150–1, cases 35, 36). The same does not apply for a congregation of men, on the basis of the doctrine that only men can lead men in prayer. Even in the hypothetical case of ignorance of the *imām*'s sex, the congregant's prayer is invalidated if they find out their *imām* is not a man. The underlying reasoning is that they neglected to confirm their *imām*'s sex, particularly when the *khunthā*'s status is considered to be well known within a community.

Each participant in a congregation has a location allocated for them during the worship. This spatial organization is dependent on function (as a prayer leader or a congregant), on age (adult men, then young men) and on sex (men first, followed by *khunāthā*, then women) (Almarri 2019:151–4, cases 37, 39, 41). Even those arriving late to a congregation have their space allocated. The location of the *imām* is typically in front of the first row in the case of men, whereas an *imāmah* leading women in prayer stands in the center of the first row. A *khunthā imām*'s location in leading *khunāthā* or women is the same as the case of a congregation of men – in front of the first row. This is precautionary, as the location itself avoids the possibility of a male standing in the row allocated for non-men. The first row in mixed congregations is reserved for adult men, followed by a row for boys, and a separate row for *khunāthā*, followed by a row for women. The specification of boys as separate from men (despite their being occasionally lumped together in rows) shows us the age hierarchy through separation. The age hierarchy manifests itself among women too; elderly women are permitted access to the mosque's congregation, while younger women and girls are allocated to a different congregation within a domestic congregation.

This spatial organization designed by the jurists alludes to a cosmological hierarchy, one where the *khunthā* is isolated from the rest of society. This isolation is magnified by their uniqueness within community spaces; however, in the case of a community with many *khunāthā* their location is allocated similarly, but with additional caveats. The allusions to a cosmological hierarchy come into play with respect to issues that arise when allotting a space to the *khunāthā* as a collective category, rather than to an individual *khunthā*. The question is whether the *khunāthā* should stand in a single row formation (ultimately the solution), or whether they should stand in a column formation with each individual *khunthā* standing alone. Both solutions have problems with respect to this cosmological hierarchy: a row formation risks the intermixing of men and women in a single row, resulting in their equality. This goes against the inherent sexual binary concept pushed by al-Isnawī and many jurists, which the former cites in the *Īḍāḥ*. The column formation, on the other hand, compounds the problem of intermixing with a second, more serious, problem: the possibility of a woman standing in the column in front of the men. This caused the column solution to be at far greater cosmological risk of inducing a *fāḥishah*; that is, a category for sexual sins that risk social disorder and the sinner's afterlife (Almarri 2019).[15] Each of these solutions allude to the hierarchies created by the jurists, and their preference of risks: they would rather risk the possible equality of men and women through the convergence of many uncertain *khunāthā*, than risk a woman standing in front of men during prayer. These hierarchies, and their maintenance through spatial organization, are an element of juridical patriarchal concern. The *Īḍāḥ's* concern with the problem of how the *khunāthā* should stand in congregations suggests that it is not concerned with the mundane practice of a person's presence in a communal space. The process of risk hedging that arises through the legal method of the jurists does not consider the everyday practice of a person's tendency to identify with a group, such as how men identify themselves as men, and how women identify themselves as women.

Each congregation at a mosque is a scheduled social event held at a specific time. This means that there are usually late arrivals to the congregation. Those arriving late, assumed by the *Īḍāḥ* to be men, are made complicit in the social isolation of the participating *khunthā*. If they need to establish a new row for the congregation, they must take care not to join a row of *khunāthā*. The solution is to find a different location to stand on their own, preferably in front of the row if it is possible for the man arriving late to skip the row altogether (Almarri 2019:153–4, case 41).

The *khunāthā* leaving 'one by one'

The clearest example of isolation imposed on the *khunthā* is when they participate in the congregation in numbers. The rule builds on a similar rule expected of congregant men when there are women in the congregation. Men are expected to remain seated and wait until the women have left the mosque. The extrapolated rule for the *khunāthā* is different in that it is almost *liturgical*. Men are still expected to wait, but a further detail on how the *khunāthā* may leave the mosque is given. It is liturgical because it is not a mere exiting of a class of congregants. It is formulaic and ritualized: 'to leave solitary, that is, one by one, however after the women, and before the men' (Almarri 2019:151–2, case 38). The *khunāthā* participating in the congregation form a row of their own during the prayers. The conclusion of the prayer separates this class of congregants from one another and they become separate individuals. Each of the now separate individuals is expected to leave the mosque on their own, 'one by one.' Each *khunthā* waits until the next *khunthā* has exited before initiating their own exit, counting down until there are none.

This process denies the *khunāthā* any autonomy of their own to leave the mosque in their own way, unlike women. The only element of similarity between the women and the *khunāthā* as two distinct classes is that men are required to wait until they have left the prayer space. The rule itself suggests that it was made by the jurists prior to application and without any consideration of the everyday practice of religion. An example of an everyday practice that might call this rule into question, and possibly subject it to modification, is when a worshipper stays back following the conclusion of a congregation for further worship. The power of the jurists in constructing religious norms is clearest when they construct a spatial practice that lacks any idea of what non-jurists may be doing in their everyday religious practice.

Conclusion

The mosque, as a microcosm for a Muslim community, is a looking-glass for the community's social relations. The community is obliged through the doctrines of the jurists' law to recognize a *khunthā* in their midst and accommodate them in the social world. However, this recognition displaces everyone, and isolates the *khunthā* from the rest of the community through the very process of accommodating the *khunthā*. This isolation manifests itself most clearly in their participation in prayer congregations at the community mosque.

The isolation produced by these doctrines of law does not stem from a condemnation of sexual diversity. In fact, it could be said that the *Īḍāḥ*, as a comprehensive legal manual describing the *khunthā* and their religious and social life in legal terms, is a recognition of sexual diversity in Muslim societies. Rather, the social isolation is a product of the jurists' anxieties about the unsupervised presence of non-male persons in public spaces as equals. This anxiety concerning juridical equality is what underlies the norms produced and required by the jurists.

The jurists are able to construct doctrines regarding the *khunthā*'s required comportment and location within public spaces. Their power to require an observant *khunthā* to fulfill these demands has the effect of isolating them from the society they work within. This isolation is not intended to impose a layer of abjection or monstrosity on the *khunthā*, but it is rather patterned on the similar spatial isolation impressed on women. The uniqueness of a *khunthā*'s life magnifies this isolation in many ways, most notably through the jurists' effective demand on the entire community to know a *khunthā* as *khunthā*, leading them to become a subject whose location is always known and understood by their presence in a row alone, or by their exit from the mosque alone. The attempts by the jurists to out a person as a *khunthā* and make this public knowledge among members of a community, in order to avoid transgressing the boundaries of the law, leads us to ask what a person subjected to such public, and possibly regular, outing might do in order to avoid the consequences imposed on them?

The juridical concerns of the classical jurists, as Hamzić observed, differed quite significantly from the concerns of the jurists of the Mamlūk and Ottoman states. The post-classical jurists were often in a different form of alliance with the state, serving not only as judges but also as functionaries of the state's bureaucracies. This alliance led them to return to questions, which the classical jurists left as private questions not needing detailed solutions, and articulate them further to create a jurisprudence complex enough for state-appointed judges to apply as the legal doctrine of the state (Hamzić 2016). Our Mamlūk jurist, in compiling the *Īḍāḥ*, is an example of this alliance; he has indeed constructed a comprehensive legal regime for the state-appointed judges to impose on the *khunāthā*. However, despite its comprehensiveness, as we see in the case of the *khunthā*'s access to the mosque, the legal regime overlooks the complexities of a *khunthā*'s everyday life, including its isolating consequences.

About the author

Saqer A. Almarri is a research fellow at New York University Abu Dhabi's Humanities Research Fellowship for the Study of the Arab World. They hold a Ph.D. in Translation Studies from Binghamton University–State University of New York (2019). Their research examines how Islamic jurists incorporate bodies that do not conform to the dominant sexual binary into frameworks of Islamic law, and the changes to epistemology when translating pre-modern scholarship into modern languages. Saqer's previous scholarship has appeared in academic publications such as *Women & Language* (2018) and *TSQ* (2016).

Acknowledgments

I would like to thank the late María Lugones for her support in thinking with me about the subject of this article. I would also like to thank the many participants of 'The Religious Body Imagined' symposium hosted at Elon University in 2019 for their engagement with the presentation that became this article, and most especially the symposium participants who read my paper in my place and took notes of the comments for me to use.

Notes

1. For a study of the *Īḍāḥ* and its author, see Almarri (2019), which contains a critical edition of the work along with translations of the chapter cited here. The notion of the *khunthā* has been carefully examined by multiple scholars, including Almarri (2016, 2018), Gesink (2018) and Sanders (1991). For further scholarship on sexual and gender diversity in Islam and Muslim societies, see Almarri (2018), Amer (2009), El-Rouayheb (2005), Fortier (2019), Habib (2007, 2009), Hamzić (2016), Ragab (2015) and Rowson (1991a, 1991b).
2. Sanders (1991) describes how the mere presence of the *khunthā* in a community is capable of desocializing everyone in the community.
3. For a discussion on how sex and gender and orientation are intertwined in Islamic jurisprudence, see Ali (2006:93–4). See Gesink (2018) for an alternative interpretation of the *khunthā* identity in Islamic jurisprudence.
4. On prayer and women's access to the mosque, see Ahmed (1992), Calderini (2011, 2013), Katz (2013, 2014), Mahmutćehajić (2006), Melchert (2006), Mohammed (1999), Renard (1996) and Sirry and Omar (2014). On the modern debate on women's access to the mosque and religious authority, see Elewa and Silvers (2010) and Hammer (2012).
5. Mernissi (1987) understands the public/domestic divide as a communal/conflictual division, where women are restricted to domestic spaces and are subject to enforced obeyance towards men. This understanding arises from specific contexts in mid- to late-twentieth century Morocco.
6. For a discussion on the tradition report, see Calderini (2013).
7. Knott developed this analytical method further in an extended study on the left hand as a space for religion. The specifics of this method are described in chapter 5 (2014).
8. Knott (2014) specifies the resistance that can be adopted, such as 'strategic incursions' and 'ironic collusion,' along with other approaches, all of which stem from practices in everyday life.
9. Citations for specific cases in al-Isnawi's *Īḍāḥ* follow Almarri's numbering of the cases used in their translation.

10   There are five legal qualifications in Sunnī Islamic jurisprudence, ranging from obligatory (*farḍ/wājib*) to prohibited (*ḥarām*). Refer to Schacht (1982), p. 121, for a general overview of the qualifications.

11   For a discussion on the free/unfree distinction in the modesty zone, refer to Hsu (1994), who describes the disagreements in the Shāfiʿī school about the unfree woman's modesty zone.

12   Modesty is not the only condition for valid prayer; others include observing other obligatory elements of prayer, correct time, ritual purity, and orienting the body and mind to the *qiblah*; see Katz (2013:44–74).

13   For more on *khunūthah* and the relationship connecting the *khunthā*, *mukhannath* and *khanīth*, see Almarri (2018).

14   An example, while not the subject of this article, is found in modern manifestations of Islam, where Muslim LGBTIQ and/or Muslim women communities have established resilient congregations for regular and Friday worship.

15   Almarri (2019) notes in footnote 514 that the term uses a superlative adjective form of *fāḥishah*.

References

Ahmed, L. (1992) *Women and Gender in Islam: Historical Roots of a Modern Debate*. New Haven and London: Yale University Press.

Elewa, A. and Silvers, L. (2010) 'I am one of the people': A survey and analysis of legal arguments on woman-led prayer in Islam. *Journal of Law and Religion* 26(1): 141–71. https://doi.org/10.1017/S074808140000093X

Ali, K. (2006) *Sexual Ethics and Islam: Feminist Reflections on Qur'an, Hadith, and Jurisprudence*. Oxford: Oneworld.

Almarri, S. A. (2016) 'You have made her a man among men': translating the *khuntha*'s anatomy in Fatimid jurisprudence.' *TSQ: Transgender Studies Quarterly* 3(3–4): 578–86. https://doi.org/10.1215/23289252-3545251

Almarri, S. A. (2018) Identities of a single root: the triad of the *khunthā*, *mukhannath*, and *khanīth*. *Women & Language* 41(1): 97–109.

Almarri, S. A. (2019) *The khunthā and the community: a study in the medieval Islamic understanding of the body and a critical edition of ʿAbd Al-Raḥīm Al-Isnawī's Īḍāḥ Al-Mushkil Fī Aḥkām Al-Khunthā Al-Mushkil*. PhD dissertation, Binghamton University, State University of New York.

Amer, S. (2009) Medieval Arab lesbians and lesbian-like women. *Journal of the History of Sexuality* 18(2): 215–36. https://doi.org/10.1353/sex.0.0052

Calderini, S. (2011) Contextualizing arguments about female ritual leadership (women *imāms*) in classical Islamic sources. *Comparative Islamic Studies* 5(1). https://journals.equinoxpub.com/index.php/CIS/article/view/11114

Calderini, S. (2013) Classical sources on the permissibility of female imams: an analysis of some hadiths about Umm Waraqa. In V. Klemm and N. Al-Sha'ar (eds) *Sources and Approaches across Disciplines in Near Eastern Studies* 53–69. Proceedings of the 24th Congress, L'Union Européenne des Arabisants et Islamisants, Leipzig 2008. *Orientalia Lovaniensia Analecta* 215. Leuven: Peeters Publishers.

Certeau, M. de. (1984) *The Practice of Everyday Life* (trans. S. Rendall). Berkeley: University of California Press.

El-Rouayheb, K. (2005) *Before Homosexuality in the Arab-Islamic World, 1500–1800*. Chicago: University of Chicago Press. https://doi.org/10.7208/chicago/9780226729909.001.0001

Fortier, C. (2019) Sexualities: transsexualities: Middle East, West Africa, North Africa. In S. Joseph (ed.) *Encyclopedia of Women and Islamic Cultures*. https://hal.archives-ouvertes.fr/hal-02448267

Gesink, I. F. (2018) Intersex bodies in premodern Islamic discourse: complicating the binary. *Journal of Middle East Women's Studies* 14(2): 152–73. https://doi.org/10.1215/15525864-6680205

Habib, S. (2007) *Female Homosexuality in the Middle East: Histories and Representations*. Routledge Research in Gender and Society 13. New York, NY: Routledge.

Habib, S. (2009) *Arabo-Islamic Texts on Female Homosexuality: 850–1780 A.D.* Youngstown, NY: Teneo Press.

Hammer, J. (2012) *American Muslim Women, Religious Authority, and Activism: More than a Prayer* (1st edn), Louann Atkins Temple Women & Culture Series 28. Austin, TX: University of Texas Press.

Hamzić, V. (2016) *Sexual and Gender Diversity in the Muslim World: History, Law and Vernacular Knowledge*. Library of Islamic South Asia 1. London New York: Tauris.

Hsu, S.-S. A. (1994) Dress in Islam: looking and touching in Ḥanafī fiqh. PhD thesis, University of Utah. https://search.proquest.com/docview/304141533?accountid=14168

Hsu, S.-S. A. (2003) Modesty. In J. D. McAuliffe (ed.) *Encyclopaedia of the Qurʾān* 3:403–5. Leiden: Brill.

Katz, M. H. (2003) Nudity. In J. D. McAuliffe (ed.) *Encyclopaedia of the Qurʾān* 3:548–9. Leiden: Brill.

Katz, M. H. (2013) *Prayer in Islamic Thought and Practice. Themes in Islamic History*. Cambridge and New York: Cambridge University Press. https://doi.org/10.1017/CBO9781139034333

Katz, M. H. (2014) *Women in the Mosque: A History of Legal Thought and Social Practice*. New York: Columbia University Press. https://doi.org/10.7312/katz16266

Knott, K. (2012) Spatial theory and method for the study of religion. *Temenos: Nordic Journal of Comparative Religion* 41(2). https://doi.org/10.33356/temenos.4778

Knott, K. (2014) *The Location of Religion: A Spatial Analysis*. London: Routledge. http://search.ebscohost.com/login.aspx?direct=true&scope=site&db=nlebk&AN=1052333; https://doi.org/10.4324/9781315652641

Mahmutćehajić, R. (2006) *The Mosque: The Heart of Submission* (1st edn). Abrahamic Dialogues Series, No. 3. New York: Fordham University Press. https://doi.org/10.5422/fso/9780823225842.001.0001

Melchert, C. (2006) Whether to keep women out of the mosque: a survey of medieval Islamic law. In B. Michalak-Pikulska and A. Pikulski (eds) *Authority, Privacy and Public Order in Islam* 59–69. Proceedings of the 22nd Congress, L'Union Européenne des Arabisants et Islamisants. *Orientalia Lovaniensia Analecta* 148. Leuven: Peeters Publishers.

Mernissi, F. (1987) *Beyond the Veil: Male–Female Dynamics in Modern Muslim Society* (revised edn; 1st Midland Book edn). Bloomington: Indiana University Press.

Mernissi, F. (1991) *Women and Islam: An Historical and Theological Enquiry* (trans. M. J. Lakeland). Oxford: Blackwell.

Mohammed, K. (1999) The foundation of Muslim prayer. *Medieval Encounters* 5(1): 17–28. https://doi.org/10.1163/157006799X00231

Ragab, A. (2015) One, two, or many sexes: sex differentiation in medieval Islamicate medical thought. *Journal of the History of Sexuality* 24(3): 428–54. https://doi.org/10.7560/JHS24304

Renard, J. (1996) *Seven Doors to Islam: Spirituality and the Religious Life of Muslims*. Berkeley: University of California Press.

Rowson, E. K. (1991a) The categorization of gender and sexual irregularity in medieval Arabic vice lists. In J. Epstein and K. Straub (eds) *Body Guards: The Cultural Politics of Gender Ambiguity* 50–79. London; New York: Routledge.

Rowson, E. K. (1991b) The effeminates of early Medina. *Journal of the American Oriental Society* 111(4): 671. https://doi.org/10.2307/603399

Sanders, P. (1991) Gendering the ungendered body: hermaphrodites in medieval Islamic law. In N. R. Keddie and B. Baron (eds) *Women in Middle Eastern History* 74–95. New Haven and London: Yale University Press.

Schacht, J. (1982) *An Introduction to Islamic Law*. Oxford; New York: Clarendon Press.

Sirry, M. and Omar, A. R. (2014) Muslim prayer and public spheres: an interpretation of the Qurᵃānic verse 29:45. *Interpretation: A Journal of Bible and Theology* 68(1): 39–53. https://doi.org/10.1177/0020964313508736

Tucker, J. E. (2008) *Women, Family, and Gender in Islamic Law* (1st edn). Themes in Islamic Law 3. Cambridge and New York: Cambridge University Press. https://doi.org/10.1017/CBO9780511841316

Part III
Migrating bodies

5   Lope's *El Hamete de Toledo*: The infidel's body as conquered land

Mina García

Abstract

Set in the aftermath of the 1609 expulsion of the Moriscos decreed by King Philip III of Spain (r. 1598–1621), the play *El Hamete de Toledo*, by Lope de Vega, has found a new relevance on stage and in political debates linked to the current immigration crisis. This article aims to rethink the current victimization of Muslims, as presented in the production of AlmaViva Teatro, a Spanish theater company which used the Early Modern Spanish tragedy to connect to a contemporary audience, thirsty for social justice. To this end, I will focus on the treatment of Hamete, a Moor imprisoned in Spain, and whose body becomes the symbol of the Other, to be conquered. As such, in the course of the play, his body is vilified, dehumanized, chained, and tortured. The culmination of this process coincides with the final act of surrender, the moment of his conversion, but also of the physical dismemberment of his body, a brutal ritualistic sacrifice carried out in the name of eternal salvation.

Keywords: literature; Spanish literature; early modern; immigration; Lope de Vega; body

Introduction

El Hamete de Toledo, by Lope de Vega, one of Spain's most famous playwrights, is one of those plays that has found a new relevance both on stage and in political debates. Its immediacy made AlmaViva Teatro, a Spanish theater company founded with the mission to present works around themes of social justice that can connect to a contemporary audience, choose this play as only the second title in their repertoire, and it was brought to the stage in

2010. Set in the aftermath of the expulsion of the Moriscos decreed by King Philip III of Spain in 1609, Lope's play explores the fate of those individuals who were feared for their difference, and who found themselves in the middle of nowhere, no longer welcome in the land where they came from and strangers in their new home, individuals who travelled aimlessly in the hope of taking control of their own destiny. However, they met with the fear of difference in their destinations, an irrational feeling that equated safety with their expulsion. This scenario describing the situation of Spain in the late sixteenth and seventeenth centuries is unfortunately very relevant today, in particular in the post-9/11 United States, in relation to the worldwide refugee crisis and to President Trump's travel ban directed mainly toward Islamic countries. This perceived fear of the representatives of a particular religion implicitly dictates who belongs and who doesn't to a particular system, increasingly excluding diversity and normalizing policies of discrimination on the basis of religion.

The fear of difference is not a new phenomenon, and neither are population movements. What this play does is to bring the topic of difference or immigration, as presented in AlmaViva's rendition, to the forefront of the debate, arguing that migrants are not negative in themselves, but rather that it is the treatment that these new arrivals receive which is crucial to their assimilation. As shown in Lope's play, this can result in an inescapable destiny. Violence breeds violence, and negative behavior only leads to negative outcomes, or to use Lope's words: *Los buenos con agravios se hacen malos* (2007:v. 2391) ('Good people with grievances turn bad'; author's translation).

This study is an examination of a literary work, a play by Lope de Vega probably written between 1606 and 1612, in which the treatment of the body of the Moor – the main character – becomes the principal focus of attention (Dean 2004:4). His body is presented as a space to be conquered, and his way of living, as codified in the movements of his body, the enemy to eradicate. I will present the Moor as the *Other* for the Spanish state in formation, using the wide spectrum of cultural studies and the door that they open to interdisciplinarity, to political, social, literary, historical, and religious discourse. I take literature to include any text, any cultural message whose meaning we can interpret, and, therefore, I include within texts a wide variety of cultural products as testimonies to a particular culture and time. I shall therefore analyze the play itself and the body of the Moor as cultural objects, and explore how these artifacts relate to wider structures of power.

As stated above, *El Hamete de Toledo* was probably written between 1606 and 1612, most likely in 1609; that is, just as the Edict of Expulsion was enacted and an important portion of the population was forced to leave Spain.

These were tumultuous times. In a period of just two decades, Lope de Vega had witnessed the promulgation of laws against the Morisco culture (*Pragmática*, 1567) by the previous King Philip II, the subsequent uprising and War of the Alpujarras (1568), the Battle of Lepanto (1571), and the terrible loss of the Spanish Armada, in which Lope himself participated (1588), to mention just a handful of events. All of these incidents took place during the years preceding this play, and they left a permanent imprint on the lives of the Moriscos, and on Spain's relations with North Africa. Therefore, although Hamete is not technically a Morisco (i.e. a Spanish Muslim descendant from the Moors left behind after the fall of Granada and who converted to Christianity), Lope's play deals directly with the Morisco problem in Spain, the consequence of 'more than a century of official bungling and inept social policies on the part of the Christian majority' (Case 1999:194). As a result of the Spanish Crown's discriminatory policies, Moriscos became a subclass under the Christian rulers, an oppressed minority which was suffocated until their final expulsion in 1614.

The expulsion was not necessarily a popular act, as Domínguez Ortiz and Vincent (1978) explain.

> los servicios de los moriscos eran apreciados. La hostilidad rara vez llegaba al extremo de enfrentarse con las armas en la mano. La expulsión de la minoría no era un hecho inevitable, no era una exigencia de la mayoría cristiana. Era una medida impuesta desde arriba y aceptada sin entusiasmo (1978:155).

> *The work of the Moriscos was appreciated. Hostility seldom reached the point of an open confrontation with weapons drawn. The expulsion was not inevitable. it was not a demand from the Christian majority. It was a measure imposed from above and was accepted without enthusiasm.* (author's translation)

Perhaps due to this lack of enthusiasm, Lope de Vega opted not to present the expulsion on stage, but rather to dramatize the tension of the historical moment and the internal struggle that the clash between cultures produced, even though Hamete was only a Morisco of sorts, a noble Moor from North Africa captured and enslaved, and not a natural born member of the group facing expulsion.

The first act starts by emphasizing the traditions that both Christians and Muslims share rather than pointing out the differences. This common point of departure is the celebration of the Nativity of St John the Baptist (24 June), which is venerated in both religions (sura 19:1–38 in the Qur'an) with festivities on both sides of the Mediterranean. On the Christian side, Don

Juan Castelví, of the order of San Juan, courts Doña Juana before sailing off to Malta with his fleet. This emphasis on all things 'Juan' to the point of exaggeration does not go unnoticed by his servant Beltrán, who makes a play on words around the word 'Juan' on the saint's day (Lope de Vega 2007:vv. 10–14).[1]

> Beltrán: A ser aquestos galanes
> Que han de cantar también Juanes,
> y llamarse Juan Beltrán
> y tener todos juanetes
> era linda Juanería.
>
> *Since these gallants*
> *Who are about to sing are also Juanes,*
> *to be named Juan Beltrán*
> *and have all bunions*
> *was a very cute Juanería.*

Just as Juan Castelví promises to bring Juana a Moorish slave as a gift, she is approached by Don Luis. Challenged by another suitor, Don Juan does not hesitate to kill Don Luis, the first act of senseless violence that we will witness in the play. Therefore, what started as a celebration turns violent very quickly. It is important to notice that the first act of violence we experience on stage does not come from Hamete or any of the Moors, but rather it comes from a Christian, who will soon capture Hamete and be his first role model in the Christian world. It is Hamete's first experience of the way things are dealt with in the new world he is about to enter.

Meanwhile, on the coast of Argel, Hamete admits his devotion for the saint, as he recalls a bloody encounter with Christians in the past and asserts his hate for them. Soothsayer Dalima tells Hamete about the tragic future that awaits him, but he refuses to believe it. Zaide and Hamete prepare to attack a Christian ship believed to have treasure on board. His bride Argelina accompanies him. The act ends with a battle at sea and the capture of Hamete and Argelina by Don Juan and his uncle Don Cristóbal. This concludes an act that combines peaceful celebrations and shared devotion with violence, piracy, war, and captivity.

In Act II, we see Hamete as a slave changing masters very rapidly and finally being taken to Toledo, thus separating him from his wife. During the whole journey, Hamete appears as a devout Muslim who is willing to explain his religion to whoever will listen, and thus he is portrayed as a man rooted in his beliefs and loyal to his culture.

In preparation for the wedding between Don Gaspar and Doña Leonor, a bull gets loose and Hamete stops it with his bare hands, displaying his impressive physical strength. Páez, a servant who has grown to know him, allows Hamete to handle his master's sword as his interest is peaked by Christian weaponry. Hamete, as a corsair, weapon in hand, is tempted to retaliate against his captors, but his better judgment counsels him to remain calm. However, when he witnesses the love between the couple he serves, his strength starts to crumble as he thinks of the life he could have had with Argelina, and which was stolen from him. In his sleep, he calls out for the lovers' deaths, which frightens Doña Leonor.

In the final act, Doña Leonor's fears become a reality. Hamete suffers from melancholy and finds it harder and harder to control his temper. In contrast with Hamete's increasing anger, the lovers exchange vows. Ana, a servant, thinks that Hamete may have been drinking because he is no longer acting like himself. When Hamete enters Don Gaspar's quarters, the master feels threatened and beats him. Humiliated and hopeless, Hamete begins a violent rampage, killing Ana and her father, followed by Doña Leonor and several innocent people he comes across as he flees. Several peasants finally subdue him. Hamete is brought to justice in chains, and his cruel and merciless execution is announced. He is paying for the individual murders he has committed, but he is also the catalyst for the release of all the pent-up rage against the Islamic religion. The soothsayer's premonition has been realized: gallows, fire, and chains with Hamete at the center. Just as he is about to die, a friar reminds him of St John the Baptist, whose significance in both religions has already been noted, and of the good thief on the cross who obtains Christ's mercy at the end of his life, bringing the play full circle. Hamete decides to convert to Christianity, expecting no mercy in return, and Don Gaspar becomes his godfather in baptism just before his death.

Unlike other heroes, Hamete, as portrayed in the play, is a very complex character, a man full of contrasts. On the one hand, he is the admired noble Moor, proud, eager to defend his honor, his bride and his religion, a strong warrior, knowledgeable about weapons and horses, skeptical when it comes to superstitions, and always ready for action. Hamete is thus the image of the perfect hero, as becomes obvious at the moment of his capture (Lope de Vega 2007:vv. 895–903).

Hamete: No soy tan corsario, no.
           Hamete soy.

Don Cristóbal:	¿De qué parte?
Hamete:	Galán soy de Meliona,
	de los moros Benarajes
	que de España procedieron.
Don Cristóbal:	¿Dónde ibas?
Hamete:	No a buscarte,
	aunque te halló mi desdicha.
Don Cristóbal:	En la persona y el talle
	pareces hidalgo moro.

Hamete:	*I'm not so much a corsair. I am Hamete.*
Don Cristóbal:	*Where are you from?*
Hamete:	*I am a gentleman from Meliona, of the Benarajes Moors from Spain.*
Don Cristóbal:	*Where were you going?*
Hamete:	*Not to find you, although my bad luck found you.*
Don Cristóbal:	*In personality and appearance you look like a Moorish nobleman.*
	(author's translation)

His noble ways are apparent even to the Spaniards at the moment of his capture, and so is his pride in his lineage. But Ignacio Arellano notes that Hamete does not quite fit the *maurofilia* vision of the Moor, and points out a whole new dimension of his personality that makes him unique (Arellano 2015:18). Those around him recognize his qualities and comment on them, acknowledging his value and attributing his condition as a slave to unfortunate circumstances (Lope de Vega 2007:vv. 1545–51).

Gaspar:	¿No hubo esclavo?
Laurencio:	Y el mejor
	de Berbería.
Gaspar:	No dudo
	las partes de su valor,
	escogido de tal gusto.
	¿Es hombre fuerte?
Laurencio:	Es robusto,
	trabado, moreno, bravo
	y muy galán, aunque esclavo.

Gaspar:	*Was there no slave?*
Laurencio:	*The best from Berbería.*
Gaspar:	*I don't doubt the details of his courage, chosen for this purpose. Is he strong?*

Laurencio: He is robust, muscular, dark, brave and very gallant, although a slave.
(author's translation)

As we can see, his masters are aware of his qualities and remark on his attributes extensively, appreciating his value and noting his misfortune. It is this contrast between his past and his present that make Hamete's situation harder to deal with: *Estoy triste porque vengo / de un alto a un humilde estado* ('I am sad because I have dropped from a high status to a low one'; author's translation) (vv. 1646–7).

Arellano argues that the confluence of these circumstances makes him a very different type of hero. Hamete thus achieves a dramatic individualization that goes beyond the typical portrait of the protagonist, including the very positive traits of the hero mentioned above. But some very negative traits are also mentioned: pride, greed, violence, desire for revenge, etc., which paint a portrait of the marginalized infidel that can only lead to tragedy and death (Arellano 2015:18). He is, therefore, not a typical hero, but rather an individual driven to a very cruel death by his personal greed and excessive pride, but also through the bad treatment he has suffered, not only at the hands of his master, but also as a result of the endemic conflict between two worlds at war (2015:22). Seen in this light, although he is not a typical tragic hero, Hamete is undoubtedly the owner of his own tragedy.

Hamete's unusual strength is often the focus of comments of the people around him. This strength clearly makes him different from the rest; it sets him apart and contributes to creating an image of Hamete as one who does not blend in, the foreign element, one that does not fit. Therefore, whether as the noble Moor or as the indomitable slave, Hamete is a unique individual even among captives, an exotic and valuable asset to his masters, whose differences (physical, religious, or otherwise) are emphasized every step of the way. Hamete is thus used not only as a symbol of what is different, but he also becomes the unifying principle that organizes the Christians around how much they are not like the Moor. Perceval explains it as follows: *se afirmó un tipo de morisco o de 'lo morisco', necesario para unificar y cosificar la comunidad, pudiendo así expulsarla, como un todo, del cuerpo social* ('It confirmed a type of Morisco, or rather a type of the Morisco that was needed to objectify the community, therefore allowing its expulsion as a whole, from the social body'; author's translation) (Perceval 1997:185).

As the counterpoint of the Spanish nation in formation, Hamete appears as the enemy that needs to be fought, as the representative of a community that no longer fits in the new nation-building project and who needs to be expelled for the sake of the prosperity of the plan in progress.

An important element in this process of orientalizing the Moor is his community's reliance on superstitious practices, and although Hamete himself seems to disdain these beliefs, this is how Moors are depicted in the opening scene, when soothsayer Dalima is reading their fortunes. For Pedro Ciruelo – mathematician, famous demonologist, Philip II's tutor, and author of 'A treatise reproving all superstitions and forms of witchcraft' – the belief in this kind of superstition is the ultimate criterion for deciding who should belong to or be excluded from a particular system, therefore eliminating diversity and normalizing policies of discrimination on the basis of religion. He phrased it as follows.

> Que estas hechicerías y supersticiones, se deben mucho castigar por los prelados y jueces, y echarlas de la tierra de los cristianos como cosas muy malas y ponzoñosas, y muy perjudiciales a la honra de Dios, y muy dañosas y peligrosas a las ánimas; y finalmente provocan la saña de Dios sobre las tierras y ciudades y pueblos donde consienten (Ciruelo 1977 [1551]:33).

> *These sorceries and superstitions must be severely punished by prelates and judges, and be cast off Christian lands as very evil and toxic things and very damaging to God's honor, and very harmful and dangerous for the souls; and finally, they incite God's wrath over the lands and cities and villages that allow them.* (author's translation)

Therefore, from the very first scene, the Moors are presented as the *Other* that is impossible to assimilate, as the radically different one, and thus the one that does not belong and could not ever belong. But it is important to remember Hamete's disbelief of Dalima's fortune-telling, his lack of trust in these superstitions, a factor that sets him apart from the other Moors and plants the seed of his final conversion. In a way, Hamete is different from the other Moors; however, he does not quite belong with the Christians either, although he is admired and valued by them. This peculiarity is what allows him to cross between cultures and religions, although this process is incomplete, and he ends up not fully belonging to either camp.

From this point of view, Hamete thus becomes the image of the worthy opponent, the strong Moor firmly holding to his convictions, an enemy impossible to beat or to convert. Of course, this admiration of the opponent only makes the Christian victory that much harder and more impressive, magnifying the importance of the final scene. This Moor, a representative of his community and a symbol of what Christian Spain must conquer, becomes devoid of content, of individual essence, and if he appeared at the beginning of the play as a complex character, attractive and full of contradictions, he evolves more into a vessel for what others want to see in him; less of a well-defined person and more like a caricature of himself.

As the play progresses, Hamete, once the image of the noble Moor, starts blending in with the animals on stage: *Haz cuenta que Berbería / es un caballo* ... ('Imagine that Barbary is a horse ...'; author's translation) (Lope de Vega 2007:vv. 332–3) is the first reference to this process of animalization that Hamete goes through as he loses his humanity, a connection that is reinforced multiple times. Thus, Herrera, one of his masters, is in need of a slave to take care of his horses (vv. 787–92); the Berber Coast, where Hamete is from, is admired as the place of origin of good horses (vv. 1231–5); Hamete is what Don Gaspar brings home instead of horses (vv. 2096–2101), and he shares the barn at night with the horses as he tends to them. It seems clear that Hamete is progressively losing his own individuality to become one of his master's animals, increasingly losing the attributes that make him human.

In this process, Hamete is applauded for controlling with his bare hands an out-of-control bull, brought to celebrate Gaspar and Leonor's wedding. This bull, feared by everybody on stage and running around aimlessly, is the direct antecedent of Hamete's violent rampage in Act III, where the Moor is presented as another out-of-control creature, which is finally tied down by chains and restrained like a violent animal. So, if Hamete was once capable of killing lions in Africa, as he brags in Act II, by the end of the play he himself will become the wild animal that must be put to death (vv. 1176–83).

This idea is especially well conveyed in AlmaViva's production (Lope de Vega 2010), where the stage is covered in sand and simulates the bullfighting ring prepared for the wedding celebration. But once again, as in Act I on St John's day, the festivities end in violence, developing a parallel structure. From the beach where Hamete was first captured, to the sand of the bullring's defeat and torture, AlmaViva Teatro has understood the development of Hamete's character as a ritual with a sacrifice at the end to seal the transformation from noble human to wild beast, arriving at a place of complete loss of his humanity. This dramatic apprehension is shown in the image from the 2010 AlmaViva production (Figure 5.1).

This Moor who has lost his humanity along the way is trapped like an animal and chained like a beast. In this sense, the stage acts as a catalyst and amplifies the fear of this perceived threat, making it cruel, violent, and diabolical. As a matter of fact, the emphasis on the violence that he displays during his maddening rampage is so excessive and so unfocused that Hamete becomes a ridiculed *Other*, a figure so far removed from the people around him who is now impossible to relate to, or to think that there was ever a possibility of admiring this individual. He has become completely empty of content, of

Figure 5.1: Photo courtesy of AlmaViva Teatro.

values; he is now nothing more than the representation of the excess that the new state in formation needs to purge, in order to move along. Only when the character of the Moor is taken to the extreme and the minority element is presented on stage as a distorted group, does redemption become a possibility.

There are multiple speculations about what caused this extreme change in Hamete, and multiple too are the hints that are scattered all over the play. We are witness to a blow to the head in Act II so severe that it made him lose consciousness and could be to blame for his recent change in character (Lope de Vega 2007:vv. 1619–24).

> Hamete: Heridas son que en Orán
> de cristianos recebí,
> y estas que frescas están
> es que a tu puerta caí,
> que al ir a entrar tropecé
> y me quedé sin sentido.

> *Hamete: These wounds I received in Oran by Christians' hands, and these fresh ones are from when I fell at your door and lost consciousness.* (author's translation)

In these lines, Lope could be presenting a case of concussion as the possible source of Hamete's change in behavior. However, the blow to the head is not stressed after these lines and is not mentioned again as the cause for his violence.

Another possible culprit might be found in the Christian food and drink, specifically pork and wine, which the Moors considered to be harmful and almost poisonous for them.[2] Therefore, if Hamete had ingested one of these poisons, he could be affected in ways that he would be unable to control. Ana, one of the servants in Don Gaspar's home, suspects that wine could be involved in Hamete's change (Lope de Vega 2007:vv. 2277–83).

Ana:	Bueno vienes.
	Como no tienes costumbre,
	yo apostaré que algún trago
	ha hecho en ti más estrago
	que en Beltranillo una azumbre.
Hamete:	¡Vive Dios!
Ana:	Perro, ¿tú a mí
	la mano alzada? ¡Pues calla!

Ana:	*You come prepared. Since you are not used to it, I will bet that a drink has had more effect on you than two liters on anybody else.*
Hamete:	*Goodness!*
Ana:	*Dog, you are raising your hand at me? Enough!*

(author's translation)

In this passage, we can read how the suspicion of wine poisoning is mentioned immediately before Hamete's violent hand is raised. But there is no evidence that Hamete actually ingested wine (or pork) apart from Ana's suspicions.

There is one more element that contributes to Hamete's unleashing of rage and it is the abandonment of his faith. He expresses it using the words *Blasfemo de Mahoma* (v. 2380) as a clear sign that he has reached rock bottom and feels that he has nothing else to live for. Vilified and denigrated, Hamete cannot even find comfort in the religion that he defended all along in the play, the faith that he held dear and was educating Christians about in Act II. Hamete is now portrayed as a man who lacks direction and a moral compass, and who is suffering from a depression, that is, *fieras melancolías* (v. 2130).

Several factors contribute to his doom and gloom: first, his lack of freedom and being forced to serve others, which constitutes a humiliation on his part due to his noble origins; second, his lack of hope of ever going back to his initial status; and third, the loss of his love, Argelina, and the jealousy that causes in the presence of the two lovers, which proves to be too much to bear. All these factors contribute to Hamete's melancholy, a common disease that Sebastián de Covarrubias defines as *enfermedad conocida y passión mui ordinaria, donde ay poco contento y gusto* ('known disease and very ordinary passion where there is little joy and pleasure'; author's translation) (2006:1264). To this definition Thomas Case adds that 'Melancholy was the result of an imbalance of humors and that had its origin in the spleen (*bazo*)' (1999:202). Therefore, any disease, including a mental one like melancholy, would be the result of an imbalance of corporeal fluids, that is, the humors.

To this dangerous cocktail of possible culprits we have to add two definitive blows. One appears in the form of a letter from Argelina accusing him of having forgotten her. This is the moment when Hamete accepts that he suffers from the melancholy only mentioned by others up to this point (Lope de Vega 2007:vv. 2292–301).

> Hamete: ¡Qué fiera melancolía!
> ¡Ay, mi patria! ¡Ay, cielo santo!
> Ojos ha bañado el llanto
> que el mismo fuego solía.
> Eterna tristeza mía,
> ¿qué tienes hoy más que ayer?
> De mi amo y su mujer
> creo que nace esta rabia,
> no porque nadie me agravia,
> pero por verlos querer.
>
> Hamete: *What fierce melancholy! Oh my land, oh my goodness! My eyes that were fire are now covered in tears. Eternal sadness, what do you have today more than yesterday? I believe this rage is born from my master and mistress, not because they offend me, but because of their display of love.* (author's translation)

Jealousy, melancholy, despair, and captivity are all addressed in these lines. But the second and final blow is actually physical rather than emotional, and it comes from Don Gaspar, who, feeling threatened by Hamete's violent conduct in his own house, beats him with a reed (*caña*). This punishment, therefore, leaves a mark that is not only psychological but also physical, as

Gaspar marks Hamete as his property, as if he were an animal that he owns and brands accordingly (García 2016:56).

> Hamete: ¿Palos a mí, que general he sido?
> ¿Palos a mí, galán de Meliona?
> ¿Palos a mí, que tantos he vencido
> en los campos de Orán por mi persona?
> ¿Al bárbaro más noble y bien nacido
> de cuantos hoy el África corona?
> ¿Palos con una caña, y en España,
> donde es mayor la infamia con la caña.
>
> (Lope de Vega 2007:vv. 2366–73)

> Hamete: *Blows to me, who has been a general? Blows to me, noble from Meliona? Blows to me, who has defeated so many in the fields of Oran? To the wildest noble and most noble birth that rule Africa? Blows with a stick, in Spain, where is the biggest infamy?* (author's translation)

Hamete's outrage has no bounds, as shown in this soliloquy. He can hardly believe that he has ended up in this situation. When Don Gaspar uses violence against him and marks him as his property, he just cannot endure such humiliation and he simply snaps. This marks the beginning of his spiral down into a path of destruction. But he does not react as a slave beaten by his master, but rather as a disrespected noble, and he takes offense at Don Gaspar's behavior because it fails to recognize his status (Arellano 2015:21).

Hamete's beating with the *caña* is a moment of no return, the inflection point that leads to the final tragedy. It is the ultimate humiliation. To the actual physical blow we have to add the significance of the prestige that the use of reeds had in both the Muslim and Christian worlds.

The game of reeds, or *juegos de cañas*, was an equestrian game of Arab military origin that had been warmly embraced by Spanish nobles. The reed, or *caña*, actually came to serve as a symbol that represented Spain.

> Because they were distinctively Iberian, they represented Spain in a way that the more common jousts or classical pageants ubiquitous in Renaissance Europe (including Spain) never could. (Fuchs 2009:96)

The importance of the game and its prestige as an activity destined for noblemen in the representation of their country make the humiliation of Hamete all the greater, as he is beaten down by the symbol of Spain triumphant after the *Reconquista* using a game of Arab origin. This game that served in the Early Modern period to boost the Spanish sense of honor at home and abroad also becomes the last straw in Hamete's process of losing his own honor, and thus the start of his rampage.

From this point on, the ill-treatment that Hamete has received during his time in Spain turns into violence shown at many different levels. As we saw at the opening of the play, gratuitous violence is present from the very first scene, when Don Juan kills Don Luis in a senseless duel. Violence, too, dominates the capture of Hamete in the context of a century-long war between Spain and the Turks and Moors in the Mediterranean. We also must not forget that Hamete himself was a corsair, and thus one of the inflictors of violence in this war. But nothing can prepare the audience for the final display of violence as Hamete runs away. His rebellion against his master starts by attacking his master's wife. So, just as his wife was taken from him, inflicting the worst pain imaginable, Hamete's attack on his master aims to kill Doña Leonor, killing everyone who will step in his way. His unleashed fury then evolves into killing at random. This excess of violence only finds its parallel in Hamete's unnecessarily cruel torture right before his death.

In any case, it becomes obvious that Hamete's life is destroyed from the moment of his capture. Since then, he has been depressed, treated like an animal, humiliated, and beaten. All of those circumstances push him to become violent, bringing out a side of him that was completely unknown, or to remind us of Lope's words: *Los buenos con agravios se hacen malos* (2007:v. 2391). Therefore, the voyage in Hamete's case does not lead him to find himself, but to find a completely different person, unknown even to him, and capable of the most horrendous crimes, a person with nothing to lose.

The final humiliation takes place after his capture, when Dalima's premonitions come to pass and he finds himself restrained by the chains he dismissed at the beginning. This is when Hamete's losses move to center stage. From the beginning of the play, the Moor has lost his freedom, his dignity, his bride, the rest of his community and his culture, his religion, his sanity and his status as a person, the control over his life and destiny, and now he is about to lose parts of his body as his hands are cut off at the request of the *corregidor* (a local administrative and judicial authority appointed by the king, equivalent to mayor or judge). Hamete is literally required to lose himself (or parts thereof) in the process of becoming a Christian during his *auto-da-fé*, as his body is dismembered after his baptism. Only his death as a Christian citizen, paying for his terrible crimes, allows his incorporation into the Christian hegemonic project.

This ritualistic aspect is reinforced by the fact that the *auto-da-fé* takes place in the Plaza de Zocodover, the main plaza in Toledo, which was the setting used to buy and sell animals, to run with the bulls, and also as the stage for the Inquisition's trials or the *auto-da-fé*, the final ritualistic act in a long process of dehumanization of the accused; it provides a fitting backdrop for the ultimate animal sacrifice.

Only at this point, when Hamete has seemingly lost everything, does the reference to St John the Baptist, who was also persecuted and murdered, resurface to serve as a symbol of reconciliation with God (venerated in both religions) and mitigate the horror of the preceding violence, allowing the possibility of a new beginning. This also marks the point when we, as an audience, can appreciate Hamete again, and can connect with him once more following his violent outburst. Hamete, once humiliated by Don Gaspar, becomes a sympathetic character again. Before his rampage, he had deserved our pity and compassion, but only after his repentance does he regain the admiration of the audience.

From this position, Hamete holds on to the last connection between the two worlds of Christianity and Islam (St John the Baptist) and prepares to die in the hope for the life he did not have on earth, for the salvation of his soul, which, after his crimes, is only possible after his death as a Christian citizen. Therefore, Hamete fully embraces the waters of baptism, not hoping to save his life after receiving the sacrament, and expecting nothing in return. The tragedy is complete. Lope de Vega has managed to make us suffer Hamete's internal struggle, the harsh circumstances of the historical moment, and the lack of options. Violence only breeds violence and the results are equally damaging for everybody involved. Only the Christian message in Lope's play leaves room for redemption and a happy ending, as long as it is not in this world.

When asked about the play, César Barló, director of AlmaViva Teatro and responsible for the 2010 production, answered that the message he wanted to leave the audience with was a profound feeling of injustice. When adapting it for a twenty-first-century audience, the company was attempting to challenge the idea that there are superior and inferior people depending on their place of origin or religion. This is a particularly relevant topic because of the migrant crisis we are living with today. In their view, the play shows how Spain, a country with a tremendous tourist industry, warmly welcomes migrants from the first world; but when those immigrants come from Africa, they are viewed as inferior and as a problem that needs to be dealt with. This is the issue that the AlmaViva Teatro production wanted to raise for debate. In this context, they argue that migrants do not come to take over our country, but that they are forced to act through political or economic circumstances. In their opinion, only intolerant attitudes can destroy a culture and people's lives, not the physical arrival of others.

This concept also caused the company to dramatically change the way they presented their performance. They insisted on making the stage one single space shared by all the actors (from both religions and both sides of the Mediterranean). They were also able to change characters if necessary, showing that crossover was a possibility. But the most important element was to make the stage feel like a place where a ritual was taking place, to give the idea of a space ready for a sacrifice – a bullfighting ring with sand, where a poor unfortunate was going to be tried by the very same people who had pushed him to an extreme level of violence, a ring with no escape or options, a place of total surrender.

In the end, the conflict does not achieve closure. As baroque art, it is unsettling and reflects a painful reality, displaying open wounds and revealing an insecure and unstable social fabric. César Barló expressed it as follows: *Cuando chocan las culturas desaparecen los seres humanos* ('When cultures clash, human beings disappear'; author's translation). In the current context of a worldwide refugee crisis, and with President Trump's travel ban directed mainly at Islamic countries, how we treat other cultures becomes a topic of newly found relevance.

About the author

Mina García is a Professor of Spanish in the Department of World Languages and Cultures at Elon University (North Carolina, USA) and specializes in continental and colonial Spanish literature of the 16th–17th centuries. Her first book *Magia, Hechiceria y Brujeria: Entre La Celestina y Cervantes* (*Magic, Sorcery and Witchcraft: Between La Celestina and Cervantes*) (Renacimiento, 2011) was followed by her second book *Idolatry and the Construction of the Spanish Empire* (University Press of Colorado, 2019). Her most recent book *Social Justice in Spanish Golden Age Theatre* is an volume co-edited with Erin Cowling, Tania de Miguel Magro and Glenda Nieto-Cuebas (University of Toronto Press, 2021). Throughout her numerous articles and chapter contributions, García explores the role of literature in the expansion of the Spanish empire, Early Modern Spanish literature, transatlantic studies, Latin American colonial culture and literature, the relation between society and superstition in the early modern period, and the spiritual and territorial conquest of the Americas.

Acknowledgements

I would like to thank AlmaViva Teatro, and especially César Barló, for their invaluable help, for providing images of their performance and anything that I asked for, But above all, for creating experiences that keep alive our shared search for social justice through classical theater made contemporary and relevant again.

Notes

1. Margaret R. Greer also noted this play on words in reference to *El Tuzaní de la Alpujarra* (2006:127).
2. In lines 2233-4, Hamete takes a plate of food from Ana. Similar to the references to the wine, we are to assume that the food is poisonous to him, that is, it contains pork and so can be regarded as one of the contributory factors to his rage.

References

Arellano, I. (2015) *El Hamete de Toledo* y el tratamiento del moro esclavo en el Siglo de Oro. *Iberoromania* 81(1): 16–31. https://doi.org/10.1515/ibero-2015-0004

Case, T. (1999) Violence and reception in Lope's *El Hamete de Toledo*. *Revista de Estudios Hispánicos* 26(2): 193–205.

Ciruelo, P. (1977 [1551]) *Reprobación de las supersticiones y hechicerías*. Barcelona: Glosa.

Covarrubias, S. de (2006) *Tesoro de la lengua castellana o española* (I. Arellano and R. Zafra, eds). Pamplona, Spain: Universidad de Navarra.

Dean, M. (2004) A critical and annotated edition of Lope de Vega's *El Amete de Toledo*. PhD dissertation, University of California Riverside.

Domínguez Ortiz, A. and Vincent, B. (1978) *Historia de los moriscos. Vida y tragedia de una minoría*. Madrid: Revista de Occidente.

Fuchs, B. (2009) *Exotic Nation. Maurophilia and the Construction of Early Modern Spain*. Pennsylvania: University of Pennsylvania Press. https://doi.org/10.9783/9780812207354

García, M. (2016) *El (H)amete de Toledo* en el contexto de las expulsiones: ecos a ambos lados del Atlántico. In A. A. Gómez Yebra (ed.) *Patrimonio Literario Andaluz V* 55–63. Malaga, Spain: Servicio de Publicaciones Fundación Unicaja.

Greer, M. (2006) The politics of memory in *El Tuzaní de la Alpujarra*. In R. Pym (ed.) *Rhetoric and Reality in Early Modern Spain* 113–30. Woodbridge: Tamesis.

Lope de Vega, F. (2007) *El Hamete de Toledo*. In M. Presotto (ed.) *Comedias de Lope de Vega, Parte IX*. Lérida: Milenio.

Lope de Vega, F. (2010) *El Hamete de Toledo* (A. Sansano and C. Barló, dir.). AlmaViva Teatro.

Perceval, J. M. (1997) *Todos son uno. Arquetipos de la xenofobia y el racismo. La imagen del morisco en la monarquía española de los siglos XVI y XVII*. Almeria: Instituto de Estudios Almerienses.

6 The embodied palimpsest: Dancing kinesthetic empathy in bharatanatyam

Katherine C. Zubko

Abstract

In the South Asian dance style of bharatanatyam, the devotional bodies of dancers and the gods they portray model a performative porosity about 'religious bodies.' But what embodied resonances of religiosity transfer when the intention of the dancer or topic is not marked as devotional? Apsaras Arts' *Agathi: The Plight of the Refugee* (2017) offers an ethnographic case study through which I aim to deepen the theory around the porosity of bodies by developing the theoretical construct of an embodied palimpsest: a framework that allows previous 'erased' layers to become present and interactive with later layers. I demonstrate how the choreographed gestures and *rasas*, or aesthetic moods, utilized to embody certain Hindu myths inform this danced portrayal of migrant experiences, but also note how the interactive layers of the palimpsest reshape classical theories about *rasa*, in particular *karuna rasa*, the mood of compassion, and can be used to particularize theories about kinesthetic empathy.

Keywords: dance; kinesthetic empathy; *rasa*; refugees; aesthetics; embodied religion

Introduction

As I open the newspaper and skim through social media feeds, headlines about refugees fleeing from war torn countries who are dying at sea appear regularly. As these stories slowly recede from front pages and top posts, hidden among flashier news stories, the experiences of refugees disappear into the peripheries of our awareness as our attention is caught up elsewhere. In this ebb and flow of information, something draws our interest, capturing us with an emotional hook in our shared humanity. Instead of a headline that we have become numb to, such as 'More than 100 migrants die at sea in wreck off Libya, survivors say' (Pianigiani 2019), a more substantial tug may come from a single photograph of a dead child, Aylan Kurdi, lying face down on the beach in Turkey,[1] or *Sea Prayer* (Hosseini 2018), an animated documentary and children's book utilizing bold watercolor brushstrokes to juxtapose the pre-idyllic nostalgia and post-terror aftershocks of trauma,[2] or, as this article will focus on, the embodiment of refugee experiences in the dance production of *Agathi: The Plight of the Refugee*.

The power of art as an expression of and response to individual and social suffering often serves as the primary scholarly lens employed to examine the impact of these multifaceted and multimodal works in connection to social change, civic engagement, and ethics. In an edited volume on artistic citizenship, for example, the editors frame art-making as conscious of advancing social good, through creating the conditions for 'active reflection and critically reflective action guided by an informed ethical disposition to act rightly, with continuous concern for protecting and advancing the well-being of others' (Elliott, Silverman and Bowman 2016:6–7). Within the broader literature, many case studies focus on the role of theater and dance in socially responsive movements, including performance related to refugees or involving refugees specifically (see Balfour 2013). While aware of these frameworks, this study aims to bring embodiment, and more specifically bodily porosity, to the forefront of not only the conversation on art and ethical impact, but also to inform theoretical work on bodies across disciplines. To ground this work, I focus on choreographic sequences from Apsaras Arts' *Agathi: The Plight of the Refugee* (debuted in Singapore in 2017), performed in the idiom of bharatanatyam, a South Asian dance style that traditionally embodies narratives of Hindu gods and their devotees. While the company is based in Singapore, it is composed of dancers mostly trained under institutions and gurus in South India.

My argument expands on experiences and expressions of bodily porosity by developing the theoretical construct of an embodied palimpsest: a framework that allows previous 'erased' layers to become present and interactive with later layers. How do performative bodies demonstrate an affective bodily porosity that draws on Hindu religious narratives and aesthetics in the service of raising awareness of social crises and human suffering? What embodied resonances of religiosity transfer when the intention of the dancer or topic is not marked as devotional, but instead focuses on a humanitarian crisis? To address these and other questions, I investigate how choreography commonly utilized to embody particular Hindu myths and the expectations of physical-emotional gestural enactment behind the creation of *rasas*, or aesthetic moods, permeate this danced portrayal of migrant experiences. The interactive layers of the palimpsest that come into focus through this analysis engage with and expand on classical theories about *rasa*, in particular *karuna rasa*, the mood of compassion, but also serve to particularize theories about kinesthetic empathy.

My organizational aim for this study on religious embodiment takes the form of a scholarly palimpsest. I will layer concepts of body, ethnographic descriptive vignettes focusing on narrative enactment, South Asian aesthetics in theory and practice, and embodied performance with ethical imperatives as refracted through theories of kinesthetic empathy. These layers, while divided by their own headings, are intended to perforate, blend, disrupt, and inform each other.

Multi-layered embodiments: theorizing at the peripheries and interstices of performative bodies

While much has emerged from different disciplines regarding the study of 'body' and embodiment within religious studies, I will not be rehearsing that history and its many issues, subtopics, and critiques, which can be found elsewhere in more detail (e.g., see Vasquez 2011). Instead, I will work from an ethnographic and performance analysis approach, by examining what the processes of embodiment in a particular case study offers to our ongoing intellectual curiosity and theorizing about religious bodies. After viewing *Agathi* in Chennai, India (2017) and London, United Kingdom (2018), interviewing performers and audience members, and reviewing performance documents, I became intrigued by the ways in which religious-aesthetic practices and ideas punctuate the experience of this unusual secularized theme. Centering marginalized aspects of embodied practices entails inviting examples from the outskirts of more established systems, such as the expected bharatanatyam repertoire, to lead in offering categories 'to think with.' This shift changes the questions we ask, reveals hidden assumptions, and can push theory to become even more inclusive of diverse epistemologies which try to account for and translate embodied knowledges that still struggle for authority within academic contexts.[3]

The dancing bodies of *Agathi* performing at the peripheries of themes and traditional purposes are positioned to illuminate the blurrier edges of embodiment, namely, their porous, relational, and intersubjective dynamic defining processes. Here, I am building on ethnographic studies on transactional, fluid constructions of embodied personhood rooted in localized cosmologies and cultures (Csordas 1993; Lamb 2000; Nabhan-Warren 2005; Sklar 2001; Trawick 1990), but through a performative aesthetic lens. Just to highlight one vivid example of this processual characteristic, Sarah Lamb details how the bodies of widows in Bengal are constructed through shifting interactions with food, clothing, the substance of homes and environments, and the postural composure and grammar of familial exchanges. In Lamb's study, a body is not individually or rigidly bounded, but is defined as a dynamic relational nexus in which the processes of 'material and emotional' exchanges are intentionally cooled, dried, and minimized during widowhood through changes to bodily praxis (Lamb 2000:13–14). I suggest that the theoretical construct of an embodied palimpsest, as evidenced in the performative case study of *Agathi*, is a useful and transferable framework for expanding on these porous, relational aspects of bodies.

Palimpsests

I was reintroduced to the concept of a palimpsest during a workshop on campus by Beth Berila, a facilitator known for her work on anti-oppression pedagogy (see Berila 2015). We were asked to remember an oppressive, difficult, or challenging experience in our teaching or other work contexts, and then to take each of four layers of partly transparent vellum paper and identify words that came to mind about the event, emotions, and how our body felt or sensory responses on the first three sheets, and on the fourth paper, to include drawings or other non-verbal aspects. These thin papers were then stacked on top of one another, creating the effect of the emotional, sensory, and non-discursive layers underneath the words bleeding through to various degrees, in order to create a holistic representation of the difficult or oppressive experience.

As a processual activity, it was particularly effective in its attempt to untangle various embodied components of experience. In its more usual contexts, a palimpsest is a term most often used in relation to archeological work on ancient and medieval manuscripts, in which previous texts have been scraped and written over, but still retain traces that emerge either naturally over time or are discovered through other interventionist chemical or radiation technologies. Manuscript palimpsests include religious (Biblical and Qur'anic), legal, political, and literary texts. The term has also been used as an analytical lens for interpreting fiction and poetics, and employed in literal (archeology) and metaphorical (literary cityscapes) dissections of places (see Battles 2015; Haines-Eitzen 2012; Thomas 2010).

In the *Poetics of the Body*, Catherine Cucinella imports the concept of a palimpsest into conversations about embodiment in relation to her analysis of the poetry of Marilyn Chin. As Cucinella explains,

> [t]he body often serves as the visual site of this collision or overlap [of identities] because the body as depicted by Chin must continually negotiate among various cultures – American, Chinese, and Chinese American. Because of this continual negotiation and because of the bicultural aspects of being an immigrant in white America, the body manifests as a palimpsest, in both senses of the word. Chin often marks her poetic bodies with multiple layers of inscriptions and previous experiences remain legible and readable. The body also becomes the object that reflects personal, familial and cultural histories. Thus, in Chin's poetry, we read history, dislocation, grief, anger, as well as subjectivity both on the body and through the body (Cucinella 2010:81).

In Cucinella's description, national identities, histories, and emotions are all interactively layered in the poetic expressions of a female Chinese immigrant whose body is ambiguous, porous, multilocational, and multitemporal. Cucinella asserts the co-existing possibilities for both claiming and disavowing both particularized bodies and cultural bodies as part of the fluid emergence of various embodied experiences in the palimpsest model (Cucinella 2010:19).

While Cucinella applies the palimpsest to poetic embodied imagery about experiences, her understanding, further aligned through its application to immigrant artistic expression, has transferable resonances for the performance context of *Agathi*. Working from individual and particularized refugee experiences in interaction with South Asian religious and aesthetic contexts produces insights into palimpsests not on paper but embodied even more directly on stage. The negotiation between and expression of various identities (e.g., familial, lover–beloved, religious), sacred and contemporary histories, and experiential and aesthetically framed emotions exist at the core of *Agathi*'s presentation.

Bharatanatyam, an Indian classical dance form

Bharatanatyam is a South Asian classical dance style constructed in the 1930s from temple and court dance traditions as part of an emerging Indian nationalist art movement prior to Independence from the British Empire (Allen

1997; Srinivasan 1985). Hereditary dance knowledge(s) of *devadasis*, women dedicated to temple service, transferred to a mostly upper class and caste set of exponents, and were reshaped through an emphasis on ties to a 2000-year-old Sanskrit dance-drama compendium, the *Natyasastra*, which, as Coorlawala notes, 'Sanskritized' the physical techniques, the portrayal of gods and devotees, and reasserted a sacredness on both dancer and dance form as performed in the new concert venues (Coorlawala 2005:173–94). Because dancers have fully embedded the Sanskrit technical and aesthetic terminologies of the *Natyasastra* as a respected authoritative framework for their dance practices on their websites, program notes, and during lectures, I will also be including references to the *Natyasastra* as part of this analysis (Salinas 2016).

In its current iteration, as a designated classical dance of India, bharatanatyam is known for its complex rhythms, gestured storytelling related to embodying Hindu gods and their devotees, and its stylized aesthetic abilities for dancers to cultivate *bhakti rasa*, or a devotional mood. The experiencing of *rasa*, or aesthetic mood, is the primary technical focus of stagecraft by dancers at the center of ideal audience receptivity. *Rasa* is based on the combination of emotional nuance depicted through physically enacted contextual cues, physical responses that coordinate gesture, posture, and speed and timing of movements, and a weaving together of more subtle, fleeting emotions. This formula delineated in the *Natyasastra* creates one of eight, eventually nine primary *rasas* (i.e., love, humor, anger, heroism, fear, wonder, compassion, disgust, and peace), which are highly valued in South Asian dance-drama.

Social themes

Bharatanatyam dancers have explored other social thematic threads outside of or through the reframing of Hindu mythological characters and stories.[4] These have tended to coalesce around issues related to unequal treatment of or violence toward women, caste and/or religious discrimination or other bases for ostracization or bullying, environmental devastation, or raising awareness of ways to enact social altruism. One early pathbreaking artist was Mrnalini Sarabhai (1918–2016), the founder of the Darpana Performing Arts Academy in Ahmedabad, Gujarat, and carried forward by her daughter, Mallika Sarabhai, the current director of the school and touring company. Mrnalini was known for addressing themes related to dowry deaths, Dalit discrimination, and pollution of the Ganga in a variety of productions that mixed bharatanatyam with kathakali, Tagorean theater, and regional Gujarati *sutradhar* storytelling techniques.

While one strand of the development of classical dance forms in India aligned with primarily Hindu religious frameworks in the service of an emerging national identity (see Allen 1997; O'Shea 2007; Srinivasan 1985), the artistic path of Mrnalini Sarabhai, influenced by her work with Rabindranath Tagore and partnership with Ram Gopal, reflects another more hybridized strand in the technical and thematic practices of Indian dance forms of the time. These works were intended for either localized renaissances (Tagore) or global representation of 'Asian' dance for elite Euro-American audiences (Gopal), in both cases adapting themes across religious and social positioning including Candalika, a Dalit who encounters Buddhism, and depictions of the suffering crucified body of Jesus. Mallika Sarabhai absorbed and made several of these themes her own, notably in *Sita's Daughters*, a globally toured multimedia production focused on the experience of women trapped between the ideal role of the modest, devoted woman, modeled after the primary female heroine of the *Ramayana*, and the realities of domestic abuse, rape, and gender-based discrimination founded on their second-class existence.

While trained in bharatanatyam, Candralekha is another noteworthy example of the rejection of conservative or traditional approaches to the construction of Indian classical dance, preferring her own unique modernist choreography that would embody a different pathway of social critique in both form and theme. Much of her choreographic œuvre critiqued gender hierarchies and roles through distilling movement into a more abstracted focus on physical postures, lines, and energetic exchange centered on female power, *sakti*.

In contrast to the Sarabhais and Candralekha, several dancers have engaged only bharatanatyam techniques in their choreography on social themes. The range includes individual dancers creating an exploratory item or two as part of their extensive traditional repertoire, to established choreographers building full-length productions around social critiques, such as M. V. Narasimhachari's final work, *Karuna Sakti: The Power of Compassion* (2015). This program highlighted a series of contexts evoking the need for compassionate response, from harmonizing relationships between humans and their environmental care of trees, animals, and the land, to reframing the experience of living with the stigmatizing illness of AIDS/HIV (see Zubko 2018).

Agathi: The Plight of the Refugee

While it is now more common for bharatanatyam dancers to explore thematic threads outside Hindu mythology, very few have highlighted the contemporary realities of refugee or (im)migrant experiences, as performed in the ethnographic case study at the center of this article, *Agathi: The Plight of the Refugee*.[5]

The idea for *Agathi* emerged out of artistic director Aravinth Kumarasamy's own experiences as a refugee fleeing from the Sri Lankan civil war (1983–2009). As will be discussed further in the later section on aesthetics, the process of absorbing the experiences of refugees into the dancers' bodied portrayals involved an intentional process of building trust in taking artistic risks as an ensemble, engaging with the poetry of refugee children, and studio lab exercises allowing dancers to experiment with difficult movement-emotion connections. The production consists of three main acts. The first act is an idyllic portrayal of pre-war life, with cows nurturing their calves and couples falling in love. The second act examines various calamities, including natural and human-driven conflicts that cause people to live in fear and flee their homelands, with an extended depiction of refugees caught up in the many dangers of trying to escape by boat. A third act explores how refugees, if they survive the journeys out of their homelands, meet with many challenges in their new lives – from citizens in their newly adopted countries resistant to their very presence, to missing their own cultures, foods, and customs. Music and dance become symbols of healing, as people strive to make their way in new contexts in which 'they will never be the same again' – the constant lyrical refrain sung in Tamil throughout the program. These three acts are introduced by a narrator. Throughout each item, poetry-inspired lyrics, translated into English from Tamil, are displayed on screens at the side of the stage.

The two contexts in which I viewed this performance differed in important ways. In Chennai, India, *Agathi* was performed as part of the Chennai Music and Dance Season during the Tamil month of Margazhi (mid-December–mid-January), an auspicious or particularly favorable month for artistic performances. At over 30 auditoriums throughout the city, and now also in Mamallapuram (60 km south of Chennai), there is a full slate of amateur to professional programs from morning to night. Besides performances, there are also conferences and workshops, including the Natya Kala Conference at Krishna Gana Sabha, the Music Academy lecture and panel series, and Kartik Fine Arts' Natya Darshan hosted by the religious-cultural community organization of Bharatiya Vidya Bhavan. While most of the conferences involve lecture-demonstrations by a variety of well-established senior artists from different classical and folk styles, panels on hot topics, and dance scholars, historians, and critics delivering keynotes, the Natya Darshan festival, begun in 2001, has aimed to create a venue for edgier themes and styles in conversation with traditional topics over the past few years.[6]

It was at the coveted final evening timeslot as part of the Natya Darshan Conference in December 2017 that *Agathi* had its Chennai premiere at Bharatiya Vidya Bhavan. The audience included a broad generational representation and several senior artists, who sat in a slightly offset row of more comfortable chairs at the very front of the auditorium. Bharatiya Vidya Bhavan is located in the heart of Mylapore, one of the oldest and most conservative areas of the city, next to the Kapaleeshwarar Temple dedicated to the Hindu god Siva, and surrounded by high-end jewelry, sari, *puja* and dance supply stores, vegetarian eateries and sweet shops, as well as street stalls and pop-up evening markets, all circled around the temple water tank. Auto-rickshaws and scooters now compete with personal mid-size vehicles and Uber services that circumambulate the area, adding to the flow of pedestrians especially prominent in the evening hours after the sun has set.

In contrast, the London program, also at a Bharatiya Vidya Bhavan which occupied the building of a former congregational church in London, drew a smaller audience with a multicultural mix of ethnicities, a handful of children, and at least one London-based bharatanatyam dancer in contrast to an auditorium full of dancers and teachers. Replacing the pulpit, choir, and altar at the front was now an elevated concert stage, with curtains and lights. At the top of the arches intended to draw eyes upwards, former stained-glass windows lining both sides of the topmost part of the nave were covered with blackout curtains. Graduated stadium seating at the ground-floor level and in the balcony completed the transformation to a concert venue.[7] The London performance was part of the multi-week Milapfest highlighting South Asian concert arts. Most of the audience members would have travelled from many different parts of London to attend, rather than come from the West Kensington cosmopolitan residential neighborhoods, whereas the Chennai audience included 'Mylapore maamis and maamas,' or aunts and uncles appreciative of classical arts, alongside teenage students, and junior and mid-career dancers based within the vicinities of the dance institution hubs of Mylapore and further south in Adyar.

The Q&A sessions that followed both programs reflected differences in audience interests and levels of technical expertise, although both included emotional responses to the subject matter of refugees. As Kumarasamy noted, in Chennai, the Q&A went to nearly 11 p.m., with audience members lingering to comment on the ways they were emotionally moved, rather than critiquing the costumes, the steps, or making other more surface observations: 'They were focused on the message and not just the technical aspects of the dance' (interview with author, June 10, 2018). To look more closely at this affective dimension, I will focus on one of the most evocative scenes in Act

II of *Agathi*, which portrays refugees fleeing by boat, as a choreographic case study to examine how these narratives surface and change the reception of difficult immigrant experiences. After providing a performance description, I will engage in a performance analysis of how the concept of an embodied palimpsest helps to make sense of the ways narratives and aesthetics interact and reshape the expression and reception of this creative endeavor.

The boat scene
After performing a handful of vignettes in trios that provide a window into some of the reasons people flee their homelands, from earthquakes and tsunamis, to fires and political violence, the stage goes dark except for a central spotlight. The urgent co-ordinated rhythm of all of the dancers' feet underlie each individual emerging into the spotlight, depicting some component of fear in their lives, whether it is witnessing the horrors of human tragedy of others or being subject to harassment themselves. As the group comes together communally in a single line, they begin to call out for help, waving their hands toward the audience, while also shielding themselves from the imagined onslaught coming at them from each side of the stage. The stridency is well exhibited through leg and arm movements striking swiftly out on opposite diagonals, influenced by the Keralan martial art of kalaripayattu. There is a constant rhythm and rocking motion to this choreography, imitating the instability of the ground under their feet due to their circumstances, and foreshadowing the rocking of the boat they now call out to with their hands.

Jumping into the illusory boat one by one, the dancers hold onto the sides as the vessel lists, others cross their arms over themselves with wide-open eyes, and one mother holds a baby trying to steady herself and anxiously tries to calm the child. All but the mother rise and clasp hands, morphing into the oblong shape of the boat surrounding the mother and child. Rocking, leaning, tilting high on one side and then the other, the people-boat navigates the rough waters. Hands unclasped, the boat turns back into individual people, being tossed around as the dancers roll into each other on the ground, eventually showing distinct moments of sickness, fear and anxiety. The lead male dancer tries to use an oar to row, but in exhaustion faints and is revived by water tossed on his face.

As the rains come, the people shiver, crossing their arms to stay warm, just as the mother begins to shake her child who is not moving. Even with the mother transferring her breath, the lack of response from the child induces panic, the mother signaling for help from the person next to her, who also is unable to evoke a response from the child. The male dancer takes the unresponsive child into his arms, shakes the child a bit, hesitates, shakes his head, but then with a pained look, tosses the corpse into the water to the scream of his mother and anguish of the others who cover their mouths in shock. The mother faints, and the rest of the dancers stand and become the boat

Figure 6.1: *Agathi* boat scene: dancers creating the structure of the boat. (Photo credit and permission: R. Prasana Photography. Courtesy of Apsaras Arts Dance Company.)

again. Rocking back onto one leg and lurching forward a few times, the boat breaks into several pieces and the people roll around, crawling, grasping pieces of splintered wood and each other to keep afloat, while others are not moving, leaving only three survivors. One dancer points in the distance, hoping for land or rescue, even as the tragedy of loss and separation continue to surround them before transforming into the next scene of grief and lament.

Permeating the surface: traces of Hindu narrative frameworks

One of the defining features of many traditional bharatanatyam repertoire genres,[8] storytelling, is at the heart of this boat scene. In Sanskrit terminology, *natya*, or dance, includes both *nrtya*, in which gestures are utilized for narratives, and *nrtta* as 'pure dance' or decorative, rhythmic dance without a story feature. *Nrtya* is more commonly referenced by dancers as *abhinaya*, or narrative sequences utilizing mimetic hand gestures, facial expressions, and postural stances.

However, it is not a typical story in several ways. Historically in religious contexts, *devadasis*, women dedicated to the service of the god of the temple, performed dances that embodied stories about the attributes and actions of the gods in interaction with their devotees as part of ritual offerings of entertainment to *murtis*, or physical images/forms of the gods, ranging from anthropomorphized carved statues to trees or rivers (see Marglin 1985; Soneji 2011). After the shift in roles and perceptions of *devadasis* under the British Empire led to the Anti-Nautch Movement's successful decentering of hereditary dancers and their embodied knowledge about the stories of gods, the emergence of a newly 'reformed' art in the 1930s that could bolster national identity led to changes in narrative emphasis, along with techniques. During this period, as Matthew Allen describes, certain gods and stories became central to the repertoire, especially stories related to Siva as Nataraja, Lord of the Dance, Krishna's childhood feats, and to a lesser extent, Murugan, a more localized Tamil-identified son of Siva (Allen 1997). Other items, learned from hereditary dancers, explored the emotional dimensions of female heroines, or *nayikas*, in union with and separation from their beloveds. The newly invested Brahmins learning dance, such as Rukmini Devi and her later influential Kalakshetra institutional lineage, often stripped away what was perceived as overt sensuality in both gesture and narrative, and refocused on interpretative frameworks of lover–beloved mysticism between the divine self (*atman*) and god, or devotional experiences.

In today's narrative contexts for bharatanatyam, items about many different gods and goddesses are performed, including some from non-Hindu religions (see Zubko 2014). Alongside dance-dramas based on traditional Sanskrit plays and segments of the *Ramayana* and *Mahabharata* epics, there are also religious and secular thematic productions. *Agathi* falls into the thematic category, utilizing bharatanatyam to focus on experiences of refugees within a more secular framework. However, the religious themes are still present and influential in the layers below the surface. This is partially due to the expectations of the dance form and its technical narrative tools not always being tied to direct lyrical elaboration, as the boat scene has no lyrics, but instead relies on several other strategies.

For example, the first narrative present below the surface in the boat scene is the 'Churning of the ocean.' This narrative focuses on the Hindu god Vishnu's *avatar* as the tortoise Kurma. As the gods and *asuras* (titans/demons) sought *amrita*, the nectar of immortality, they were told they must churn the ocean of milk to locate it. Mount Meru would be used as a churning stick, with Vasuki the snake as a rope wrapped around the mountain with two loose ends, each end being pulled and retracted in turn by a group of gods on one side and a group of *asuras* on the other, in order to turn the mountain back and forth on a single pivot point. Because a steady base was needed for this collaborative plan to work, Kurma volunteered and descended to the bottom of the ocean to allow the mountain to rest on his back. This set-up is an imitation of how a butter-churner in ancient rural India would operate.

Amrita did eventually arise out of the ocean, along with its opposite, poison, but more dramatic shenanigans follow before the nectar is secured by the gods. According to the *Natyasastra*,[9] it is the very first narrative performed in the newly initiated art of dance, but when *asuras* in the audience saw how they were being depicted, they stormed the stage and disrupted the first dance-drama. The god Brahma then intervened by giving an educational rationale:

> O faultless Daityas [*asuras*] do not be angry, cast away your worries. I have made the Natyaveda as containing instructions to both you and the Devas [gods], to distinguish between good and bad in the realm of action, character and heredity. (I:105–6) … The drama will portray the activities of people who are of exalted, low and middle class and will contain instructions for their benefit … It will provide solace to the afflicted, fatigued, miserable ones and ascetics tired of religious ceremonies. The art of drama will promote virtue, bring fame and longevity, provide benefit, increase the intelligence and contain proper advice to the world (I:113–16).

Since all types of characters would be depicted, no offense should be taken. Instead, the very intention of dance-drama is to provide moral edification on all topics to the audience. *Agathi* aligns well with this missive through the portrayal of those who are low, afflicted, and miserable, in order to 'promote proper advice to the world.'

In addition to this moral backdrop, the 'Churning of the ocean' narrative permeates other dimensions of *Agathi*. Both the boat and the people in the boat are on a tempestuous ocean, roiled by storms to the point of being broken up on the sea. It may not be gods and *asuras* creating the choppy conditions, but the depiction invites a metaphorical turn. As the refugees attempt to escape from death, the search for *amrita*, or immortality, becomes the search for a better life and the ability for their children to be able to live. *Asuras* embody the political, climactic, and discriminatory causes for fleeing, as well as the apathy of response toward their difficulties. In the boat scene, dancers employ a narrative technique that layers a matrix of related stories and multiple perspectives (*sanchari bhavas*).[10] In *Agathi*, the performers engage in this technique as an ensemble rather than as a solo dancer oscillating between different roles as part of telling a story within a dance item. The dancers' transition between inhabiting individual people in the boat, linking hands to become the boat listing on the surging swells, and when the boat breaks up, the rolling of the people invoking turbulent waves diminishing to ripples as they sink into and become the ever-changing sea. *Agathi* invites new meanings for interpreting the narrative of the 'Churning of the ocean,' while also drawing on its moral context and metaphorical resonances for enhancing the way in which the boat scene is engaged.

A second narrative cycle evokes in audiences the relational interactions between the Hindu god Krishna as a child and his adopted mother Yashoda. The most often depicted child in bharatanatyam is Krishna in all his daring divine escapades and youthful human antics, from being carried across the river to safety out of his evil uncle Kamsa's fort, to stealing buttermilk, dancing on the river-snake Kaliya's head, and eating dirt in order to prompt Yashoda to ask him to open his mouth, a playful device which allows Krishna to reveal the entire universe to her for a fleeting moment. Yashoda's motherly chiding and affection shapes understandings of *vatsalya bhakti*, a parental devotional model of love for God. In *Agathi*, as the woman holds on tightly to the child, trying to soothe and protect the child amidst the unstable rocking of the boat and pouring rain, this mother–child pair emerges into heightened attention when all the other dancers rise to use their bodies to form the boat around this pair, to make sure they do not just blend into the other refugees. After the dancers turn back into the other people on the boat and the oarsman is revived, the sequence focusing on the mother–child pair builds to its shocking, although not unexpected climax, heightened further by its tragic focus on the events surrounding the death of the child on the boat.

While the audience should be prepared for the high likelihood of death in relation to refugees, bharatanatyam rarely shows death on stage, let alone performative responses to a child's lifeless body being thrown overboard as other dangers quickly emerge. The scene was effective due to its realistic, no-nonsense depiction rooted in sympathetic necessity within the confined space of the boat. But I would also argue that the effectiveness of this scene relies on the fond attachment and motherly responses to 'Krishna as a child,' setting up expectations for audiences of love and humor that elevate the pathos further when *vatsalya bhakti* turns tragic. Audience members responded in both venues with a somewhat unusual stillness. While applause was common between items leading up to this point in the Chennai and London programs, the absence of applause after this scene concluded with the boat breaking up signified that observers were unsettled or deeply moved in a way that upended typical audience interactions.[11]

The aesthetics of empathy

Accompanying the intermittent permeation of resonances of Hindu narratives in *Agathi* is the use of facial expressions, gestures, and postures to evoke aesthetic moods, or *rasas*. In its most formulaic iteration in the *Natyasastra*, the eight, later nine *rasas* experienced by audience participants are created through a combination of three types of *bhavas* (physical-emotional components): (1) the physically expressed delineation of context, namely, through body gesture and not scenery/props; (2) enacted physical-emotional responses; and (3) fleeting emotions. These three *bhavas* enhance the overall primary emotion (*sthayibhava*) to be depicted by the dancer. If this combination is masterfully portrayed, the audience is thought to be able to 'taste' the overall *sthayibhava* created by the dancer as a *rasa*. In order to achieve the *rasa* of *srngara* (love), for example, the dancer might gesture (1) moonlight and the calls of night birds, (2) the sidelong glance and hands clasped coyly behind the back of a woman seeing her beloved appear in the garden for a tryst, and (3) transitory moments of shyness, curiosity, and jealousy punctuating the scene as it unfolds. Dancers and choreographers acknowledge this aesthetic theory of audience receptivity as an ideal, but in their own practice-based discourses they adopt the authoritative Sanskrit vocabulary from the *Natyasastra* that makes the most sense to them in relation to their own kinesthetic processes of stagecraft.

For example, artistic director Aravinth Kumarasamy directed the conversation toward the related mechanics of *abhinaya*, or gesture, one of the key techniques to develop the *bhavas* defined above, when asked about the choreographic processes and intended *rasas* of *Agathi*. He noted that '[t]he dancers do not have first-hand experience [of being refugees]. The process was to try to work from the inside, from emotions. In our context of the *Natyasastra*, we tried to get to the *sattvika abhinaya* [internal involuntary physical responses], so that the *angika abhinaya* [full body gestures/postures] would come' (interview with author, June 10, 2018). The *sattvika bhavas* enumerated in the *Natyasastra* are horripilation, turning pale and fainting, trembling, tears, and other 'involuntary' physical responses that arise from *manas* (mind–heart) (see 6:22–3 and 7:93–106). In this way, Kumarasamy is more interested in tapping into the underlying emotional responses that would transform the depth of execution enacted through the ensemble's interactive physical gestures and facial expressions of *angika abhinaya*. To connect the dancers to that emotional-body level, Kumarasamy told stories about his own experience as a refugee and asked them to read the poetry of refugee children,[12] in order to 'investigate and understand the body language of a refugee' (*Agathi* Program Notes 2018:4). This is a discussion about *bhava*, the physical expression of emotion on stage, as understood by dancers in their processes and performances, which leads to the potential experience of *rasa* for audience members.

Figure 6.2: *Agathi* boat scene: performing *bhavas* expressing grief, fear, and shock after the child's body has been tossed overboard. (Photo credit and permission: R. Prasana Photography. Courtesy of Apsaras Arts Dance Company.)

Based on interviews with dancers and audience members, the primary *rasas* coalesce around fear, disgust, and love within the framework of loss and separation. In taking a closer look at the boat scene, *bhayanaka rasa* (aesthetic mood of fear) is built through *bhavas* of various iterations – some dancers show their torsos caved in and protective, while others wave and push others away in trying to become visible and escape. Dancers exhibit wide-eyed disbelief, blink and tremble, close their eyes tight and hold their heads and wail, or shake their heads from side to side to indicate 'no.' Hands tucked up under their chins cover their own mouths, cover their ears, cover their eyes, and cross their hearts. It is a creative feat to be able to show this many different iterations of embodied fear and loss throughout the program without it becoming repetitive.

The lament scene that follows the boat scene is particularly effective at demonstrating the expressional variety of *bhavas* leading to *bhayanaka rasa* to illuminate how everyday relationships with dear ones are torn asunder under extreme duress, whether it is the mother who is no longer present to feed her son, the brother who witnesses his sister being raped, or the daughter whose father has been dragged away by 'bad men.' As Renjith, one of the main choreographers and lead performers explains, 'the shift to a relational perspective increases the ability to connect the audience to the experience of these refugees. It invites you to consider your mother, your sister, your wife' (interview with author, June 10, 2018). It becomes a lens to explore the wider networks of relations impacted by the experiences of refugees. The underlying emphasis on relationships is also central to the boat scene. While fear remains continuously portrayed by each individual, it is punctuated by the protective love of the mother for her child (*vatsalya bhakti rasa*) and the communal compassionate response (*karuna rasa*) toward the mother's panic, a response that remains brief as other dangers quickly arise. While this production is based on the very personal experience of the artistic director, the intentional blending of individual and communal aspects illuminates the more universalized emotions that the aesthetic theory of *rasa* aims to portray.[13]

While dancers focus their energies on *bhavas*, statements about *rasa* manifest in performance artifacts. For example, the London handbill describes the intended outcome of the choreographic process and program as ideally leading audiences to 'be able to experience the psyche of a refugee ... and encourage[s] an inclusive community for refugees seeking shelter' (*Agathi* Program Notes 2018:4). This statement points us to the primary overall intended *rasa* for the program, *karuna rasa*, or the compassionate or empathetic mood, while simultaneously transgressing more traditional understandings of *rasa* in its ability to instigate reflective action, and not just be educational but also enjoyable entertainment.[14]

Expanding *karuna rasa*

There is often a primary overall *rasa* for a thematic program, to which other *rasas* may contribute. In the case of *Agathi*, fear, disgust, and love support the dominant *rasa* of *karuna*. In the *Natyasastra*, *karuna rasa* is connected to the *sthayibhava* of *śoka*, or sorrow. Its *bhavas* provide appropriate contexts, responses to be enacted, and transitory emotions to utilize, as noted in the primary explanatory verses in chapter VI:

> [*Karuna rasa* is produced by] ... the despondency of the dear one separated on account of curse, loss of wealth, loss of life, imprisonment, flight, misfortunes, etc. It should be represented by shedding tears, lamentation, parched throat and mouth, paleness, change of voice, drooping of limbs, sighing and loss of memory. Its transitory feelings are self-disparagement, debility, reflection, longing, flurry, confusion, distraction, weariness, fear, sorrow, depression, sickness, stupefaction, madness, dementedness, alarm, indolence, death stupor, trembling, paleness, tears and change of voice [sic].

Other traces of information about *karuna rasa* include an additional verse reiterating 'the sight of the death of the dear one, or the hearing of unpleasant words' as contexts, the more detailed exposition of *śoka* through variations on forms of crying based on gender, class, and motivation (chapter VII:21–6), and in the earlier parsing of *srngara*, or the erotic *rasa*, the difference between love during separation which always retains a space for reunion with the beloved, and the more permanent experiences of loss without hope for restoration that fuel *karuna* (chapter VI:58).[15]

These statements point to situations, responses, and emotions that at first appear relevant to the depiction of fleeing refugees in the boat scene. The contexts grounded in loss resonate, along with the many physical and emotional responses possible; however, it is important to note that *karuna* functions from a place of witness of the beloved who has suffered these forms of loss, and through that only secondarily causes the painful irreversible state of separation for the witnessing hero or heroine. On stage, *karuna* is most often used by heroes surveying the aftermath of battle and/or the more permanent, ongoing suffering of others as a way to bolster the appropriate characteristics of the hero.

Agathi utilizes *karuna* differently as dancers embody the forms of loss directly, and are engaged in 'flight' themselves, although there is an implied sense of witnessing the loss and death of beloved family members and friends. The very climax of the boat scene enacts a witnessing of the baby's death by the people in the boat, creating immediate proximity to the causes of loss. The theory of *rasa* relies on a certain distancing from directly experiencing any of the nine aesthetic moods as internalized human emotion, in order to create space for enjoyable engagement at witnessing the enactment of those moods as an audience member. When watching a program, one does not experience terror or disgust, but enjoys how artists enact characters being frightened or repulsed.

The enactment of *karuna rasa* in *Agathi* aims to break down that aesthetic distance which pushes beyond the original intent of the formulas of the *Natyasastra* in pivoting the role of direct witness to the audience, rather than viewing the hero enacting a compassionate response, and with the added expectation of evoking the experience of real compassion in the audience members. Kumarasamy reflected on how different the Q&A sessions were than for other productions, not only in the length of time people stayed to make comments, but also the nature of what they focused on: 'Rather than costumes and *jatis* (step sequences), the audience focused on the message' (interview with author, June 10, 2018). One Chennai-based audience member observed, 'You made us silent,' with others nodding and vocalizing assent. Another audience member from Houston affirmed how the depiction aligned with what she had heard from refugees in a resettlement community in Texas and declared, 'When I go back home, I will be volunteering, especially to help the children.' In London, raising awareness was the focus of audience comments, with one audience member stating, 'For people who don't know, it is a powerful way to tell the stories and does keep it moving forward to the next generation so that they know.'

Rather than technical assessments, which are very common in response to bharatanatyam programs, audience members demonstrated their own responses and considerations of how the program might impact their real-life behaviors toward refugees. For today's dancers, the mechanics of *rasa* often cannot maintain its universalized, distanced position. Instead, it becomes personalized for the dancers and audience members, either creating direct devotional experiences, or in the case of *Agathi*, an empathetic, ethical motivation to reflect and take action, in alignment with the educational framework at the beginning of the *Natyasastra*.

Kinesthetic empathy

Kinesthetic empathy entails the evoking of compassionate responses through embodying and/or watching the embodiment of physical-emotional movements that may or may not have intentional narrative aspects. The development of this concept is based on ongoing interdisciplinary conversations across disciplines such as philosophy, neuroscience, and dance studies. I propose that this case study of *Agathi*, with its palimpsest approach to performative narrative and aesthetic empathetic processes, provides insight into the creation and experience of kinesthetic empathy. Scholars have previously identified aesthetic theories of audience receptivity as a productive area for examining how the workings and efficaciousness of kinesthetic empathy might be explored. However, the dynamic applications of *rasa*, as one of the most ancient yet evolving aesthetic theories on audience receptivity tied to dance, has not been part of the conversation that I hope this analysis of *Agathi* adds to.[16]

The earliest Western-focused discussions of aesthetic theories of audience receptivity are interested in empathy in relation to the arts more broadly, with some delineation of embodied responsiveness to visual arts (see Jones 2012). Narrowing the field for the purposes of this article, scholars juxtaposing empathy explicitly within the context of dance arts often cite the 1930s dance critic John Martin, who posits the ability of audiences to directly feel the emotions of the dancer through an 'inner mimicry' (Martin 1939:47–53). Dance scholar Susan Foster notes Martin's formulation of kinesthetic empathy as a form of 'contagion' that is based on problematic assumptions about psychological access to the experience of others and a universalizing of empathetic processes that ignores cultural specificity (Foster 2008, 2011). I agree with this critique, in that Kumarasamy used his own refugee experiences and those expressed by children in poetic form to inform the choreographic process for *Agathi*, but the dancers themselves should not be assumed to be able to fully access the individual and cultural specificity of those experiences, even with the improvisational emotional work explored in the studio work sessions. Neither should psychological access be assumed of audience members.

Instead, Foster and others reframe discussions about kinesthetic empathy to include a variety of interdisciplinary insights, which I think bring us closer to the workings of kinesthetic empathy. They take seriously neuroscientific studies on 'mirror neurons' that light up in brains not just when a person is doing a particular action, but also when witnessing that action in others (see Reason and Reynolds 2012:17–25). In addition, attention is paid to more finely parsing distinctions between emotion and affect, namely, their processes and locations related to artistic production and reception. For example, Dee Reynolds problematizes the centering of emotion in conversations in which she suggests affect is a more apt framework for analysis. Because emotion attains cognitively discursive levels of categorization, Reynolds notes, affect better captures the experiential non-discursive level of 'being moved,' but without naming any particular emotion. Affect does not require narrative to become aware of particular emotions (Reynolds 2012:124).

Many of these more recent inquiries into kinesthetic empathy depend on delineations of dance as relying on porous, processual understandings of bodies and embodiment. Building on the work of Brian Massumi and Elizabeth Grosz, who outline the ways in which affect exists in the interface, neither wholly in the subject or object, but rather unfolding in the in-between as process, Reynolds argues that

> dance is a movement through and across bodies rather than being an attribute of the dancer's body. I want to suggest that the dance spectator can be invested as both subject and object in a shared materiality and flow of choreographed movement across dancers' bodies. … Affective empathy does not take as its object a perceived other, such as a dancer, but rather the dance's body, which is neither 'self' nor 'other'. The impact of affect on the body intensifies sensation such that the 'dance's body' [what is created in the intersubjective processual interface between dancer and spectator] as object of vision is also felt from within, 'enfolded' through kinesthesia. (Reynolds 2012:129)

First, this notion of 'body' shifts attention from falsely rigid boundaries to embracing transactive processes as the defining quality of embodiment. Second, Reynolds focuses particularly on how embodied intensity created in this in-between kinesthetically impacts the communal 'body' inclusive of dancer and spectator emergent in a dance event (Reynolds 2012:132).

An embodied palimpsest model of analysis, as I have engaged in with *Agathi*, attempts to center process and communal creation, a type of intercorporeality, in tracing the performative emergence of possibilities for kinesthetic empathy. Embodiment as a palimpsest productively disrupts the habituated analysis of reifying unique boundaries between dancers and spectators, and brings to the center the layers of flow and process happening in the interactions in the in-between, the communal 'dance's body.' In the 'dance's body' that is the boat scene in *Agathi*, the physically enacted turmoil of refugees fleeing also intentionally evokes the embodied affective resonances of the push-and-pull battle between gods and *asuras* and its potential for life and death from the 'Churning of the ocean' narrative, among other individual and cultural layers of affective experiences of fear, flight, or conflict. The embodied affections and intimacies between a mother and child, connected to resonances of Krishna and Yashoda, but also dancers and spectators' own experiences of play, nurturing, and protective love, contribute to the multilayered process of potential kinesthetic empathy creation. The embodied palimpsest of the 'dance's body' being created in each moment is shaped and engaged by all the affective resonances of those participating in the performance process in the room, without everyone having had direct refugee experiences themselves. How does *rasa* uniquely inform this approach to kinesthetic empathy?

Embodied palimpsests center the non-discursive affective contributing layers that an understanding of the dimensions of *rasa* is particularly good at making visible, especially when illuminating the particularity of situational physical-emotional vignettes. At the same time, *rasa* by its very nature operates at an aesthetic distance, whose universalizing tendencies would seem to work against the creation of actual empathy. I would suggest that *rasa*'s universalizing aspects instead embed an adaptability related to the location, experience, and performance of physical-emotional expression, which allows multiple, shared affective contributions to the 'dance's body' that can create the potential for particularized situations of empathy. Rose Parekh-Gaihede suggests in her analyses of the links between empathy and ethical awareness in performance that '[aesthetic] distance and empathy do not necessarily work in opposition to each other' (Parekh-Gaihede 2012:177). I would agree that in the case of *Agathi*, *rasa* functions to guide the emergence and experience of an intracorporeal palimpsest, which hinges on the adaptability of aesthetic distance to invite multiple affective contributions from dancers and spectators, in order to create the 'dance's body' in process together. Traces of an efficacious process of kinesthetic empathy is evident in the dancers and spectators' comments about being affectively moved in relation to the particular experiences of refugees. The boat scene highlights the potential for understanding embodiment as a palimpsest, as well as the workings of kinesthetic empathy.

Concluding thoughts

I suggest in this article that the construct of a palimpsest explains the ways bodies carry forward the expectations around the aesthetics (*rasas*) and gestures of previous staged encounters, including the narrative resonances of Hindu mythologies and affective human–divine relationships, even when the main theme of the production is not explicitly about the gods. The first layer of the palimpsest is the choreographic focus on refugees. The next layer sees the narratives of the 'Churning of the ocean,' a story related to an avatar of Vishnu, and the relationship between Krishna and his adopted mother Yashoda influence the reading of the boat scene in *Agathi*. The use of *sanchari bhavas*, or the embodiment of multiple, interrelated narrative perspectives, and the presence of a mother and child as a central feature set up an audience familiar with bharatanatyam to expect particular roles and outcomes that deepen the pathos of the refugee experience.

A third layer of the palimpsest involves the development of *rasa*, or aesthetic moods to be enjoyed by the audience, created by the physical-emotional stagecraft employed in the boat scene. *Rasa*, as an ancient audience receptivity theory, has also been interpreted as a model by the Indian philosopher Abhinavagupta (eleventh century) for attaining divine bliss – 'to taste *rasa* is to taste Brahman,' or the divine essence (Gnoli 1968). In *Agathi*, the *rasas* of *vatsalya* (parental love), *bhayanaka* (fear), and *karuna* (compassion) are conveyed through gesture sequences, in which the tropes around the physical expressions involved in creating these *rasas* powerfully reframe the refugees through emotional experiences related to separation, loss, and empathy. *Agathi*'s use of *rasa* reflects both classical theoretical understandings from the 2000-year-old dance-drama compendium, the *Natyasastra*, and changes how the limited opportunities for *karuna rasa*, usually restricted to warrior heroes on the battlefield and *nayikas*, may be expanded in new moral-somatic directions related to refugees.

This case study of an embodied palimpsest, with its layers of Hindu narratives and *rasas* that shape the portrayal and expectations of immigrants' experiences, adds new dimensions to the conversation within aesthetics/dance studies on kinesthetic empathy (Foster 2011; Reason and Reynolds 2012). By analyzing the palimpsest of the performers' embodied experience holistically in *Agathi*, the universalized notions of the workings of *rasa* shift to an intercorporeal, process-centered partnership with affective particularities of dancers and audience members participating in the experience of the 'dance's body' created communally in the interactive in-between. Kinesthetic empathy does not exist bounded in the dancer or audience, but rather the potential is created interstitially and through a multi-layered bodily porosity, an embodied palimpsest. This one example from *Agathi* will hopefully spark further research at the intersection of body, movement, ethics, and aesthetics.

About the author

Katherine C. Zubko is Professor of Religious Studies and NEH Distinguished Professor of the Humanities (2018–23) at the University of North Carolina, Asheville. Her areas of expertise include aesthetics, ritual, performance, and embodied religion in South Asia. Zubko is the author of *Dancing Bodies of Devotion: Fluid Gestures in Bharata Natyam* (2014), and co-editor with George Pati of *Transformational Embodiment in Asian Religions: Subtle Bodies, Spatial Bodies* (2019). Current research interests include exploring the role of embodied gestures of compassion and hospitality in performances on conflict transformation, and inclusive, interdisciplinary curriculum design as part of the scholarship of teaching and learning.

Notes

1. See *New York Times* articles and photos on September 2–3, 2015 of Aylan Kurdi.
2. See 360 film at: https://www.unhcr.org/khaled-hosseini.html
3. There is now a well-established cohort of dance scholars committed to not just studying and developing theories about bodies, but also involving their own embodied knowledge in their research process. In Indian classical dance forms, this cohort of dance scholars includes Meduri, Kersenboom-Story, O'Shea, Chakravorty, Soneji, Coorlawala, Kamath, Devarajan, P. Srinivasan, and Zubko. Learning bharatanatyam has changed both my ethnographic relationships with

the dancers of *Agathi* and the types of knowledge I bring to analyzing the aesthetics and gestures of this performative case study.

4   There are debates about the adaptability of the constructed dance form of bharatanatyam in relation to its Hindu participants, themes, and contexts. For one viewpoint that delineates bharatanatyam as solely a Hindu practice, see Malhotra and Neelakandan (2011:113–20).

5   See Nadhi Thekkek and Ruby Tut, *Broken Seeds (Still Grow)*, 2017–19, an ongoing multimedia work that juxtaposes narratives of survivors of Partition in 1947 between India and Pakistan with current immigrant experiences during the American Trump presidency.

6   Anita Ratnam's 'The Other Festival,' focused on Indian contemporary dance existing on the peripheries of the Chennai arts festival, begun in 1998 and offered a dozen times since then, was ahead of its time in bringing contemporary dance performances to more conservative Chennai audiences. Natya Darshan was probably able to incorporate less traditional work due to the earlier festivals hosted by Ratnam. Natya Kala is one of the longest running conferences focused solely on dance, and only recently has been more open to folk styles and difficult topics, such as the inclusion of issues related to #MeToo raised during the December 2017 and December 2018 programs. The Music Academy still tilts more heavily to programs related to music, but one week in January is fully devoted to dance.

7   The Bharatiya Vidya Bhavan in West Kensington is an example of a spatial palimpsest.

8   The contemporary concert repertoire traces its roots to the nineteenth-century Tanjore Quartette, four brothers under the patronage of the king of Thanjavur in Tamil Nadu, who systematized the genres contained in a *margam*, or concert, as performed in court settings. While *padams*, *sabdams*, *javalis*, and the *varnam* feature the performance of narratives, *alarippu*, *jatiswaram*, and *tillana* genres typically do not. See Allen (1997) for more history.

9   All references to Bharata's *Natyasastra* are quoted from Ghosh (1950–67), although many other translations are available, which is why I include chapter and verse numbers.

10 An example of *sanchari bhavas*: if the primary focus of the story is to describe the physical features of a god's form, such as the blue color of Krishna's body, the gesture matrix might include depicting the blue of a monsoon cloud, which then leads to a gestured set of references about Krishna holding up a mountain to shield devotees from monsoon-like rains.

11 Kumarasamy notes that in other programs, the lack of applause after the scene startled him at first, as he recollected thinking that the dancers were pouring their hearts into this scene and the audience was unappreciative, but he later

realized that the audience did not want to interrupt the emotional moment they were experiencing (interview with author, June 10, 2018).

12 Kumarasamy utilized the following organizational source: *A Book of Poems: Expressions of Our Youth* (Toronto: Costi Immigrant Services and UN High Commissioner for Refugees, 2011).

13 William Mazzarella has explored the relationships between the universal and intimately personal in reference to affect within modernities and public cultures in ways that illuminate ongoing tensions and assumptions within this dynamic (Mazzarella 2009). It is beyond the scope of this study to address the ways in which *bhava* and/or *rasa* might be a type of affect as defined through multiple lenses, but this topic is worth consideration as a separate essay.

14 *Bhavas* and *rasas* have never been stagnant in concept or practice. For example, Pallabi Chakravorty provides a study of the shifting of *bhavas* and *rasas* within the context of Bollywood and reality show dance choreographies, positing a *bhava*-remix model, in which the 'emotion of aspiration that creates a cosmopolitan hybrid Indian identity' drives the creation of 'dancing bodies [that] remain porous and flexible to learn new techniques and embody images that may appear from any visual world,' rather than the traditional codified possibilities from classical aesthetics (Chakravorty 2017:138). Because of the intentional distancing from the classical model Chakravorty indicates in her development of the *bhava*-remix model, I have decided not to import it into this analysis of the aesthetics of *Agathi*, even though the porosity that the *bhava*-remix creates is an allied processual foundation point.

15 *Agathi* also breaks with this understanding of the difference between *srngara* and *karuna* forms of loss. For example, in the first and the third acts, the dancers Renjith and Vijna perform duets on love and separation that can be found in typical repertoires of *nayikas* (female heroines) or *astapadis*, short dance items from Radha's perspective based on the *Gita Govinda*. In this production, they aptly redirect their skills in developing the pain of separation to portraying the difficulties of refugees who are separated from their families and lovers. Instead of a solo dancer depicting both perspectives, the duo, sitting at opposite ends of the stage, develop lines of the song with accompanying gestures to reflect the distinct perspective of each individual. They have effectively created a bridge between *srngara* and *karuna rasas*.

16 See Aristotle, *Rhetoric, Poetics and the Nicomachean Ethics* (trans. T. Taylor; London: Valpy, 1818) for another ancient (fourth century BCE) audience receptivity theory foregrounding the use of mimesis and the importance of catharsis in relation to speech-making, poetry and dramatic tragedy. While rhythm is part of tragedies, Aristotle does not focus on dance to the same extent as South Asian dance-drama systems do, including Bharata's *Natyasastra*.

References

Agathi Program Notes (2018) *Agathi: The Plight of the Refugee*. A Dance-Theatre Production by Apsaras Arts, June. UK Program published by Apsaras Arts and Milapfest.

Allen, M. H. (1997) Rewriting the script for South Indian Dance. *Drama Review* 41(3): 63–100. https://doi.org/10.2307/1146609

Balfour, M. (ed.) (2013) *Refugee Performance: Practical Encounters*. Bristol: Intellect.

Battles, M. (2015) *Palimpsest: The History of the Written Word*. New York: Norton & Co.

Berila, B. (2015) *Integrating Mindfulness into Anti-Oppression Pedagogy: Social Justice in Higher Education*. New York: Routledge. https://doi.org/10.4324/9781315721033

Chakravorty, P. (2007) *Bells of Change: Kathak Dance, Women and Modernity in India*. London: Seagull Press.

Chakravorty, P. (2017) *This is How We Dance Now! Performance in the Age of Bollywood and Reality Shows*. London: Oxford University Press. https://doi.org/10.1093/oso/9780199477760.001.0001

Coorlawala, U. (2005) The birth of bharatanatyam and the Sanskritized body. In Avanthi Meduri (ed.) *Rukmini Devi Arundale, 1904–1986: A Visionary Architect of Indian Culture and the Performing Arts* 173–94. Delhi: Motilal Banarsidass.

Csordas, T. J. (1993) Somatic modes of attention. *Cultural Anthropology* 8(2): 135–56. https://doi.org/10.1525/can.1993.8.2.02a00010

Cucinella, C. (2010) *The Poetics of the Body: Edna St. Vincent Millay, Elizabeth Bishop, Marilyn Chin, and Marilyn Hacker*. New York: Palgrave. https://doi.org/10.1057/9780230106512

Elliott, D., Silverman, M., and Bowman, W. (2016) Artistic citizenship: introduction, aims, and overview. In D. Elliot, M. Silverman, and W. Bowman (eds) *Artistic Citizenship: Artistry, Social Responsibility, and Ethical Praxis* 3–21. New York: Oxford University Press. https://doi.org/10.1093/acprof:oso/9780199393749.003.0001

Foster, S. (2008) Movement's contagion: the kinesthetic impact of performance. In T. C. Davis (ed.) *The Cambridge Companion to Performance Studies* 46–59. Cambridge: Cambridge University Press. https://doi.org/10.1017/CCOL9780521874014.004

Foster, S. (2011) *Choreographing Empathy: Kinesthesia in Performance*. New York: Routledge. https://doi.org/10.4324/9780203840702

Ghosh, M. (trans.) (1950–67) *Nāṭyaśāstra, A Treatise on Hindu Dramaturgy and Histrionics Attributed to Bharata*. Calcutta: Royal Asiatic Society.

Gnoli, R. (trans.) (1968) *The Aesthetic Experience According to Abhinavagupta* (2nd edn, revised and enlarged). Banaras: Chowkhamba Sanskrit Series.

Haines-Eitzen, K. (2012) *The Gendered Palimpsest: Women, Writing, and Representation in Early Christianity*. New York: Oxford University Press. https://doi.org/10.1093/acprof:oso/9780195171297.001.0001

Hosseini, K. (2018) *Sea Prayer*. New York: Riverhead Books.

Jones, A. (2012) Foreword. In M. Reason and D. Reynolds (eds) *Kinesthetic Empathy in Creative and Cultural Practices* 11–15. Bristol: Intellect.

Lamb, S. (2000) *White Saris and Sweet Mangoes: Aging, Gender, and Body in North India*. Berkeley: University of California Press. https://doi.org/10.1525/9780520935266

Malhotra, R., and Neelakandan, A. (2011) *Breaking India: Western Interventions in Dravidian and Dalit Faultlines*. Delhi: Amaryllis Publishers.

Marglin, F. A. (1985) *Wives of the God King: The Rituals of the Devadasis of Puri*. London: Oxford University Press.

Martin, J. (1939) *Introduction to the Dance*. New York: Dance Horizons.

Mazzarella, W. (2009) Affect: what is it good for? In S. Dube (ed.) *Enchantments of Modernity: Empire, Nation, Globalization* 291–309. New York: Routledge. https://doi.org/10.4324/9781003071020-13

Nabhan-Warren, K. (2005) *The Virgin of El Barrio*. New York: NYU Press.

O'Shea, J. (2007) *At Home in the World: Bharata Natyam on the Global Stage*. Connecticut: Wesleyan University Press.

Parekh-Gaihede, R. (2012) Breaking the distance: empathy and ethical awareness in performance. In M. Reason and D. Reynolds (eds) *Kinesthetic Empathy in Creative and Cultural Practices* 177–92. Bristol: Intellect.

Pianigiani, G. (2019) More than 100 migrants die at sea in wreck off Libya, survivors say. *New York Times*, Section A10, January 20.

Reason, M., and Reynolds, D. (2012) Introduction. In M. Reason and D. Reynolds (eds) *Kinesthetic Empathy in Creative and Cultural Practices* 17–25. Bristol: Intellect.

Reynolds, D. (2012) Kinesthetic empathy and the dance's body: from emotion to affect. In M. Reason and D. Reynolds (eds) *Kinesthetic Empathy in Creative and Cultural Practices* 123–36. Bristol: Intellect.

Salinas, A. (2016) Building a Natya Shastra: individual voices in an evolving public memory. In M. Anoop and V. Gulati (eds) *Scripting Dance in Contemporary India* 61–84. Maryland: Lexington.

Sklar, D. (2001) *Dancing with the Virgin: Body and Faith in the Fiesta of Tortugas, New Mexico*. Berkeley: University of California Press.

Soneji, D. (2011) *Unfinished Gestures: Devadasis, Memory, and Modernity in South India*. Chicago: University of Chicago Press. https://doi.org/10.7208/chicago/9780226768113.001.0001

Srinivasan, A. (1985) Reform and revival: the devadasi and her dance. *Economic and Political Weekly* 20(44): 1869–76.

Thomas, A. (2010) *Prague Palimpsest: Writing, Memory, and the City*. Chicago: University of Chicago Press. https://doi.org/10.7208/chicago/9780226795416.001.0001

Trawick, M. (1990) *Notes on Love in a Tamil Family*. Berkeley: University of California Press. https://doi.org/10.1525/9780520912809

Vasquez, M. (2011) *More Than Belief: A Materialist Theory of Religion*. Oxford: Oxford University Press.

Zubko, K. C. (2014) *Dancing Bodies of Devotion: Fluid Gestures in Bharata Natyam*. Maryland: Lexington Press.

Zubko, K. C. (2018) Christian themes and the role of the *nayika* in *bharatanatyam*. *International Journal of Asian Christianity* 1(2): 269–89. https://doi.org/10.1163/25424246-00102006

Part IV
Microcosmic bodies

7 Religion and the imperial body politic of Japan

Pamela D. Winfield

Abstract

This article offers a religious history of the Japanese emperor's body as it was discursively constructed, visually imagined, and ritually reinforced as the larger body politic. It demonstrates that the Shintō-inflected notion of the imperial body politic (J. *kokutai*) technically only emerged during the early modern period in Japan. It therefore draws attention instead to the important premodern Buddhist precursors that first equated the emperor's own body with the greater state polity of Japan. Buddhist teachings about the world-body of Buddhahood (*dharmakāya*), the monumental bronze Buddha body of Birushana in Nara, and Buddhist ritual activity throughout Japan's provincial temple system all helped to construct Emperor Shōmu (r. 710–56) as the all-protecting head of the family-state (*kokka*). Later esoteric Buddhist teachings about 'becoming a Buddha in this very body' (*sokushin jōbutsu*) and elaborate state-protecting rites performed before Kūkai's (744–835) multi-headed and multi-armed figures all helped to protect the body of the emperor (or his clothes), and by extension, the health and wellbeing of the country at large. Finally, modern reformulations such as Kiyozawa Manshi's (1863–1903) 'hand metaphor' and Minobe Tatsukichi's (1873–1948) 'organ theory of government' continued to resonate with these pre-existing Buddhist corporeal tropes, as well as with newly imported Western philosophical constructs. As a result, this premodern Buddhist analysis of the emperor's rhetorical, artistic, and ceremonial body-state demonstrates the centrality of the human body in imagining religious authority and political power in Japan.

Keywords: Japan; emperor; body politic; Buddhism

Introduction

This article offers a religious history of the Japanese emperor's body as it was discursively constructed, visually imagined, and ritually reinforced as the larger body politic.

It first examines the ancient Chinese texts, architectural structures, and ritual procedures that equated the emperor's body with the larger 'country-body' (C. *guoti* 國體).[1] This term's simplified form in Japan (J. *kokutai* 国体) technically only emerged during the early modern period, when Japan's seventeenth-century nativist School of National Learning (J. *kokugaku* 国学) resuscitated it and theorized that Japan's essential character depended upon the emperor's unbroken lineage descending from the mythic sun goddess Amaterasu. This line of thinking reached its most extreme expression during World War II.[2]

This article then proposes the novel argument that premodern Buddhism had long provided important precursors for thinking about, seeing, and ritually performing the emperor's body-as-state. During the Nara period (710–84), Emperor Shōmu (r. 710–56) commissioned a monumental statue of Birushana Buddha at Tōdaiji temple in the ancient capital of Nara. On the visual and discursive levels, this massive bronze Buddha-body personified the universal world-body of Buddhahood (*dharmakāya*), where the term -*kāya* literally means 'body' in Sanskrit. This colossal image also symbolized Shōmu's unified, centralized state, which was likened to a 'country-family' (J. *kokka* 国家) with Shōmu at its head. On the ritual level, furthermore, Shōmu commissioned Buddhist state-protecting rites to be performed at Tōdaiji headquarters and throughout Japan's provincial system of regional temples (J. *kokubunji* 国分寺). Metaphorically speaking, this Buddhist infrastructure served as a sort of circulatory or immunological system for the protection and pacification of the familial body politic (J. *chingo kokka* 鎮護国家).

Furthermore, during the Heian period (794–1333/36), esoteric Buddhist ideas, images, and rituals also ensured the emperor's – and by extension, the entire country's – physical health and wellbeing. On the doctrinal level, Kūkai's (774–835) key teachings on 'becoming a Buddha in this very body' and his instructions for embodying the universal *dharmakāya*'s body, speech, and mind through the practitioner's mudrās hand gestures, mantra recitations, and mandala visualizations placed unprecedented emphasis on the physical body as a vehicle for awakening. Ritually speaking, it also discusses Kūkai's esoteric practice of *kaji* mutual empowerment between self and Buddha. Visually speaking, finally, it examines how these esoteric teachings and techniques were leveraged to protect the emperor-as-state, either in the

Benevolent Kings ceremony before the sculptural mandala at Tōji temple, or in the image-filled Latter Seven Day Rite within the imperial palace grounds itself.

Finally, the epilogue considers modern Buddhist iterations of the long-standing equation between the emperor's physical and national bodies. It analyzes the philosophical argument of the True Pure Land Buddhist reformer Kiyozawa Manshi (1863–1903), who maintained that individual citizens of the nation work together like the fingers of a hand. As a result, he proposes that personal freedoms must already be incorporated into the state's whole body, and must therefore automatically be aligned with the king's law (*ōhō*). It also reconsiders Minobe Tatsukichi's (1873–1948) so-called 'organ theory of government' in light of these Buddhist precedents, and suggests that Buddhism's rich heritage of ideas, images, and ritual institutions continued to resonate with political forms well into the modern period. This analysis of the emperor's rhetorical, artistic, and ceremonial body-state thus locates its analysis at the intersection of Buddhist doctrine, state–sangha relations, art history, and ritual studies.

The emperor-as-state in China and Japan

Chinese origins: the 'country-body' *(guoti* 國體*)* and imperial ritual

The original Chinese notion of the body politic was first mentioned in records dating from the Han dynasty (206 BCE–220 CE). A second-century BCE commentary on the Spring and Autumn Annals called the *Guliang zhuan* 穀梁傳 identifies the *dafu* 大夫 high minister as the *guoti* 國體 or official embodiment of the entire country. Later, the first-century CE *Book of Han* also uses the term *guoti* as a collective singular for all the laws and officials of the Confucian government. However, it is Ge Hong's 葛洪 (283–343 CE) early fourth-century Daoist alchemical text called the *Book of the Master Who Embraces Simplicity* (*Baopuzi* 抱朴子) that most clearly equates the ruler's bodily cultivation with the realm's wellbeing. Ge Hong writes,

> The body of an individual can be pictured as a state. The diaphragm may be compared with the palace; the arms and legs, with the suburbs and frontiers. The bones and joints are like the officials; the inner gods are like the sovereign; the blood is like the ministers of state; the *qi* [energy] is like the population.
>
> Therefore, anyone able to regulate his own body can regulate a state. To take good care of the population is the best way to make your state secure; by the same token

to nurture the *qi* is the way to keep the body whole, for when the population scatters, the state goes to ruin; when the *qi* is exhausted, the body dies (Kohn 2006:8).[3]

In its archaic form, this two-character compound for the Chinese polity or 'country-body' (*guoti*) includes the word for 'body' (-*ti*體). This character is composed of two elements: the root radical for 'bones' (骨) as well as the character for 'abundant' (豊). Given the ideographic nature of Chinese language, human bones are therefore automatically evoked to indicate the country's skeletal framework for its elaborate government structures. The healthy functioning of this corporeal government structure depended upon proper Confucian statecraft, regulated by the emperor at its head. For this reason, '[t]he body of the emperor and the body politic was [also] formalized in the medical treatises of the Han dynasty; which applied the principles of government to the flows of *qi* [energy] in the body: the same Chinese word *zhi* [治 to treat] refers to healing and government' (Palmer 2007:10).

This metaphorical equation of the emperor's human body with a healthy state polity applied to religious activity as well. During the Han dynasty, state-sponsored rituals reinforced the notion that the proper standing of the emperor's own body directly equated to the wellbeing of his larger empire. For example, the usurper Wang Mang 王莽 (r. 9–23 CE) used state ritual to heal the state's internal discord and to legitimate his interregnum between the Former Han (206 BCE–9 CE) and Latter Han dynasties (25–220 CE). During his annual ceremonies in the ancient capital of Chang'an (present day Xian), Wang Mang made his ritual progress through a specially constructed ritual complex called the Ming Tang 明堂 or 'Bright Hall.' In a kind of symbolic and distributive logic, Wang Mang's miniature parade through the rooms of the Ming Tang's microcosmic structure symbolically mirrored his imperial inspection tours throughout all the lands of the Han empire. In addition, his final processional arrival in the penthouse observatory of the Ming Tang established him as the Son of Heaven, ostensibly aligned heaven and earth, and thereby maintained the peaceful regulation of the cosmos. His location at the center of the ritual *axis mundi* as the embodied Son of Heaven guaranteed the timely rotation of the heavens, which in turn ensured the proper rotation of the agricultural seasons, and sufficient crops throughout the land. It also ritually prevented inauspicious celestial omens that could supposedly result in pestilence, epidemic, famine, or any number of other societal ills. The emperor's own body was therefore inextricably linked to the health and wellbeing of the larger country-body, and later Chinese emperors replicated these annual rites at the Temple of Heaven and at the Temple of Soil and Grain (Earth) in future capitals, including present day Beijing.

Amaterasu and the body politic (*kokutai* 国体) in early modern Japan

Technically, the two-character Chinese compound *guoti* does not appear in Japan until the early modern period, when the Japanese proto-nationalist Aizawa Seishisai (会沢正志斎 1782–1863) resuscitated the Chinese term *guoti* and read its simplified characters with the Japanese pronunciation *kokutai* 国体. In the early modern and nativist context of Aizawa's so-called School of National Learning (J. *kokugaku* 国学), the term *kokutai* came to mean the Japanese state's distinctive character, essence, or fundamental personhood. The simplified character for 'country' (J. *koku* 国) includes the character for jewel 玉 and/or king 王 enclosed within the country's borders 囗. The simplified character for 'body' (-*tai* 体) also includes two elements: the radical 亻 to the left derives from the character for a person 人 or the people of the Japanese state, and the character 本 indicates 'origin' or 'root,' as it literally has a root at the base of a tree 木. As a result, the School of National Learning constructed the fundamental 'essence' or 'character' of the Japanese people, collectively singularized as the *kokutai* body politic. In the context of their proto-nationalist agenda, the School of National Learning inextricably linked this purported Japanese essence with the Shintō sun goddess Amaterasu's imperial line and lands.

Amaterasu, the female solar deity, is perhaps the best-known Shintō *kami* 神 (sacred presence) both inside and outside of Japan. She first appears in two mythic histories of Japan: The *Record of Ancient Matters* (J. *Kojiki* 古事) written in 712, and the *Annals of Japan* (J. *Nihon Shoki* 日本書紀) written in 720. Both of these politically motivated texts were commissioned by the reigning emperors of their day, and constructed Amaterasu as the progenitrix of their imperial line. Specifically, according to the *Nihon Shoki,* Amaterasu's grandson Ninigi begot a great grandson Jimmu, who became the semi-mythological first emperor of Japan (legendary reign dates c. 660–585 BCE).

Interestingly, the ability to read the archaic Chinese characters and properly pronounce the names of all the Japanese *kami* mentioned in the *Kojiki* and *Nihon Shoki* had been almost completely lost by the eighteenth century in Japan. It was only by virtue of scholars like Motoori Norinaga (本居宣長 1730–1801) and the *kokugaku* school that these texts were taken up and understood once again by contemporary Japanese audiences. Relying upon their scholarly reconstructions, early English translators introduced the proper names of all the various *kami* quite literally. For example, Basil Hall Chamberlain's 1882 English translation of the *Kojiki* takes the sun's namesake 'Ama-terasu [no] ō-mi-kami' 天照大御神 and renders it quite literally as the gender-neutral 'Heaven-Shining Great-August-Deity' (Chamberlain

Figure 7.1: Amaterasu emerging from her cave. Woodblock print, Utagawa Toyokuni III, 1857 (Creative Commons).

1919:section 16:65). It is only later, with William George Aston's first English translation of the *Nihon Shoki* in 1896, that Amaterasu is explicitly referred to as 'The Sun Goddess' during 'The Age of the Gods' (J. *kami-yo* alt. *jindai* 神代) section of the 30-chapter work (Aston 1896:49).

In perhaps her most famous mythic episode during this primordial age, Amaterasu's obnoxious storm god brother Susanoo defecates in her palace and breaks down her rice paddy divisions. In righteous indignation, Amaterasu withdraws into a cave and effectively plunges the islands of Japan into a solar eclipse. Light and order are eventually restored, however, when Amaterasu is lured out of her cave again by her own dazzling reflection in a mirror, by beautiful comma-shaped *magatama* 勾玉 jewels hung in a nearby tree, and by the sounds of a raucous party (Figure 7.1). After she emerges from her cave, another quick-thinking *kami* closes off the cave with a boulder and Amaterasu is restored to her proper role as the reliable rising sun. As a result, the entire country-body of Japan, the Land of the Rising Sun (*nihon* 日本 lit. 'sun-origin') is mythically and inextricably symbolized and personified by the shining sun-body of the female goddess Amaterasu.[4] As a result, in Shintō ritual halls throughout Japan, the mirror that lured her light out of the darkness becomes enshrined as a material symbol of Amaterasu's 'divine body' (J. *shintai* 神体). Shintō ritualists today therefore typically use the honorific prefix -*go* 御 to refer to Amaterasu's mirror as the *goshintai* 御神体 in order to indicate the mirror's sacred status as the divine body of the *kami* (Figure 7.2).

Symbolically, Amaterasu's divine mirror, her *magatama* comma-shaped jewel, and her brother Susanoo's 'grass-cutting sword' (J. *Kusanagi no tsurugi* 草薙の剣) constituted the three imperial regalia of Japan, as they embodied

Figure 7.2: Shintō mirror; the material 'spirit body' of the *kami* (*goshintai*) and one of the three imperial regalia of Japan. Photograph by the author.

the virtues of wisdom, benevolence, and valor, respectively.[5] Historically, furthermore, these three sacred material bodies were directly associated with the emperor's larger political body, especially during the contested period of the Southern and Northern Courts (J. *Nanboku-chō* period 南北朝時代 1333–92). Most notably, the fourteenth-century Japanese courtier and historian Kitabatake Chikafusa (北畠 親房 1293–1354), who was sympathetic to Emperor Go-Daigo's (後醍醐天皇 r. 1319–39) southern regime, explicitly claimed in his *Chronicles of the Authentic Lineages of the Divine Emperors* (J. *Jinnō Shōtoki* 神皇正統記) that Go-Daigo's possession of the three imperial regalia and his unbroken line of descent from the sun goddess Amaterasu together legitimated his rule over Japan. Centuries later, Kitabatake's influential history dating from 1339–43 was instrumental in shaping the so-called Mitō ideology (J. *mitōgaku* 水戸学) of the late Edo period (1600–1868). This school's positions on isolationism, Shintō nativism, and respect for the emperor helped to dismantle over 600 years of the shōgun's military dictatorship over Japan, and helped to 'restore' the Meiji emperor to the throne in 1868.[6]

Amaterasu and the *kokutai* in World War II

Historically speaking, in premodern Japan, Amaterasu's human descendants were never considered to be divine. Technically, the imperial progenitrix Amaterasu simply functioned much like any other heaven-dwelling *kami*, in that she was imagined to be the lineage parent and protector of an aristocratic clan (J. *ujigami* 氏神). This simply legitimated the rule of the emperor's clan over all the other clans by virtue of Amaterasu's superior status to all the other *kami*. It did not necessarily turn imperial clan members into gods.

However, in the modern period, the purported divine origins of the imperial line did help to legitimate and sanctify the growing specter of fascist ultra-nationalism and expansionist imperialism leading up to World War II. This began with the School of National Learning, continued with Mitō ideology, and went unchecked with the rapid militarization and rabid nationalism of the 1930s, so that by the end of the war, Amaterasu's human progeny on the throne was literally considered to be divine as well.

State Shintō orthodoxy in the nineteenth and twentieth centuries attempted to construct a fabricated Shintō motherland that was forcibly and artificially purified of all continental influences, including Buddhism. Once Japan had supposedly recovered its pure Shintō 'essence,' it attempted to cleanse the rest of Asia of its foreign influences as well. Metaphorically speaking, this meant shining Amaterasu's purifying rays into the heart of Asia to purge it of Western colonialism, although Japan's Western-trained imperial army itself hypocritically began acquiring a string of colonial spoils from the Sino-Japanese (1894–5) and the Russo-Japanese Wars (1904–5) (Hardacre 1991). Sociologically speaking, Japan's expansionist bent in the early twentieth century meant that it exported female bodies into Manchuria, for example, to colonize, sexually reproduce, and physically expand the boundaries of the Japanese motherland. Culturally speaking, finally, it meant that prominent Japanese female authors such as Yosano Akiko (与謝野 晶子 1878–1942), Tamura Toshiko (田村 俊子 1884–1945), and Hayashi Fumiko (林芙美子 1904–1951) re-inscribed women's bodies into the 'essence' of Japan's *kokutai* (Horiguchi 2011).

Eventually, military officers such as Honjo Shigeru (本庄 繁 1876–1945) and ultranationalist Shintō scholars such as Hozumi Yatsuka (穂積 八束 1860–1912) and Uesugi Shinkichi (上杉慎吉 1878–1929) directly asserted Emperor Hirohito's (裕仁 1901–89) divine status as a *kami*, since he was descended from the all-illuminating Amaterasu herself (Shillony 1999:7). Accordingly, Japan's widely used national teacher's manual, the *Country-Body's Fundamental Principles* (J. *Kokutai no hongi* 国体の本義) of 1937, instructed educators to teach that the emperor was a 'manifest god' (J. *arabito-gami* 荒人

神 or *akitsu mikami* 現御神). The latter poetic expression of imperial praise originally appeared in the mid-eighth century *Manyōshū* collection of classical poetry, but it was resuscitated and interpreted quite literally in the context of State Shintō fundamentalism during World War II (Shillony 1999:4). During this period, emperor worship was sanctioned and enforced by the state under the Peace Preservation Laws, and recently established religious sects such as Ōmotokyō were severely persecuted for not including Amaterasu in their devotions. With Japan's defeat in 1945, however, and with US-led occupation forces rewriting Japan's constitution, State Shintō and emperor worship premised on Amaterasu's divine nature were dismantled.

The Shintō-inflected notion of *kokutai* as Japan's national essence still continues to live on in subtle ways, however. The postwar discourse of 'Japanese-ness' (J. *nihonjinron* 日本人論) and calls to restore Japan's 'national character' (J. *kunigara* 国柄) are still embraced by a number of conservative right-wing groups in Japan, who wish for a return to pre-war nativism. Members of the ultra-nationalist group Nippon Kaigi 日本会議, for example, regularly pay respect to the military war dead at Yasukuni Jinja 靖国神社 in Tokyo, the controversial 'Peaceful Nation Shrine' that nevertheless houses the spirits of 14 Class-A war criminals among thousands of other fallen Japanese soldiers since 1869. The figure of Amaterasu no longer dominates their discourse, but for many ultra-conservative Japanese nationalists, the notion of the *kokutai* at the shrine still resonates with passionate corporeal power. The striking testimony of an aggrieved war widow is a case in point. Iwai Masuko pleads in defense of Yasukuni Jinja during a 2002 hearing at the Osaka District Court,

> If you must dishonor Yasukuni Shrine, kill me a million times instead. Hearing just one word that disparages Yasukuni Shrine, I feel my body shredded into pieces. And all the blood of my entire body gushes out and spreads as far as the eye can see – it is the ocean created by [the] blood of the [Japanese] troops. (Quoted in Takenaka 2015:introduction)[7]

Mrs Iwai's graphic rhetoric 57 years after the end of the war attests to her consanguinity with the fallen soldiers' ocean of blood, and her con-corporality with their shredded bodies if Yasukuni's rites are no longer able to make them symbolically whole in death. The imagined community of Japan's 'country-body,' therefore, still lives on through the civic religion of Yasukuni Jinja's institutional ideology, as well as in the bodies and minds of Japan's ultra-conservative right-wing nationalists.

Buddhist correlates

It is clear, therefore, that the word *kokutai* itself has only ever been used in Japan in the context of early modern discourse and World War II agendas to promote State Shintō and emperor worship. The original thesis of this article, however, is that Buddhism in the service of the state had previously promoted several rough correlates to the idea of an imperial body-politic throughout Japanese history, although it never invoked the term *kokutai*, strictly speaking.[8]

Nara period (710–84)

The concept of a centralized state as a body, and specifically as a Buddha-body, dominated state ideology during the Nara period (710–84). Most notably, Emperor Shōmu (聖武天皇 r. 710–56) used the East Asian Mahāyāna Buddhist notion of the *dharmakāya*, or cosmic world-body of Buddhahood, as a unifying symbol for the entire country. That is, in order to symbolize the universal body (Skt. *kāya*) of dharma teachings that would unite his realm after a series of disasters (e.g., the smallpox epidemic of 735–7 and Fujiwara no Hirotsugu's 藤原広嗣 (d. 740) attempted rebellion in the southern island of Kyūshū in 740), in 743 Shōmu began to cast a colossal gilt bronze statue of Vairocana (J. *Lochana* or *Birushana*), the Great Buddha of Light. This figural personification of universal buddha nature resembled other monumental cut-rock Buddha-bodies throughout Central and East Asia (e.g., at Bamiyan in Afghanistan and at Leshan in Sichuan, China). Likewise, in Japan, Shōmu's enormous bronze Buddha figure originally measured 53 feet tall (16 meters), but was destroyed due to a series of fires beginning in 1180. The current re-cast statue dating from the early eighteenth century measures approximately 49 feet (15 meters) tall, and is still the largest gilt bronze statue in the world housed in the largest wooden structure in the world (Figure 7.3).[9]

The formal eye-opening ceremony to consecrate this massive figure was held at Tōdaiji temple in 752, at the very heart of the ancient capital of Nara. In order to gather the necessary 500 tons of materials for this monumental public works project, Shōmu appealed to his subjects to donate metal to the cause, which naturally included all weapons and armor that might be used in future rebellions against him. Shōmu's tactical metal recall not only neutralized potential military opposition to him, but it simultaneously established a peaceful, centralized state that was both materially and metaphorically unified through the enormous embodiment of the Buddha of Light. In his appeal, the Emperor writes,

Figure 7.3: Birushana/Lochana Buddha, the monumental embodiment of the *dharmakāya*. Cast bronze with traces of gold, Tōdaiji temple, Nara, Japan. Eighteenth-century restoration of 752 statue by Emperor Shōmu (Creative Commons).

[On this day in 743], we take this occasion to proclaim Our great vow of erecting an image of Lochana Buddha in gold and copper. We wish to make the utmost use of the nation's resources of metal in the casting of this image, and also to level off the high hill on which the great edifice is to be raised, so that the entire land may be joined with Us in the fellowship of Buddhism and enjoy in common the advantages which this undertaking affords to the attainment of Buddhahood. (De Bary, Keene, and Tsunoda 1958:104)

This monumental Buddha-body at the heart of Japan's earliest centralized state thus became the focal point for all state-sponsored rituals to 'pacify and protect the country-family' (*chingo kokka* 鎮護国家). The two-character compound for 'country-family' (J. *kokka* 国家) resembles the ancient Chinese notion of the 'country-body' (C. *guoti*), but draws upon Confucian family values. These directed the ruler to govern over his people like a father governs his son, thus positioning the emperor as the metaphorical *pater familias* of the body politic.

In order to ensure the proper health and safety of his country-family, Shōmu commissioned Buddhist rituals in every province. Previously in 741, Shōmu had established a regional network of provincial temples called *kokubunji* 国分寺 (lit. country-Buddha-temple). His consort-wife Empress Kōmyō 光明皇后 (701–60) likewise established a similar network of provincial convents (J. *kokubun-niji* 国分尼寺), where rituals involving the *Lotus Sūtra* (J. *Hokkekyō* 法華経) were performed. As this sutra hints at female enlightenment potential, Kōmyō is credited with including women in the larger Buddhist body politic of ancient Japan (Meeks 2010).

The imperial edicts emulated similar decrees in Tang dynasty China (618–907 CE) and Silla period Korea (57 BCE–935 CE), which were designed to unify their respective kingdoms under a single Buddhist ideology.[10] Within the centralized infrastructure of *kokubunji* temples and *kokubunniji* convents, state-sponsored Buddhist rituals were performed for what we might call today national healthcare and homeland security. In this regard, they resembled the ancient Chinese notion of *zhi*, which indicates both healing and statecraft. These were two tasks that were inextricably linked at the time, since a safe and healthy body-politic must be made up of safe and healthy bodies.

Specifically, ritual chanting of the *Golden Light Sūtra* (J. *Konkōmyōkyō* 金光明経) in Japan's *kokubunji* temples called upon the four heavenly kings (J. *shintennō* 四天王) to 'protect th[e] king and his people, give them peace and freedom from suffering, prolong their lives and fill them with glory' (de Bary, Keene, and Tsunoda 1958:98). Later in the sutra, the Buddha himself rejoins, 'If any king upholds this sutra and makes offerings in its behalf, I will purify him of suffering and illness, and bring him peace of mind' (de Bary, Keene, and Tsunoda 1958:99). As a result, the *kokubunji* temples acted as a kind of early immunological system that circulated protective ritual activity throughout Japan's early body politic. They regulated the health and wellbeing of the state, extended Emperor Shōmu's therapeutic and political influence throughout the land, and metaphorically cast him as a universal world ruler (*cakravartin*), who literally cast the unifying personification of Buddha's world-body (S. *dharmakāya*) at Tōdaiji headquarters in the capital. In this context, the Buddha's conceptual world-body, his monumental sculptural body, Shōmu's imperial body as head of the family-state, and the populace's individual bodies – protected and prolonged by the four heavenly kings' bodies – all intersected and overlapped to form a multivalent early Buddhist 'body politic' in Japan.

Heian period (794–1192)

In the classical Heian period, named after the eponymous capital at Heian-kyō (present day Kyoto), Buddhism continued to serve the body-politic, though in more elaborate esoteric ritual forms. Esoteric Buddhism was a form of Vajrayāna or Tantric Buddhism that the patriarch Kūkai (空海 735–835) brought back to Japan in 806 after studying abroad in China for two years. Kūkai's central teachings focused on 'becoming a Buddha in this very body' (J. *sokushin jōbutsu* 即身成仏). The ritual logic behind his elaborate esoteric methods presupposed that the *dharmakāya's* universal body, speech, and mind could be embodied on the microcosmic level in the individual practitioner's corresponding *mudrā* hand gestures, *mantra* recitations, and *mandala* visualizations. As Kūkai's commentary on the *Mahāvairocana Sūtra* (T18:4a–5a) states,

> Therefore the three mysteries of the Dharmakāya['s body, speech and mind] and [those of] sentient beings correspond, making it possible for sentient beings to be blessed and empowered by the Dharmakāya. When, having observed this meaning, the practitioners of Mantrayāna [i.e., esoteric Buddhism] form mudrās with their hands, recite mantras with their mouths, and fix their minds in *samādhi* [meditative absorption], then their three mysteries become immersed in those of the Dharmakāya, resulting in the attainment of great perfection. (Trans. Abe 2000:129).[11]

This interpenetration of the larger Buddha-body and the practitioner's self-body was a meditative state known as *kaji* 加持, or mutual empowerment, in which the practitioner senses that 'Buddha enters me; I enter Buddha' (J. *nyūga ganyū* 入我我入). Historically, priests initiated into these esoteric practices performed rituals with mudrās, mantras, and mandalas, and ostensibly channeled universal forces into the ritual hall for the pacification and protection of the family-state.

For example, beginning in 823, Kūkai performed imperially sponsored esoteric rites at Tōji 東時 temple in Kyoto to protect the country under the relatively new Heian regime. Consequently, Tōji was known as the temple dedicated to 'The King of the Sutras That Defend the Country' (J. *kyō-ō gokokuji* 経王護国寺). This preeminent 'King of the Sutras' refers to the newly imported *Benevolent Kings Sūtra* (J. *Ninnōkyō* 仁王経 T246), a third state-protecting scripture that Kūkai popularized to supplement the old *Golden Light* and *Lotus Sūtras* used during the Nara period. Charles Orzech observes that the *Ninnōkyō* was a kind of urtext or 'charter for a national Buddhism of protection in China, Korea and Japan' that persisted well into the twentieth century (Orzech 1998:3). He also remarks that Tōji's sculptural *Ninnōkyō mandara* 'is a striking reminder of the imperial Buddhism that dominated China, Korea and Japan for a millennium and which contributed much to the present political dispositions of all three nations. It is also a reminder of the power of religion to transform the political world' (Orzech 1998:3).

In Amoghavajra's Chinese version of the *Ninnōkyō* dating from 765, the Buddha warns the Indian King of Kosala to uphold the dharma, lest seven kinds of disasters befall his kingdom (anomalies in the sun and moon, stars and planets, fires, floods, storms, drought, and war). To help ward off such misfortunes, in 826 Kūkai installed a Golden Hall at Tōji temple, where officiants would recite the sutra, perform esoteric ritual sequences, and consecrate the emperor's clothes (to be discussed below) before a three-dimensional sculptural mandala of larger than lifesize Buddha-bodies. The figural mandala has three sets of five images each. The center grouping features a sculpture of the 'Great Light' Buddha Mahāvairocana (J. *Dainichi nyorai* 大日如来) with four attendant wisdom Buddhas. Another grouping of benign bodhisattvas appear to the spectator's right. Another wrathful group of the Five Great Wisdom Kings (J. *godai myōō* 五大明王) appear on the left. Figure 7.4 illustrates the latter grouping, excepting the central King of Immovable Wisdom (J. *Fudō myōō*, 不動明王).

The wrathful countenances, flaming aureoles, multiple arms, heads, and hand-held implements of these figures all indicate that they are former demons-turned-dharma protectors. Yet, even in their domesticated Buddhist aspects, these Wisdom Kings nevertheless still embody the terrifying power to protect the state as they 'stand ready to defend Buddhist rulers (and others) from invasions, bandits, and meteorological disasters' (Orzech 1998:3). Furthermore, according to Cynthea Bogel's art historical analysis of the Tōji arrangement,

> The *Benevolent Kings Sūtra* [thus provides] the visual and conceptual guides for making mandalas for rites of key importance to the state. *Abhiśekha* [consecration] rituals … and Mikkyō [i.e., esoteric Buddhist] rites related to the *Benevolent Kings Sūtra* were distinct, but both deployed mandala altars, both called out the divinities of the mandala universe, and both concerned the same goals – including the protection of the state. (Bogel 2009:285)

By the end of Kūkai's life in 835, esoteric rites to protect the emperor's body-as-state had infiltrated into the innermost sanctums of the imperial palace itself. During the second week of the New Year, following a week of prayers to the *kami*, Kūkai's Latter Seven Day Rite (J. *goshichinichi mishuhō* 後七日御修法) was performed in a specially constructed palace chapel called the Shingon'in 真言院. The elaborate altar arrangement for this esoteric Buddhist rite was recorded in the late twelfth-century *Handscroll of Annual Ceremonies* (J. *Nenjū gyōji emaki* 年中行事絵巻). The illustration shows individual offertory stands before hanging scrolls of the five wrathful Wisdom Kings,

Winfield *Religion and the imperial body politic of Japan*   167

Figure 7.4: Four wrathful Wisdom Kings surrounding Fudō myōō (not pictured). Tōji temple, Kyoto, Japan. Commissioned by Kūkai in 826 (Creative Commons).

who as mentioned above, defend the ruler against invasions, meteorological disasters, and other misfortunes. Two side altars before suspended images of the Womb and Diamond World mandalas on the right and left, respectively, were also prepared for fire ceremonies (J. *goma* 護摩).[12]

This elaborate week-long ritual sequence was designed to protect and empower the emperor's physical body as a synecdoche for the country's larger body politic. It also protected his imperial robes as a stand-in substitute for his physical presence (Rambelli 2002), and it paid devotional attention to a Buddhist relic, the so-called wish-fulfilling jewel (S. *cintamani*), because it was both 'the symbol of the Dharmakāya ... [and] the natural body of all the

Tathāgatas [i.e., Buddhas]' (Abe 2000:349).¹³ As such, it was believed to have special state-protecting abilities (Ruppert 2000).

Specifically, the ritual began with five sets of offerings to Mahāvairocana Buddha and various Buddhist and Shintō deities, then three sets of *goma* fire ceremonies to prevent calamities, to increase fortune, and to defeat enemies.¹⁴ Finally, a series of three *kaji* empowerments followed, in which a high-ranking priest (J. *daiajari* 大阿闍梨 S. *mahācharya*) performed specific mudrās, mantras, and mandala meditations to channel the *dharmakāya's* universal energies into scented water, into the emperor's robes, and into the emperor's own body (Rambelli 2002:431). On the first and last nights of the ceremony, this *kaji*-empowered water was directly sprinkled onto the emperor's body (J. *gyokutai kaji* 玉體加持). This liturgically constructed him as an immutable 'jade or jewel body' (J. *gyokutai* 玉體), and discursively conflated him with the relic of Buddha's own body in the form of the *cintamani* wish-fulfilling jewel (玉). In addition, the consecrated water was also indirectly sprinkled onto the emperor's robes (J. *gyoe kaji* 御衣加持), which eclipsed the direct blessing of the emperor's body after the Meiji Restoration (Rambelli 2002:431 n. 13). This sartorial segment was also present in the *Benevolent Kings* rites at Tōji temple mentioned above. In addition, during the last three days of the ceremony, more *kaji*-empowered water was delivered from the Shingon'in chapel to the palace residence to bless the emperor further with physical health and longevity.

Japanese scholar Hayami Tasuku 速水侑 directly connects these Buddhist rites for the imperial body to the wellbeing of the larger imperial body politic, especially during the late Heian period, when the powerful Fujiwara regents and supposedly retired (but still politically active) emperors wielded considerable influence at court. Rambelli observes,

> If Hayami is correct, that implies that in the tenth and eleventh centuries the 'jade body' of the emperor ... was actually a collective body including the protagonists of the political scene, analogous to what early modern European theorists of the 'king's two bodies' called [the] 'body politic.' In other words, the [*mishuhō*], rituals that started as forms of religious protection for the emperor and his possessions, became tools for the defense of the entire political system. (Rambelli 2002:441)¹⁵

This annual Buddhist rite for the imperial state cult was historically held in the palace, but after a series of palace fires and several periods of interruption and resuscitation (Rambelli 2002:437–45),¹⁶ it finally moved to Tōji temple in 1883 (Abe 2000:347). Today, this secret ritual continues to take place behind closed doors in the Kanjōin 灌頂院 initiation hall located in the southwest quadrant of Tōji's temple compound every January 8–14 (in the solar calendar). Visitors today may only observe the outdoor ceremonial procession of the emperor's clothing being carried into the sanctuary, and they may only enter into the Kanjōin for one hour after the rites are concluded to view the sanctuary setup. Personal observation by this author on January 14, 2002, confirms that the disposition of mandala images, altars, offertory stands, and *godai myōō* hanging scrolls in the Kanjōin conforms to the illustrated twelfth-century *Handscroll of Annual Ceremonies*.[17]

Epilogue: Meiji variations on a theme

Kūkai's esoteric *kaji* empowerments for the benefit of the emperor-as-state thus served as a template for other sectarian expressions of self-and-Buddha union. For example, during the medieval period, the Jōdo Shinshū 'True Pure Land' Buddhist patriarch Rennyō 蓮如 (1415–99) claimed that when chanting Amida Buddha's name, 'the believer and Buddha are one body' (J. *kihō ittai* 機法一体; also translated more philosophically as 'one substance'). In the modern Meiji period (1868–1912), Rennyō's slogan was reformulated by the Jōdo Shinshū reformer Kiyozawa Manshi 清沢 満之 (1863–1903), who concluded instead that 'the myriad things are one body' (J. *bamputsu ittai* 万物一体). Generically speaking, *bamputsu ittai* expresses the typical Mahāyāna Buddhist doctrine that the world-body is a Buddha-body (*dharmakāya*). Historically speaking, however, Kiyozawa's reformulation of Rennyō's motto took on added political valence in the context of the 1890 Imperial Rescript on Education that demanded allegiance to the emperor as a matter of national morality (J. *kokumin dōtoku* 国民道徳). Kiyozawa maintained that because 'all things are one body,' like the fingers of a single hand, individual members of the body politic can act with autonomy, while still fulfilling the function of the universal (i.e., national) will. Kiyozawa writes,

> Various individual actions respond to the essence and body of the one Infinite. The five fingers on each hand and their coordinated and unified movement is nothing other than this. They respond to the directives of only one mind. It is nothing but the transmission and response between this and that, this finger and that finger … The true body (*shintai*) of the finite and the source of its appearance is not a purely finite individual. We must absolutely recognize that its true body and nature is the Infinite. As its body and nature is the Infinite, it is natural to see a reflection of the Infinite in its activity. That is, though at first sight, the finite existence of 'this' and 'that,' 'self'

and 'other' appear to be independent, the reality is the same body (*dō ittai*) of the Infinite. (Trans. Fasan 2013:98).[18]

In the nation-building context of the early Meiji constitutional monarchy, Kiyozawa's body and hand metaphors reconciled the philosophical problem of individual freedom versus national duty, for '[a]s Kiyozawa saw the present social order as in fact an expression of the divine will, submission to its dictates became one with the realization of personal autonomy' (Fasan 2013:88). As a result, Kiyozawa commands, 'Take the law of the king [*ōhō*; a moniker for the national morality campaign] as the foundation and put its ethical code first. Follow the common ways of the world and deepen your faith (*anjin*) within your heart' (trans. Fasan 2013:87–8).[19]

Kiyozawa introduced his brand of organic philosophy in his 1892 *Skeleton for The Philosophy of Religion* (J. *Shūkyō tetsugaku gaikotsu* 宗教哲学骸骨) and articulates his thoughts about limited particulars in relation to the unlimited Absolute in his unpublished 1895 draft for *A Skeleton for the Philosophy of Other Power* (J. *Tarikimon tetsugaku gaikotsu shikō*, 他力門哲学骸骨試行). It is interesting to note that even Kiyozawa's 'skeleton' (J. *gaikotsu* 骸骨) titles give anatomical structure to his philosophical thought, but other than his clear analogies to the body, there was no visual culture or imperial rituals associated with Kiyozawa's abstract reasoning. He was trained in Western European philosophy at Tokyo Imperial University (present day University of Tokyo) by Ernest Fenellosa, and he was influenced by Baruch Spinoza's (1632–77) substance metaphysics, Herbert Spencer's (1820–1903) social Darwinism, and the understudied German post-Idealist Hermann Lotze (1817–81). However, 'In contrast to Spencer who argues that society *functions like* a body, Kiyozawa will submit that the Absolute Infinite *is* a body ... Kiyozawa's source for this novel understanding is not Spencer but Hermann Lotze' (Fasan 2013:96–7). In addition, Kiyozawa is heir to Buddhism's long-standing doctrine of the *dharmakāya*, the world-body of Buddhahood.

In the modern period, therefore, Western European philosophy and political science influenced leading Japanese intellectuals, who attempted to reconcile and integrate them into Japan's pre-existing religious and political institutions. For this reason, given this long and varied Buddhist history of the imperial body politic in Japan, it is perhaps worth reconsidering Minobe Tatsukichi's 美濃部達吉 (1873–1948) so-called 1911 'organ theory of government' in light of Buddhist precedents. When ultra-conservatives in the House of Peers challenged Minobe's views during the heady State Shintō days of 1934, ostensibly because Minobe's theory put constitutional limits on the emperor instead of recognizing his elevated status as Amaterasu's divine progeny, Minobe clarified his position. The Tokyo Imperial University professor of constitutional law writes,

> To say that the sovereign is an organ of the nation merely expresses the idea that the sovereign governs not for his own private ends but for the ends of the whole nation. Article IV of the Constitution clearly states that the emperor is the 'head of state.' This means that if the nation is likened to the human body, the emperor occupies the position of its head. Prince Itō in his *Commentaries on the Constitution* says in this connection: '… just as the brain in the human body is the primitive source of all mental activity manifested through the four limbs and the different parts of the body.' Needless to say, the brain is just one of man's organs, but it is the pivotal and paramount organ. In other words, the emperor-organ theory is identical in meaning with the Constitution's statement that the emperor is the head of state. It has no other meaning than that … The idea of a nation prospering or progressing assumes as its basic premise that the nation is a vital, dynamic entity comparable to a living body. The emperor is its head and occupies the position of its paramount organ. (De Bary, Keene, and Tsunoda 1958:242–3).[20]

Thus, there is a lingering affinity or family resemblance that can be discerned when comparing the history of Buddhist imperial bodies and this modern, secular endorsement of Japan's constitutional monarchy. Emperor Shōmu's eighth-century position as a Buddhist *pater familias* in charge of protecting the country-family (J. *kokka* 国家) is not exactly the same as Minobe's placement of the emperor at the head of the constitutional body politic, but many modern Meiji intellectuals did repeatedly and explicitly speak in terms of the 'family-state' (J. *kazoku kokka* 家族国家) (Gluck 1987:4, 77–8, 92, 129, 187–8, 256, 265, 259, 276). In addition, the state-sponsored Mishuhō ceremonies for the blessing of the emperor's New Year's robes were not exactly the same as the Meiji emperor's modern investiture ceremony in 1889, but the sartorial symbolism was not lost on anyone. Carol Gluck cleverly writes,

> [T]he emperor would become the ideological center of the imperial state. In 1889, however, he was not yet clothed for his new role. For the traditional vestments of the imperial office had been vaporous ones, designed for the emperor's long residence 'above the clouds,' and they would not suffice for his public presence as the ruler of a constitutional state. In terms of ideological process, it required the entire Meiji period to weave the emperor's new clothes and display them effectively before the people … [By the end of World War II], most Japanese were familiar with the cut and shape of his new imperial garments. (Gluck 1987:73)

There is thus an uncanny resonance and perhaps an under-acknowledged Buddhist intellectual lineage that runs right through these premodern and modern expressions of Japan's imperial body politic. In the modern period, these expressions were certainly complemented by the State Shintō discourse premised on ancient Chinese notions of *guoti* and cross-fertilized with European philosophical and political theory. But Buddhism's conceptual, visual, and ritual contributions to the integrity of Japan's state polity – as embodied by the emperor – should also be recognized.

Conclusion

In Japan, the notion of the imperial body politic (C. *guoti*, J. *kokutai*) technically only emerged in the early modern period with the School of National Learning. Later, in the context of late nineteenth-century Mitō ideology and twentieth-century State Shintō, the emperor eventually was revered not only as the head of the *kokutai*, but as the divine embodiment of Amaterasu in the land of the gods itself.

This study has argued, however, that prior to this, Buddhism had long provided early conceptual tropes, visual culture, and ritual enactments that likewise equated the emperor's body with his empire, such that ritually protecting the health and wellbeing of his person ostensibly ensured the health and wellbeing of the land at large. During the Nara and Heian periods especially, Buddhism had promoted doctrinal concepts such as the *dharmakāya* world-body of Buddhahood as personified by the Birushana and Dainichi nyorai statues. Its institutions facilitated ritual recitations of the *Golden Light* or *Lotus Sūtras* throughout the *kokubunji* temple system, and directly before Emperor Shōmu's monumental bronze Buddha statue at Tōdaiji. The patriarch Kūkai further provided an esoteric upgrade with the *Benevolent Kings Sūtra* recited before Tōji's five state-protecting Wisdom Kings, who also figured prominently in state-protecting empowerments during the second week of the new year. And in the modern period, Buddhist philosophers such as Kiyozawa Manshi updated medieval maxims to respond to contemporary concerns about Japan's nascent nationhood. In all of these instances, it was the figure of the emperor's body that was at the center of the ritual action, and that metaphorically cast him as a Buddhist *cakravartin* or virtuous world-ruler, who protected his realm by upholding the dharma. By attending to the numerous anatomical analogies and embodied expressions of enlightenment in both premodern and modern religio-political statecraft (J. *matsurigoto* 政),

this article has highlighted the centrality of the human body in imagining religious authority and political power in Japan.

About the author

Pamela D. Winfield is Professor of Buddhist Studies in the Department of Religious Studies at Elon University in NC. She is the author of *Icons and Iconoclasm in Japanese Buddhism: Kūkai and Dōgen on the Art of Enlightenment* (Oxford University Press, 2013) which won the AAS-SEC Book Prize in 2015. She is also the co-editor (with Steven Heine) of *Zen and Material Culture* (Oxford University Press, 2017). Her research has been supported by grants from the American Academy of Religion, the Association for Asian Studies, and the Asia Cultural Council among others, and her scholarship on the visual, material, and embodied dimensions of Japanese Buddhism have appeared in *The Japanese Journal of Religious Studies*, *Studies in Chinese Religions*, *Material Religion*, and other edited volumes with Oxford University Press, Columbia University Press, Brill, Routledge, Shambhala, Springer, and others.

Notes

1   This article translates the term *guoti/kokutai* literally and deliberately as 'country-body,' or alternatively, as 'body politic.' These translations are preferable to the common yet anachronistic mistranslation of *guoti/kokutai* as 'national polity.' The latter does not adequately grasp the premodern notion of the state before the nineteenth-century invented concept of nationhood.
2   The structure of this article as outlined above is not intended to reinforce the notion that so-called Shintō should come first as the 'indigenous' form of Japanese religiosity, and that Buddhism was a later, foreign influence. Scholarship has demonstrated that so-called Shintō only evolved in reaction to and in tandem with Buddhist influences from the continent, and that it was in fact pre-existing Buddhist notions of the body-politic that predated any early modern Shintō-inflected usage of the term *kokutai*, which only began in the early modern period.
3   DZ 1185 (18.4b) trans. Ware (1966), as cited in Kohn (2006:8).
4   In the modern period, revisionist histories and feminist retellings of these Shintō myths recast female deities in a wholly independent and empowered light. For example, Hiratsuka Raichō's (平塚 らいちょう 1886–1971) 'Manifesto' in the first 1911 issue of *Seitō* 青鞜 journal launched the eponymous Bluestocking Movement by reclaiming a new feminist genesis for Japan, declaring that, 'In the

beginning, woman was the sun' (J. *genshi, josei ha taiyō de atta* 元始、女性は太陽であった). Nearly a century later, novelist Kirino Natsuo (桐野 夏生 b. 1951) creatively reimagines the Izanagi and Izanami myth from a feminist perspective in her 2008 *The Goddess Chronicle*, which was translated into English by Rebecca Copeland in 2013.

5 According to the *Kojiki*, Amaterasu's brother Susanoo discovers the sacred 'grass cutting sword' (J. *Kusanagi no tsurumi* 草薙剣) inside the tail of a giant eight-headed serpent demon Orochi (a familiar name to many video game, manga, and animé enthusiasts today). Orochi had eaten seven daughters of a farmer, but Susanoo falls in love with the final eighth daughter and slays the dragon to save her. In so doing, he symbolically conquers the eight mythic islands of Japan and unifies the divided archipelago into a centralized state, symbolized as the single figure of the last remaining beautiful princess.

6 Scare quotes are used here to indicate that Emperor Meiji's governing powers were never fully 'restored' to premodern levels. Rather, Emperor Meiji principally acted as the public face for a small oligarchy of ruling elites who hailed from leading southern feudal clans.

7 Iwai Masuko, as quoted in Takenaka (2015:introduction). https://www.amazon.com/Yasukuni-Shrine-Weatherhead-Institute-University/dp/0824846788?asin=B0136KQ2QQ&revisionId=&format=2&depth=1. Kindle version accessed November 11, 2021.

8 Slogans throughout Japanese history have underscored the unity of state–sangha relations, and have been translated variously as: 'Chingo Kokka ("Purify and Defend the Nation"), Buppo no Furi ("Inseparability of the Emperor's Law and the Buddha's Law"), Saisei Itchi ("Unity of Religion and Government"), Kozen Gokoku ("Let Zen Prosper and Defend the Nation"), Sonno Hobutsu ("Revere the Emperor and Serve the Buddha"), Bukkyo Kokueki ("Buddhism and a Prosperous Nation"), Kyoo Gokoku ("Religion and the Emperor Protect the Nation"), Nihonkuni no Hashira ("[Nichiren as] The Pillar of the Nation"), Gokoku Aiho ("Defend the Nation and Love the Dharma"), and Gokoku soku Goho ("Defense of the Nation Is Defense of the Dharma")' (Staggs 1983:253).

9 There were numerous other sculpted Buddha bodies at the Tōdaiji temple complex besides the Great Buddha (J. *daibutsu* 大仏). For example, in 746 Emperor Shōmu installed a statue of the eight-armed esoteric manifestation of Fukukenjaku Kannon 不空羂索観音 in the Sangatsudō Hall of the temple complex. Rituals performed before this multi-limbed figure ensured that any malevolent forces that might threaten the state would be neutralized and drawn into the dharma by Kannon's eponymous 'never-empty lasso' of compassion.

10 Even today, Pulguksa 仏国寺 temple in the former capital of Kyongju, Korea, still stands as a testament to the national Buddhist temple network unifying the ancient Silla kingdom.
11 *Himitsu mandarakyō fuhōden,* KZ 1:4, cited in Abe (2000:129).
12 Reproduced widely. See Mason (1993:135, fig. 158). The caption for this illustration reads, '*Nenjū gyōji emaki,* scroll 6 section 4. 17th century copy by Sumiyoshi Jokei of the late 12th century original handscroll by Tokiwa Mitsunaga. Color on paper. Private collection, Tokyo.'
13 Abe (2000:349), citing the *Zoku gunsho ruijū* (ZG 25B:132a–b).
14 A similar week-long empowerment ceremony explicitly dedicated to subduing enemies shares many of the same altar arrangements as the Second Week Ritual. It focuses on the fierce Wisdom King Āṭavaka (J. *Daigensui mishuhō* 太元帥御修) and promises, 'if a king takes refuge in the general Āṭavaka, all generals will protect his country, all his foreign enemies will be defeated, internal rebellions will be suppressed …, in his country there will be no epidemics … all wishes of lay people and priests will be granted, be they the elimination of calamities, the acquisition of love, or the subjugation of evil' (Rambelli 2002:433, citing the last fascicle of the *Atabaku gensui shugyō ki*). This *mushuhō* rite was first performed in 846 to protect the southern island of Kyūshū from Korean pirates, and was last performed during World War II (Rambelli 2002:427, 437).
15 The 'early modern European theorists' that Hayami references include especially Thomas Hobbes, whose 1651 *Leviathan* frontispiece provides the archetypical image of a king's head atop a corporate body of citizens that rises up from the city and countryside.
16 The Shingon'in was destroyed by fire in the thirteenth century, but was rebuilt in 1429. The Mishuhō was celebrated from 1429–55 (suspended due to internal warfare), 1623–1871 (suspended during the *shinbutsu bunri* edicts separating Buddhism from a supposedly pure Shintō tradition), and then reinstated from 1883–1945 (provided the ritual only consecrate the emperor's robes, not his 'jade body' directly). The rite was resuscitated in 1968 to pray for world peace. As a result, 'In little more than a century, the GSN has changed from an official ritual for the protection of the emperor, to nationalistic ritual in support of an authoritarian regime, to a ceremony invoking world peace' (Rambelli 2002:437–45).
17 I wish to thank the Kobe College Corporation/Japan Educational Exchange (KCC/JEE) for the Margaret S. Foley dissertation grant that facilitated my research under Prof. Yoritomi Motohiro at Nichibunken from 2001–2.
18 Kiyozawa, *Tarikimon tetsugaku gaikotsu, Kiyozawa Manshi Zenshū,* vol. 2, p. 52, as cited in Fasan (2013:98).

19 Kiyozawa, 'Shūkyōteki shinnen no hisshi jyōken,' *Kiyozawa Manshi Zenshū*, vol. 6, p. 79, as cited in Fasan (2013:87-8).

20 De Bary, Keene, and Tsunoda (1958:242-3) [translation of Minobe's *Defense of the 'Organ' Theory* ('Clearing up a Misinterpretation of a Constitutional Theory') from Minobe (1934:337-47), *Gikai seiji no kentō* (*Considerations of Parliamentary Politics*). Tokyo: Nippon Hyōronsha].

References

Abe, R. (2000) *The Weaving of Mantra: Kūkai and the Construction of Esoteric Buddhist Discourse*. New York: Columbia University Press.

Aston, W. G. (1896) *Nihongi: Chronicles of Japan from the Earliest Times to A.D. 697*. London: Japan Society of London.

Bogel, C. J. (2009) *With a Single Glance: Buddhist Icon and Early Mikkyō Vision*. Seattle: University of Washington Press.

Chamberlain, B. H. (1882, 1919, 2008) *A Translation of the 'Ko-ji-ki' or Records of Ancient Matters*. Yokohama: R. Meiklejohn and Co., Printers (1882); Lexington: Forgotten Books (reprinted 1919, republished 2008). http://www.sacred-texts.com/shi/kj/kj023.htm.

De Bary, W. T, Keene, D., and Tsunoda, R. (eds) (1958) *Sources of Japanese Tradition, vol. I*. New York: Columbia University Press.

Fasan, J. (2013) Freedom in submission: Kiyozawa Manshi's organic critique of the *bunmei kaika* movement in Meiji Japan. *Pacific World: Journal of the Institute of Buddhist Studies Third Series* 15: 87–104. https://www.shin-ibs.edu/documents/pwj3-15/05Fasan.pdf

Gluck, C. (1987) *Japan's Modern Myths: Ideology in the Late Meiji Period*. Princeton: Princeton University Press.

Hardacre, H. (1991) *Shintō and the State 1868-1988*. Princeton: Princeton University Press.

Horiguchi, N. J. (2011) *Women Adrift: The Literature of Japan's Imperial Body*. Minneapolis: University of Minnesota Press.

Kohn, L. (2006) *Daoist Body Cultivation*. St Petersburg: Three Pines Press.

Mason, P. (1993) *History of Japanese Art*. New York: Harry N. Abrams, Inc.

Meeks, L. (2010) *Hokkeji and the Reemergence of the Female Monastic Order in Premodern Japan*. Honolulu: University of Hawaii Press. https://doi.org/10.21313/hawaii/9780824833947.001.0001

Orzech, C. D. (1998) *Politics and Transcendent Wisdom*. University Park: Pennsylvania State University Press.

Palmer, D. A. (2007) *Qigong Fever: Body, Science and Utopia in China*. New York: Columbia University Press.

Rambelli. F. (2002) The emperor's new robes: processes of resignification in Shingon imperial rituals. *Cahiers d'Extrême-Asie (Moines, Rois et Marginaux: Études sur le Bouddhisme Médiéval Japonais* [Priests, Kings and Marginals: Studies on Medieval Japanese Buddhism]) 13: 427–53. https://doi.org/10.3406/asie.2002.1190

Ruppert, B. (2000) *Jewel in the Ashes: Buddha Relics and Power in Early Medieval Japan*. Cambridge: Harvard University Asia Center. https://doi.org/10.1163/9781684173389

Shillony, B.-A. (1999) Divinity and gender: the riddle of the Japanese emperors. *Nissan Occasional Paper Series* 30: 1–17. https://www.nissan.ox.ac.uk/sites/default/files/nissan/documents/media/nops30_0.pdf

Staggs, K. M. (1983) Defend the nation, love the truth: Inoue Enryō and the revival of Meiji Buddhism. *Monumenta Nipponica* 38(3): 251–81. https://doi.org/10.2307/2384882

Takenaka, A. (2015) *Yasukuni Shrine: History, Memory and Japan's Unending Postwar*. Honolulu: University of Hawaii Press. https://doi.org/10.1515/9780824856939

8 Surveilled, harmonized, purified: The body in Chinese religious culture

Ori Tavor

Abstract

The human body has long occupied a central role in religious praxis across the globe. Recent decades have witnessed a change in academic studies aimed at theorizing the body and its relationship with society and the cosmos. This article adds to this discourse by demonstrating the pervasiveness of the body as a root metaphor in medieval Chinese religious culture. The notion of the body as a microcosmic replica of the social, political, and metaphysical realms, and the need to synchronize it with the natural cycles of the universe, played a key role in the emerging doctrinal and liturgical schemes of Buddhism and Daoism, China's two main organized religious traditions. Using the apocryphal medieval Buddhist scripture *The Sūtra of Trapuṣa and Bhallika* as a case study, and reading it against the backdrop of earlier religious, medical, and philosophical texts, this article argues that visions of the body as an object of surveillance by the celestial authorities, and its purification and harmonization through ethical practices and ritual means, were hailed as the most significant religious activities in Buddhist and Daoist communities alike in medieval China, a feature that continues to occupy a central place in contemporary Chinese religious life.

Keywords: Buddhism; Daoism; Confucianism; microcosmic body; celestial bureaucracy; ritual

Introduction

The human body, its cultivation, and its wellbeing have played an integral role in many religious traditions throughout human history. In the latter half of the twentieth century, the body has become a focus of systematic theorizing in the academic fields of anthropology, sociology, and religious studies. One of the key figures in this process was Mary Douglas, who stressed its significance in deciphering social structures, symbolic codes, and systems of meaning. The body, argued Douglas, functions as the basic link between humans, nature, and society, and can thus be best understood as a system of natural symbols that metaphorically reproduce social categories and concerns, a 'microcosm of society, facing the center of power, contracting and expanding its claims in direct accordance with the increase and relaxation of social pressures' (Douglas 1996:77). In her work, Douglas identifies two types of bodies: the individual human body and the compound social body that determines how physical bodies are perceived and experienced. Human bodies, she argues, are therefore 'always treated as an image of society … [and] there can be no natural way of considering the body that does not involve at the same time a social dimension' (Douglas 1996:74).

The notion of a microcosmic body has occupied a central role in Chinese religion, medicine, and philosophy. As early as the third century BCE, cosmos, body, and state were depicted as components of a set of mutually resonant systems that were intrinsically linked in shaping and transforming each other (Sivin 1995). Likewise, the idea of a 'symbolic body' that is interconnected with the cosmos and can be transformed through alchemical, meditative, and ritual procedures has been central in religious Daoism (Despeux 1996; Schipper 1993). In this article, I will expand on previous scholarship to claim that, in early medieval China, during the emergence and consolidation of the two organized religious traditions of Buddhism and Daoism, the human body became the focus of religious and philosophical investigation, and its cultivation and proper management became the center of ethical and spiritual practice. I will do so through an examination of a specific case study, a syncretic medieval Buddhist scripture titled *The Sūtra of Trapuṣa and Bhallika* (*Tíwèi Bōlì Jīng*, henceforth referred to as TWBLJ).

Despite its eponymous association with Trapuṣa and Bhallika, two wealthy Central Asian merchants who are known for offering the historical Śākyamuni Buddha a meal after his enlightenment and becoming his first lay disciples, Chinese sources indicate that the text was always regarded with suspicion and was widely believed to be apocryphal, namely, an original work written in Chinese trying to pass itself off as a translation of an earlier Indian text.[1]

The earliest reference for the TWBLJ can be found in the *Collected Records of the Tripitaka* (*Chū Sānzàng Jìjí*), a medieval catalog of the early Buddhist texts, where it is described as a two-part text compiled in the mid-fifth century CE by a monk named Tanjing. Later bibliographers expound this claim and suggest that the TWBLJ was produced in a religious community located on the northern slopes of Mount Wutai, modern-day Shanxi Province, in an attempt to revive the teachings of the Buddha after the anti-Buddhism campaign led by Emperor Taiwu (r. 424–452) of the Northern Wei Dynasty (Cao 2011:63–5).

Given the perennially negative attitude toward this text in Buddhist sources, it is hardly surprising to find that it was not included in the *Taishō Tripiṭaka*, the definitive canon of East Asian Buddhism. Moreover, since only short fragments of the TWBLJ were preserved in the canonical literature, it did not receive much attention throughout most of Chinese history. This changed in the early twentieth century, when multiple versions bearing a similar title were found in the Mogao Caves of Dunhuang in Western China. The version of the text alluded to in this article is based on two handwritten manuscripts located in the Stein collection at the British Library in London and in the Pelliot collection at the Bibliothèque Nationale de France in Paris, which have both been reproduced by Makita Tairyō and included in his study of apocryphal Buddhist sources (Makita 1976).

The TWBLJ is a moral treatise aimed at a lay audience. Written as a dialog between the Buddha and his disciple Trapuṣa, it provides a code of ethics for lay practitioners and emphasizes the role of the monastic community in providing religious instruction and healthcare services for the community. The first section of the text (Pelliot 3732) stresses the need to uphold the Five Precepts (Sanskrit – *pañcaśīla*; Chinese – *wǔjiè*) against killing, stealing, sexual misconduct, false speech, and the consumption of alcohol. The second section (Stein 2051) focuses on the Purification Rite (Sanskrit – *poṣadha*; Chinese – *zhāi*), a ritual event held in Buddhist monastic centers for the lay population, featuring a combination of fasting, chanting, confession of sins, and moral education. Both the Five Precepts and the Purification Rite were conceptualized and practiced in India long before the arrival of Buddhism to China, and have their roots in the Brahminical Vedic tradition (Haskett 2011). In the TWBLJ, however, these two imported sets of practices are articulated and theorized using pre-Buddhist Chinese ideas and terms. Central to this conceptual framework are the notions of the body as a microcosm, an entity representing the correlation between its inner geography and the bureaucratic structure of the divine realm, and the intrinsic link between moral rectitude and physical wellbeing.

The early identification of the TWBLJ as an apocryphal text and its heavy use of pre-Buddhist Chinese terminology and conceptual models have led some modern scholars to treat it as an example of 'plebian' or 'folk' Buddhism, a watered down Chinese version of doctrinal Buddhism that played a vital role in the spread of the religion during the medieval period, but which was ultimately rejected by the Tang Dynasty (618–907) and 'faded out from center stage' (Lai 1987:32).[2] In the following sections, I will argue against this position and demonstrate that the TWBLJ and its usage of pre-Buddhist jargon is in fact an important example of the centrality of the idea of the microcosmic body as a source of symbolic meaning in Chinese religious culture. By offering a close reading of key passages from this text against the backdrop of medical, philosophical, and religious texts that have often been associated with the Confucian and Daoist traditions, I hope to demonstrate the pervasiveness of the human body as a root metaphor that transcends religious traditions and identities. Its depiction as an object of surveillance by the celestial authorities, and its purification and harmonization through ethical practices and ritual means, were hailed as the most significant religious activities in many Buddhist and Daoist communities alike, a feature that continued to occupy a central place in Chinese religious life, well into the contemporary period.

Correlative cosmology and the harmonized microcosmic body

The first section of the TWBLJ (Pelliot 3732) begins with an explanation of the Five Precepts, a set of basic ethical guidelines followed by lay believers in Mahāyāna Buddhism. Unlike the highly detailed disciplinary codes for monks and nuns, the lay precepts were designed to be comprehensible and accessible to a mostly illiterate population, and are therefore often expressed as easy-to-follow injunctions, abstentions from unwanted forms of action. In medieval China, becoming a lay believer was often marked by taking the precepts in a formal ceremony officiated by a member of the monastic community (Harvey 2000:81). One of the earliest descriptions of this ritual can be found in the *Sūtra on Lay Precepts* (Sanskrit – *Upāsaka-śīla Sūtra*; Chinese – *Yōupó Sāijiè Jīng*), an Indian scripture translated into Chinese by the monk Dharmakṣema in the early fifth century CE. The text, which was widely circulated in northern China during the writing of the TWBLJ, argues that taking the precepts will allow lay believers to accrue merit, free themselves from physical and mental unwholesomeness, and break the karmic cycle of death and rebirth (*saṃsāra*) (Shih 1994:149–56). Much like other early

Indian Mahāyāna texts, the text displays an overall negative attitude toward the human body, depicting it as the source of suffering and as an impediment to enlightenment (Williams 1997:208).

The author of the TWBLJ, on the other hand, follows a different strategy in explaining the Five Precepts. Like the *Sūtra on Lay Precepts*, it draws on Indian cosmology and terminology to describe the role of the precepts in transcending bodily functions, sense perception, and mental faculties. When Trapuṣa asks the Buddha to explain the relationship between the precepts and the body, the Buddha frames his response using Indian concepts. The physical body, he states, is made from the combination of the Four Elements: earth, water, fire, and wind. Moreover, it is constituted by the Five Aggregates (Sanskrit – *pañca-skandhaka*; Chinese – *Wǔyīn*): form, feeling, perception, volition, and consciousness, the bodily and mental factors that take part in the rise of craving and attachment, as well the Six Corrupters, which are the desire-objects of the eyes, ears, nose, mouth, touch, and mind. Unlike the translated *Sūtra on Lay Precepts*, however, the TWBLJ, which was produced in China, supplements the Indian cosmological framework with a Chinese one. In fact, the majority of the first section of the text outlines an explanatory model that draws a correspondence between each of the Five Precepts and pre-Buddhist cosmological terms, such as the Five Directions, Five Celestial Bodies, Five Sacred Peaks, Five Mythical Emperors, Five Phases, and Five Depots (Tavor 2017:434–6).

The *locus classicus* for these models of correspondence can be found in the *Inner Canon of the Yellow Emperor – Basic Questions* (*Huángdì Nèijīng Sùwèn*), one of the most influential theoretical texts in the history of Chinese medicine. Compiled during the Western Han Dynasty (206 BCE–9 CE), this text outlines two interconnected models of the human body. The first treats the body as a microcosm, an entity whose inner geography mirrors that of the natural world around it. The second describes the body as an administrative unit that reflects the structural elements of the bureaucracy of the newly established unified empire. The use of administrative jargon to describe the inner workings of the body is best attested in chapter 8, in which the various organs are compared to the bureaucratic offices of the Han: the heart serves as the ruler, the lungs officiate as the chief advisor, the liver as the commander of the army, the gallbladder as the state comptroller, the spleen and stomach as the officials in charge of grain storage, and so on (Unschuld and Tessenow 2011:156–7).

The function of the spleen and stomach as granaries is significant, as one of the key features of this model is its depiction of the internal viscera as repositories of *qi*, the vital energy that animates all things in the universe. Inside the body, *qi* travels in a network of conduits that connect the various viscera. These core organs are divided into two sets: the Five Depots (*zàng*) – heart, liver, lungs, kidneys, and spleen; and the Six Palaces (*fǔ*) – the large intestine, small intestine, stomach, urinary bladder, gall bladder, and the triple burner.[3] The different functions of the depots and palaces are best described in chapter 11 of the *Basic Questions*, where the Five Depots are said to be permanent storehouses of *qi* that need to be kept full at all times, whereas the Six Palaces are depicted as temporary processing facilities. When food and drink enter the body, for example, they first fill the stomach, where they are processed, and then gradually exit the body through the small and large intestines (Unschuld and Tessenow 2011:205–7).

As a medical text, the primary function of the *Basic Questions* is to provide a theoretical model of the human body and internal structure, an etiology of the diseases that can harm it, as well as diagnostic tools and therapeutic techniques to be used by the physician. Chapter 1 begins with a discussion of the external pathogens that invade the body and damage it – insurgent winds (*zéifēng*) and depleting evils (*xūxié*). The concept of wind can be traced back to the Shang Dynasty oracle bone inscriptions (c. 1200 BCE), where, alongside ancestral spirits, they were depicted as capricious daemonic forces that can cause large-scale damage in the form of natural disasters or specific targeted damage in the form of disease. As supernatural forces, they can be placated and even controlled through ritual means – the offering of sacrifice (Kuriyama 1994). By the Western Han, when the *Basic Questions* was compiled, the Shang worldview of an unpredictable cosmos inhabited by spirits and demons was supplemented by what is often referred to as 'correlative cosmology.' According to this model, natural processes follow a set pattern and move alongside a predictable fixed pattern. The changing of the seasons, the movement of celestial bodies, and even the working of supernatural forces can be observed and categorized using the conceptual framework of *yin* and *yang*, the Four Seasons (*sìshí*), and the Five Phases (*wǔxíng*) (Lloyd and Sivin 2002).

The notion of the body as microcosm is one of the main features of Han correlative cosmology. While external pathogens such as insurgent winds and depleting evils cannot be completely eradicated, their movement and impact on the body can be predicted, as they, much like everything else in the cosmos, follow natural cycles and patterns of change. Chapter 2 of the *Basic Questions* outlines a preventative medical regimen that is based on a correlative cosmological model. Each of the Five Depots, the main viscera that store *qi* in the body, are susceptible to different external pathogens at different periods of the year. Physical health depends on harmonizing one's bodily cycles with the natural cycles of the world by following a regimen that fortifies specific bodily systems when they are most vulnerable. Neglecting to tend to this task, argues the author of the *Basic Questions*, will result in disease (Unschuld and Tessenow 2011:53).

The idea that correspondence between bodily and natural cycles can promote health and longevity had become quite pervasive by the Western Han, especially among affluent educated elites who enjoyed the resources and leisure time needed to tend to such individual regimens. A self-cultivation manual titled *The Stretching Book* (*Yǐnshū*), found in a tomb in Zhangjiashan, modern-day Hubei Province, in 1983, outlines a set of physical exercises, breathing techniques, and dietary rules designed to create a perfect state of harmony and correspondence between the practitioner's body and the daily, monthly, and seasonal cycles of the world (Tavor 2016). The *Basic Questions* develops this idea by outlining the correlation between the body's Five Depots and their corresponding counterparts. Chapter 4 offers a comprehensive table of correspondence that associates the Depots with the Five Phases, cardinal directions, celestial bodies, musical notes on the pentatonic scale, as well as smells, flavors, and location of the disease associated with each Depot. The liver, for example, corresponds with the eastern direction, the wood phase, Jupiter, the *jué* note, the eyes, sour flavor, fetid odor, and its disfunction can manifest itself as tendon pain (Unschuld and Tessenow 2011:91).

The goal of the tables of correspondence in the *Basic Questions* was to provide the physician with a diagnostic tool. In the following centuries, however, these tables, and the correlative cosmology that informed them, became a common trope in literary, religious, and philosophical texts. The *Discussions in the White Tiger Hall* (*Báihǔtōng*), a Confucian text compiled in the first century CE, features a discussion of the body that draws heavily on the administrative terminology of the Han imperial government. It is accompanied by a detailed table that equates the Five Depots with their corresponding sense organs, cardinal directions, Five Phases, and celestial bodies, but it also adds a moral dimension, associating each Depot with one of the five Confucian virtues: the liver with humaneness (*rén*), the lungs with rightness (*yì*), the heart with ritual propriety (*lǐ*), the kidneys with wisdom (*zhì*), and the spleen with trustworthiness (*xìn*) (Unschuld 2009:32). The ethicization of the Five Depots, which became a prevalent trope in this period, might explain the decision taken by the author of the TWBLJ to choose a table of correspondence to explain the five Buddhist precepts to a lay audience. Thus, while the content of the precepts did not necessarily match their corresponding Confucian virtues, the explanatory pre-Buddhist model of correlative cosmology was already an indispensable part of the philosophical and religious milieu of medieval China, making it an attractive and persuasive device to elucidate complex Indian terms to the local Chinese lay population.

Body gods and the celestial bureaucracy

The second half of the second century CE was a formative period in the history of Chinese religion. The sociopolitical instability created by the gradual decline of the Han regime produced a series of popular rebellions that challenged the existing world order. One of these uprisings eventually led to the formation of an independent theocratic state in Hanzhong, modern-day Shaanxi Province. Known as the Way of the Celestial Masters (*Tiānshī Dào*), the scriptures and practices of this movement laid the foundation for the emergence of Daoism, which eventually became one of China's main organized religious traditions alongside Buddhism. While Celestial Masters communities presented themselves as alternatives to the Han regime, their theology incorporates some of the key elements we have seen in the previous section: correlative cosmology, the notion of the body as microcosm, and the bureaucratic structure of the universe (Kleeman 2016).

One of the key features of late Han religious culture is the deification and anthropomorphization of historical figures and abstract philosophical notions. The founder of Celestial Masters Daoism, Zhang Daoling, claimed to have received a revelation given to him by the Most Venerable Lord Lao (*Tàishàng Lǎojūn*), a deified version of Laozi, the supposed author of the *Book of the Way and its Power* (*Dàodéjīng*), who lived during the Warring States period (485–221 BCE). Evidence for the worship of Laozi as someone who was born as a human but was able to achieve a deified state of immortality became more prominent during this time. Other contemporaneous textual sources go as far as claiming Laozi to be the human incarnation of the Way (*dào*), a phrase used in pre-imperial and Han texts to describe an abstract metaphysical entity or cosmic principle (Raz 2015).

A similar process of deification and anthropomorphization took place on the microcosmic level. In texts associated with the emerging Daoist religion, the Han model of the internal organs as storehouses of *qi* and as bureaucratic offices gradually gave way to a new vision of the body as the dwelling place of powerful internal spirits or gods. In the *Master of the Riverbank* (*Héshànggōng*), a late second century CE commentary to Laozi's *Book of the Way and its Power*, the Five Depots are described as the dwelling place of five spirits. The liver contains the celestial spirit (*hún*), the lungs the terrestrial spirit (*pò*), the heart the soul (*shén*), the kidneys vital essence (*jīng*), and the spleen contains the will (*zhì*). As a meditational text, the *Master of the Riverbank* provides a set of practices designed to promote physical wellbeing and longevity. By emptying the Five Depots of excessive emotions and desires, the practitioner makes room for divine spirits to descend from the heavens and reside within their body. At that point, the practitioner is tasked with protecting and preserving their body gods by following a set of moral, dietary, and religious guidelines. Failure to do so will result in illness and, in some cases, death (Chan 1991:139–47).

The self-cultivation regimen described in the *Master of the Riverbank* eventually became one of the hallmarks of the Daoist religion. While Celestial Masters communities began spreading across China, offering communal ritual services to lay followers, the post-Han period also saw the emergence of an elite form of Daoism focused on individual meditational techniques. One of the best examples of this practice can be found in the *Central Scripture of Laozi* (*Lǎozǐ Zhōngjīng*). Widely believed to be written in the third century CE, the text offers a detailed description of a meditation technique that involves the ritual visualization and actualization (*cúnsī*) of internal spirits within the human body. Attributed to the deified Laozi, the text can be read as a practical manual that offered an individual practitioner vivid descriptions of the internal geography of the body, the appearance and attributes of its divine inhabitants, and the correct procedures and schedules needed to evoke them. Drawing on these descriptions, as well as illustrations and diagrams, practitioners were tasked with visualizing, manifesting, and nourishing their body gods to maintain the alignment between their own body and the universe (Pregadio 2006:131–5).

The model of the body depicted in the *Central Scripture* draws heavily on the one found in the *Basic Questions*. With the fall of the Han, many educated literati who once served in government began to focus their attention elsewhere. Well versed in the classics, they utilized the idea of the body as a microcosm and the imperial bureaucratic terminology in their descriptions of the internal landscape of the body. Section 37 of the *Central Scripture*, for instance, describes the lungs as the imperial secretary, the liver as the imperial librarian, the heart as the minister of military affairs, the left kidney as the minister of education, and the right kidney as the minister of public works – all titles of officials in the Han government. Section 20, on the other hand, draws on the model of the body as microcosm, referring to the stomach, titled the Great Granary, as the counterpart of Heaven, the residence of microcosmic replicas of the sun, moon, and other celestial constellations, and to the navel, titled the Great Abyss, as the counterpart of Earth, the dwelling place of the Five Sacred Peaks, Four Seas, and Mount Kunlun (Lagerwey 2004).

An important component of this microcosmic model was the synchronization of bodily and natural cycles. This notion, which was one of the central features of the *Basic Questions*, is articulated in the *Central Scripture* using the new anthropomorphized cosmological framework. While *qi* still plays a central role in this model, this text supplements it with the metaphor of imperial tours of inspections. Much like the officials of the Han bureaucracy, internal gods were believed to move around the body according to a set schedule. During the daytime, for example, they resided in the abdomen, enjoying the light emanating from the sun in the navel. After dark, they migrated to the chest and spent the night cavorting and playing inside the heart. In passage 12, the author outlines a ritualistic schedule that follows the cycle of the Four Seasons and includes a series of state sacrifices that, during the Han, were performed by the emperor. The only difference is that, in the *Central Scripture*, the entire ritual is visualized by the practitioner and takes place inside their own body. The top of the head, in this model, was the location of the Suburban Altar (*jiāo*), where the Han emperor sacrificed to the supreme deity of Heaven (*tiān*), the occipital bone hosted the Ancestral Shrine (*miào*), whereas the Altars of Soil and Grain (*shèjì*), another important site in Han state religion, were located in the spleen and large intestines.

In the religious vision of the *Central Scripture*, visualizing their body gods according to the correct ritual schedule allows the adept to harness their divine power and achieve spiritual boons that once were available only to the emperor. This meditational regimen, however, was only available to a small section of the population. Not only did it require a high level of literacy, but it also involved the purchase of manuscripts, illustrations, and other expensive materials. Living in the volatile sociopolitical environment of the post-Han world, most people were concerned with the more pressing concerns of survival. These were met by the religion of the Celestial Masters, which continued to spread across China, offering material and spiritual relief to lay followers. After the initial surge of enthusiasm that followed the establishment of the first theocracy in Hanzhong, a crisis of faith emerged. In an attempt to fend off its competition, later Daoist communities began to stress a millenarian ideology, promising their followers salvation from an approaching apocalypse. These salvific promises were intrinsically linked with piety to a strict regimen of moral conduct, designed to distinguish the members of the community from the depraved outside world and ensure their ultimate salvation by the grace of the deified Way (Kleeman 2016:134).

In the etiology of the *Basic Questions*, illness was depicted as the result of external pathogens that attack the body and interfere with its normal operation. While some of the terms used to describe these pathogens, such as 'depleting evil,' had a definite moral undertone, the text did not draw a direct link between illness and immoral behavior. The notion that sinful thoughts and desires need to be expelled from the body in order to purify it and allow the spirits to reside within it, however, became one of the key tenets of Celestial Masters Daoism. This is perhaps best attested in the first section of the *Scripture of the Precepts and Codes Taught by the Celestial Master* (*Zhèngyī Fǎwén Tiānshī Jiàojiè Kējīng*), a collection of five texts that can be dated to the middle of the third century CE (Kleeman 2016:128).

The text begins with a description of an ideal past in which Heaven, Earth, and the human realm existed in a state of perfect harmony. When this harmony was broken, it impacted on the natural cycle of *yin* and *yang*, resulting in a series of natural disasters. Written in the decades following the fall of the long-standing Han Dynasty, the text outlines the impact of disharmony on the state, the family, and the individual. The complete breakdown of the sociopolitical order had left believers in a precarious state, susceptible to harm by external forces such as marauding invaders, feuding bloodlines, and malicious demons. The only way for them to survive was to follow the precepts and codes handed down by the deified Way, which are described in detail in the following section. These included a combination of Confucian values, such as filial piety, humaneness, and rightness, Daoist religious guidelines, such as venerating the Way and following the commands of the Celestial Masters, injunctions against murder, illicit sexual behavior, gluttony, and deceit, and a variety of moral imperatives such as charitability and respect toward fellow community members.

These regulations are followed by a more detailed description of the five key precepts that apply to members of the Celestial Masters communities. While these are not as simple, comprehensible, and easy to follow as the five Buddhist precepts described in the TWBLJ, they do cover the basic moral injunctions against harming others, engaging in deceitful behavior, succumbing to greed, and indulging in alcohol and other illicit activities. Moreover, this passage also expands on the relationship between the precepts, the celestial bureaucracy, and the body. In the precept that warns against harboring evil thoughts and intents, we find that doing so will unsettle the spirit that resides within the heart. As the heart is the ruler of the Five Depots, upsetting its spirit will cause a chain reaction, encouraging all the other body gods to leave the body, thereby reducing one's lifespan. This claim, which reflects the anthropomorphization process we first saw in the *Master of the Riverbank* commentary, is expanded in the following passage.

Second precept: do not let your emotions and temperament succumb to violence and anger, filling your heart and leaking out of your mouth. Do not raise your voice and curse or engage in blood oaths and incantations. This will agitate Heaven and shake Earth, startle the spirits and terrify demons. Committing multiple violations without changing your ways, you will accumulate rancor inside you, harming and depleting your Five Depots. Once the Five Depots are harmed, disease cannot be cured. Those who revere the Way know that inside the body there are celestial bureaus, emissaries, and soldiers. Every time you commit a violation or let anger take over you, your inner spirits will stop protecting you and the emissaries and soldiers will submit a memorial to the celestial bureaus revealing your sins and transgressions. As those accumulate, you will be taken off the registry of the living and put on the registry of the dead. Those with small transgressions will bring sin on their own bodies, while those whose sins are many will also bring calamity on their descendants. (Kohn 2004:13–14, with some alterations)

The idea that emotional excess can harm the Five Depots and inflict physical damage was prevalent in early medical sources. This passage, however, makes it clear that the medical etiology of *qi* was replaced in religious Daoist texts with a different model of the body that, in the words of Christine Mollier, 'is congenitally inhabited with demons and spirits' (Mollier 2006:75). According to this framework, the various bureaucratic officials that dwell inside the body are entrusted by the Way to keep a record of one's moral conduct and submit it to their celestial counterparts. This comprehensive ethical model, which draws on earlier notions of the body as a microcosm, the physical effects of sinful behavior, and the correspondence between earthly and celestial bureaucracy, has become one of the key tenets of medieval Chinese religious culture. In the final section of this article, we will see how the author of the TWBLJ weaves together all of these non-Buddhist elements into a palpably Buddhist religious vision that stresses obedience to the Five Precepts and posits the Buddhist monastic community, through their role in the performance of the Purification ritual, as the key for maintaining the physical and spiritual wellbeing of the lay population.

Ledgers, calendars, and watchful eyes

In his seminal *Discipline and Punish*, first published in 1975, Michel Foucault famously describes the human body as the key site where social and political power relations are played out. 'In every society,' he argues, 'the body was in the grip of very strict powers, which imposed on it constraints, prohibitions, or obligations' (Foucault 1995:136). Foucault defines the various disciplines used to mark, train, shape, and manipulate the body as 'projects of docility' designed to enhance its social utility and aptitude at the expense of individual autonomy. The main focus of this study is the emergence of new institutions of power in eighteenth-century Europe, such as the factory, the school, the hospital, and the prison, which together enabled the emergence of a new 'political anatomy,' an effective mode of producing subjected and docile bodies. While the effects of each institution differed, argues Foucault, they all used some shared common tools and techniques aimed at establishing control over human activity.

Some of these devices were temporal in nature, such as the timetable. Used in factories and schools, as well as in modern armies, adherence to a strict schedule allowed these institutions to establish rhythms, impose particular activities, and regulate the cycles of repetition (Foucault 1995:149). Other forms of control were spatial, with the panopticon serving as the most well-known example. Docility, claims Foucault, can only be achieved through continuous inspection and surveillance. In the past, compliance with the monarch's law was motivated by a fear of corporal punishment. Public spectacles of bodies punished, tortured, and even killed were seen as symbolic representations of the sovereign's authority. In the modern prison system, he argues, such displays were replaced by a new system that sought to monitor, manage, and transform bodies instead of simply punishing them. Central to this new institution was the panopticon, a ring-shaped building of cells where prisoners were always open to surveillance from a central watchtower, without ever knowing if they are being watched. Being under the constant gaze of an invisible overseer was meant to encourage prisoners to monitor themselves and exert self-control over their own actions without physical coercion (Foucault 1995:200–9).

Foucault uses the term Panopticism as a metaphor for the modern disciplinary society, a mode of political control based on surveillance and meticulous record keeping (Turner 2008:82). Given the central role of the bureaucratic paradigm as one of the key organizing categories of Chinese religious culture, I believe that Foucault's theory can offer us some important insights into the cosmological and ethical vision depicted in the TWBLJ. When the feuding warring states were unified by the Qin Dynasty (221–206 BCE), the new regime launched a series of economic reforms that involved the standardization of weights and measures, the system of currency, and the sprawling infrastructure of the emerging empire to facilitate commerce. This was accompanied by political reforms, which sought to replace the old aristocratic political system with a new bureaucratic model based on the circulation of written administrative and legal documents between the central government and the various commanderies and provinces.

The rapid demise of the Qin regime and its replacement by the Han Dynasty did not change this policy. During the following four centuries, bureaucracy gradually pervaded all aspects of social and individual life. As we have already seen, the idea of the body as a collection of interacting administrative units that mirrored the structural elements of the empire was central to the physiological and moral vision of Han texts such as the *Basic Questions* and the *Discussions in the White Tiger Hall*. The bureaucratic paradigm was also highly influential in the realm of religion, where it was used to explain the interaction between the human and divine realms, and the structure and organizing principles of the afterlife. Anna Seidel's analysis of Han funerary texts reveals that, even before the arrival of Buddhism and the emergence of Daoism as an organized religion, the idea of celestial and netherworld bureaucracies that surveilled human activity and judged their postmortem destiny accordingly was already quite pervasive (Seidel 1987). With the introduction of Buddhism, Indic cosmological notions, such as the karmic cycle of death and rebirth and the Six Realms of rebirth and existence (Sanskrit – *ṣaḍgati*; Chinese – *liùqù*), and the detailed depictions of hell associated with them, were gradually combined with the pre-existing Chinese models (Teiser 1994:4–5). The TWBLJ serves as a stellar example for the pervasiveness of the bureaucratic framework and the intermingling of Indic and Chinese ideas during the medieval period. Its panoptic model of a moral universe, which revolves around celestial surveillance and adherence to a strict ritual timetable, can thus serve as a valuable case study that demonstrates the centrality of the body in Chinese religious culture.

We have already learned that the first section of the TWBLJ (Pelliot 3732) focuses on the Five Precepts, the basic ethical guidelines for lay believers in Mahāyāna Buddhism. While the text draws on some Indic terminology, it mostly follows the paradigm set in Han texts, equating the precepts with indigenous sets of five (cardinal directions, Confucian moral virtues, sacred mountains, and internal organs, to name just a few) and stressing the correspondence and need for harmonization between bodily and natural cycles. Moreover, much like its contemporaneous medieval Daoist texts, the TWBLJ promotes an anthropomorphized vision of the human body, in which each of the Five Precepts and the Five Depots associated with them are governed by designated deities known as emissaries (*shǐzhě*). The precepts against killing, for instance, are associated with the emissary that resides in the liver and are in charge of the circulation and dissemination of *qi* inside the abdomen (Tavor 2017:435). The five emissaries, however, are only one part of a larger network of body gods whose names and titles are based on the administrative system of the Han, such as the Commander-in-Chief (*sīmǎ*), the Minister of Education (*sītú*), and the Minister of Public Works (*sīgōng*).[4] While the specific location of the bureau of each deity is not identical to that found in the aforementioned Daoist *Central Scripture*, the overall list bears a close enough resemblance to assume that we are dealing with a fairly standardized pantheon of body gods based on Han state religion. By the fifth century CE, the system of imperial rites and sacrifices performed by the emperor and his court officials and ritualists was incorporated into the rituals of organized religions such as Daoism and Buddhism, and transposed from the macrocosmic realm of the empire into the microcosm of individual human bodies.

The ritual regimen depicted in the *Central Scripture*, which involved the visualization and actualization of body gods for the purposes of personal gains such as longevity or even immortality, was aimed at highly educated elites. As such, it did not address any ethical concerns. The TWBLJ, however, much like the Daoist *Scripture of the Precepts and Codes Taught by the Celestial Master*, was written with a popular lay audience in mind, and thus focused on the promotion of a set of ethical prescriptions. Hence, it is hardly surprising that its detailed description of the various body gods and their location within the human body ends with the following conclusion.

> The human body is part of the same system as Heaven and Earth and the myriad things. The gods are recording your actions, so you should avoid violating [the Five Precepts]. You should know that Heaven cannot be deceived, and Earth cannot be betrayed. Thus, you must cultivate yourself, be vigilant in your actions, and refrain from idleness. (Tavor 2017:436)

The lay practitioner, much like the subjects of the Chinese imperial bureaucratic state, lived in a world of constant surveillance (de Crespigny 1981). However, whereas the state apparatus could only monitor social interactions and compliance with the laws of the land, the celestial bureaucracy was able to keep track of the practitioner's personal dispositions and inner mental states. It did so with the help of one's own body gods, which acted as the eyes and ears of the divine authorities, functioning as an internal panopticon designed to prevent immoral behavior and ensure obedience to the precepts of the religious community.

As seen in the previous section, in medieval Chinese religious culture, body gods were conceived as personal guardians that can shield the practitioner from external demonic attacks. Their protection, however, was not guaranteed. Any form of immoral behavior could offend and unsettle these deities, resulting in their departure. The second section of the TWBLJ (Stein 2051) outlines the potential disastrous results of such insubordination.

> Those who neglect to observe one precept will suffer the Five Evils, and five good spirits will leave [their body]. Those who neglect to observe all five of them will suffer twenty-five evils and twenty-five good spirits will leave [their body]. All the gods and good inner spirits will be aggrieved and discontent, the Director of Destiny will reduce their lifespan allotment, and all the demons will lay siege to their bodily orifices, inflicting them with disease … The worldly and base unenlightened masses who do not understand the Dharma proclaim to serve the Buddha, but their actions will only result in misery and death. They do not understand that their behavior sets them apart from those who practice [the Buddhist Dharma], nor do they cherish the services of an enlightened teacher or uphold the precepts and prohibitions. Attached to their own thoughts and desires, they only bring calamity and misfortune upon themselves. (Tavor 2017:437)

The opening sentences of this passage draw on themes that are by now familiar – the connection between moral behavior and physical wellbeing, the imperative to keep one's body gods placated, and the bureaucratic surveillance apparatus that keeps meticulous records of the believer's actions, rewarding or punishing them accordingly. The conclusion of this passage, however, is particularly significant, as it positions the Buddhist monastic community and the educational and religious services they provided to the predominantly illiterate lay population as a key component for one's personal wellbeing and spiritual salvation. The major venue in the medieval period at which lay believers learned about the Five Precepts and other elements of the Buddhist doctrine was the Purification Rite, a communal ritual event that took place at Buddhist centers on a regular basis (Hureau 2009:1224).

The second section of the TWBLJ offers a detailed outline of this ritual, which originated in India but quickly became the main religious event in the lives of Chinese monastic and lay communities alike, even driving Daoist liturgists to come up with their own version (Lü 2009:1285). Faced with competing versions of the Purification Rite, the author of the TWBLJ sets out to demonstrate the superiority of their ritual, warning against the worship of false deities and fake scriptures, attacking the corrupting influence of Daoist and Confucian liturgists, and stressing the vital role of the Buddhist monastic community in providing the correct moral guidance and ritual services to their lay followers. The latter, in the form of the Purification, is especially important as it functions as a course-correction of sorts, allowing transgressors to regain the trust and favor of their inner deities by cleansing their bodies and re-establishing a state of harmony with the cosmos.

The syncretic nature of the TWBLJ, which combines the imported liturgical procedures of the Indian *poṣadha* ritual with the Chinese pre-Buddhist model of correlative cosmology, is best articulated in the opening paragraphs of the second section.[5] In response to Trapuṣa's query about the meaning of the Purification Rite, the Buddha explains that the timing of the ritual must correspond with the natural cycles of the year, as it allows the participants to harmonize their *qi* with the cosmos.

> Spring is when the myriad things are born; summer is when they grow; autumn is when they are harvested; winter is when they are stored. Things are born and die in accordance with the Way. Heaven and Earth have their great prohibitions. For this reason, disciples of the Buddha take joy in avoiding these prohibitions and upholding the Purification Rite, thereby saving their soul. (Tavor 2017:438)

Without the final sentence, which identifies the text as Buddhist, the Buddha's entire explanation could be mistaken for the work of Han Dynasty literati. Read against the backdrop of the medieval texts surveyed above, it suggests that by the fifth century CE, the model of the body we first saw in such texts as the *Basic Questions* had become an integral feature of Chinese religious culture as a whole, utilized by Daoist and Buddhist authors and liturgists alike.

This passage, however, is only the first part of the Buddha's answer. Dissatisfied with this initial account, Trapuṣa asks for further clarification. In response, the Buddha offers yet another explanation, this time drawing on a bureaucratic cosmological framework. Human moral conduct, he argues, is reported to the celestial authorities on a regular basis by their internal bodily emissaries. Moral deeds are rewarded by such deities as the aforementioned Director of Destiny and the Four Heavenly Kings (Sanskrit – *caturmahārāja*; Chinese – *sìtiānwáng*), while evil-doers can be sent to hell and punished by King Yama (Chinese – *yánluówáng*) and his officers. The only way to guarantee a favorable outcome, claims the Buddha, is to participate in the Purification Rite on the same days in which the reports are sent, thereby placating one's body gods and ensuring that a favorable evaluation is sent to the celestial authorities. This passage weaves together all the various themes surveyed in this article by identifying the human body as a site of bureaucratic surveillance, harmonization, and purification. It therefore demonstrates the pervasiveness of the body as a root metaphor in medieval Chinese religious culture.

Conclusion

By the Tang period (618–907 CE), the Purification Rite, which was the most significant religious event in the lives of lay believers in the medieval period, was supplemented and eventually replaced by other rituals, such as the Buddhist Ghost Festival. In religious Daoism, it was ultimately incorporated into the Offering Rite (*jiāo*), an annual ritual of cosmic renewal that is still practiced among followers of Celestial Masters Daoism (Pregadio 2008:1217). The TWBLJ, much like other apocryphal texts, was excluded from the Buddhist canon, limiting its exposure to new generations of readers. Other literary genres aimed at lay followers, such as miracle tales and vernacular Transformation Texts (*biànwén*), soon took their place (Mair 1989). Yet the notion of the microcosmic body, and its correspondence with the social and political realms, remained central in Chinese religious culture. The theoretical framework and practices described in such texts as the *Basic Questions* and the *Central Scripture* provided the foundation for inner alchemy (*nèidān*), a highly complex form of meditation designed to achieve physical immortality. The diagrams and charts that helped to guide practitioners through the process of inner alchemy often featured a side view of the human body and depicted it as a miniature replica of the cosmos (Pregadio 2008:767–770). Seated meditation was popular with Buddhist monastic and lay practitioners, as well as among neo-Confucian literati, and a wide variety of body cultivation techniques, from martial arts to breathing exercises and mantra recitation, were adopted by practitioners of popular sectarian groups and redemptive societies throughout Chinese history.

In the twentieth century, a new form of bodily practices known as *qigong* was promoted by the Communist regime as a science-based secular regimen that can help produce healthy bodies and a healthy nation (Palmer 2006). The doctrine of the Falungong, a movement that infused more religious Buddhist and Daoist terminology into *qigong* practice, draws on elements from correlative cosmology and posits as its ultimate goal the need to create a correspondence between the human body and the cosmos through a process of purification that removes contaminated 'black matter' and eventually achieves a 'milk-white body' that is not susceptible to physical harm, disease, or aging (Penny 2012:198). For these reasons, while body cultivation and the relationship between purity, sin, and wellbeing are certainly not unique to China, the model of the microcosmic and symbolic body surveyed in this article, which has been so dominant in the Chinese religious culture across its various traditions for many centuries, can thus provide us with new and exciting ways to imagine, analyze, and understand the religious body.

About the author

Ori Tavor is a Senior Lecturer in Chinese Studies and the Director of the MA Program at the department of East Asian Languages and Civilizations, University of Pennsylvania. His research focuses on the history of Confucianism and Daoism, the relationship between religion and wellbeing, and Chinese ritual theory. His work has featured in *Dao: A Journal of Comparative Philosophy*, *Body and Religion*, and the *Journal of Ritual Studies*.

Notes

1. For more about the 'apocryphal' corpus of native Buddhist literature in China, see Buswell 1990.
2. The only other substantial English-language study of the TWBLJ is a PhD dissertation (Tokuno 1994).
3. The Triple Burner (*sānjiāo*) does not refer to a specific internal organ. Unschuld describes it as an innate source of warmth responsible for changing temperatures in the human organism and hypothesizes that it might have been a foreign concept introduced to China during the Han period (see Unschuld 2003:140).
4. Known as the Three Dukes (*sāngōng*), these were the highest officials in the imperial government during the Eastern Han period (see Loewe 2006:19–20).
5. This passage is the only fragment of the TWBLJ that was preserved in the transmitted canon. It can be found in the Buddhist encyclopedia *Forest of Gems in the Garden of the Dharma* (*Fǎyuàn Zhūlín*), compiled in the seventh century CE.

References

Buswell, R. (ed.) (1990) *Chinese Buddhist Apocrypha*. Honolulu: University of Hawai'i Press.

Cao, L. (2011) *Zhongguo Fojiao Yiwei Jing Zonglu*. Shanghai: Shanghai Guji Chubanshe.

Chan, A. (1991) *Two Visions of the Way: A Study of the Wang Pi and the Ho-Shang Kung Commentaries on the Lao-Tzu*. Albany: State University of New York Press.

De Crespigny, R. (1981) Inspection and surveillance officials under the two Han dynasties. In D. Eikemeier and H. Franke (eds) *State and Law in East Asia: Festschrift Karl Bünger* 40–79. Wiesbaden: O. Harrassowitz.

Despeux, C. (1996) Le corps, champ spatio-temporel, souche d'identité. *L'Homme* 137: 87–118. https://doi.org/10.3406/hom.1996.370037

Douglas, M. (1996) *Natural Symbols: Explorations in Cosmology*. New York: Routledge.

Foucault, M. (1995) *Discipline and Punish: The Birth of the Prison*. New York: Vintage Books.

Harvey, P. (2000) *An Introduction to Buddhist Ethics: Foundations, Values and Issues*. Cambridge and New York: Cambridge University Press. https://doi.org/10.1017/CBO9780511800801

Haskett, C. (2011) Uposatha and Posaha in the early histories of Jainism and Buddhism. Śramaṇa 62(1): 39–52.

Hureau, S. (2009) Buddhist ritual. In J. Lagerwey and P. Lü (eds) *Early Chinese Religion, Part Two: The Period of Division (220–589 AD)* 1215–54. Leiden: Brill. https://doi.org/10.1163/ej.9789004175853.i-1564.140

Kleeman, T. (2016) *Celestial Masters: History and Ritual in Early Daoist Communities*. Cambridge: Harvard University Press. https://doi.org/10.1163/9781684170869

Kohn, L. (2004) *Supplement to Cosmos and Community: The Ethical Dimension of Daoism*. St Petersburg, Florida: Three Pines Press.

Kuriyama, S. (1994) The imagination of winds and the development of the Chinese conception of the body. In A. Zito and T. Barlow (eds) *Body, Subject, and Power in China* 23–41. Chicago: University of Chicago Press.

Lagerwey, J. (2004) Deux écrits taoïstes anciens. *Cahiers d'Extrême-Asie* 14: 139–71. https://doi.org/10.3406/asie.2004.1205

Lai, W. (1987) The earliest folk Buddhist religion in China: *T'i-wei Po-li Ching* and its historical significance. In D. Chappell (ed.) *Buddhist and Taoist Practice in Medieval Chinese Society* 11–35. Honolulu: University of Hawai'i Press. https://doi.org/10.1515/9780824887438-003

Lloyd, G. and Sivin, N. (2002) *The Way and the Word: Science and Medicine in Early China and Greece*. New Haven: Yale University Press.

Loewe, M. (2006) *The Government of the Qin And Han Empires*. Indianapolis: Hackett.

Lü, P. (2009) Daoist rituals. In J. Lagerwey and P. Lü (eds) *Early Chinese Religion, Part Two: The Period of Division (220–589 AD)* 1245–1349. Leiden: Brill.

Mair, V. (1989) *Tang Transformation Texts: A Study of the Buddhist Contribution to the Rise of Vernacular Fiction and Drama in China*. Cambridge: Harvard University Press. https://doi.org/10.2307/j.ctt1dnnbfr

Makita, T. (1976) *Gikyō kenkyū*. Kyōto: Kyōto Daigaku Jinbun Kagaku Kenkyūjo.

Mollier, C. (2006) Visions of evil: demonology and orthodoxy in early Taoism. In B. Penny (ed.) *Daoism in History: Essays in Honor of Liu Ts'un-yan* 74–100. London and New York: Routledge.

Palmer, D. (2006) Body cultivation in contemporary China. In J. Miller (ed.) *Chinese Religions in Contemporary Society* 147–73. Santa Barbara: ABC-CLIO.

Penny, B. (2012). *The Religion of Falun Gong*. Chicago: University of Chicago Press. https://doi.org/10.7208/chicago/9780226655024.001.0001

Pregadio, F. (2006) Early Daoist meditation and the origins of inner alchemy. In B. Penny (ed.) *Daoism in History: Essays in Honor of Liu Ts'un-yan* 121–58. London and New York: Routledge.

Pregadio, F. (ed.) (2008) *Encyclopedia of Taoism*. New York: Routledge.

Raz, G. (2015) What is Daoism and who is its founder? In P. Gray (ed.) *Varieties of Religious Invention: Founders and Their Functions in History* 83–111. New York: Oxford University Press. https://doi.org/10.1093/acprof:oso/9780199359714.003.0005

Schipper, K. (1993) *The Taoist Body*. Berkeley: University of California Press.

Seidel, A. (1987) Traces of Han religion in funeral texts found in tombs. In K. Akitsuki (ed.) *Dōkyō to Shūkyō Bunka* 21–57. Tokyo: Hirakawa.

Shih, H. (trans.) (1994) *The Sutra on Upāsaka Precepts*. Berkeley: Numata Center for Buddhist Translation and Research.

Sivin, N. (1995) State, cosmos, and body in the last three centuries B.C. *Harvard Journal of Asiatic Studies* 55(1): 5–37. https://doi.org/10.2307/2719419

Tavor, O. (2016) Authoring virile bodies: self-cultivation and textual production in early China. *Studies in Chinese Religions* 2(1): 45–65. https://doi.org/10.1080/23729988.2016.1131464

Tavor, O. (2017) Correlative cosmology, moral rectitude, and Buddhist notions of health: selections from the Sūtra of Trapusa and Bhallika. In C. P. Salguero (ed.) *Buddhism and Medicine: An Anthology of Sources* 433–40. New York: Columbia University Press. https://doi.org/10.7312/salg17994-046

Teiser, S. (1994) *The Scripture on the Ten Kings and the Making of Purgatory in Medieval Chinese Buddhism*. Honolulu: University of Hawai'i Press.

Tokuno, K. (1994) *Byways in Chinese Buddhism: The Book of Trapusa and Indigenous Scriptures*. PhD dissertation, University of California, Berkeley.

Turner, B. (2008) *The Body and Society: Explorations in Social Theory* (3rd edn). London: Sage.

Unschuld, P. (2003) *Huang Di Nei Jing Su Wen: Nature, Knowledge, Imagery in an Ancient Chinese Medical Text*. Berkeley: University of California Press. https://doi.org/10.1525/9780520928497

Unschuld, P. (2009) Yin-yang theory, the human organism, and the *Bai hu tong*: a need for pairing and explaining. *Asian Medicine* 5: 19–38. https://doi.org/10.1163/157342109X568928

Unschuld, P. and Tessenow, H. (2011) *An Annotated Translation of Huang Di's Inner Classic – Basic Questions*. Berkeley: University of California Press.

Williams, P. (1997) Some Mahayana Buddhist perspectives on the body. In S. Coakley (ed.) *Religion and the Body* 205–30. Cambridge and New York: Cambridge University Press.

Part V
Sensational bodies

9 Seeing, imagined, and lived: Creating *darshan* in transnational Gaudiya Vaishnavism

Anandi Silva Knuppel

Abstract

Scholarship on Hindu traditions and practices proposes the practice of *darshan* as fundamental to Hindu traditions, particularly in temple worship, observing that devotees seek out images of deities primarily to see them and "receive" their *darshan*. These works typically gloss the definition of *darshan* with a sentence or two about seeing, exchanging glances, and/or receiving blessings. In this paper, I focus on the ways in which *darshan* is ideally imagined in conjunction with other bodily sensory practices through sources of authority, such as texts and senior devotees, to create a specific sensory experience and expectation in the transnational Gaudiya Vaishnava community. I then look to the lived realities of *darshan* in this tradition, specifically how devotees negotiate the structures created through sources of authority in their daily lives. Through this juxtaposition of idealized and lived *darshan*, I argue that we need a new approach towards theories of practice to take into account the complexities of *darshanic* moments in this and other religious practices.

Keywords: darshan; religious practices; visual and material culture; Hinduism

Scholarship on Hindu traditions proposes that the practice of *darshan* is fundamental to Hindu traditions, observing that devotees seek out images of deities primarily to see them and 'receive' their *darshan*.[1] These works often gloss the definition of *darshan* with a sentence or two about seeing, exchanging glances with, and/or receiving blessings from a deity, most often in a temple setting. *Darshan* is described as something that 'is' or something that devotees 'do,' 'take,' or are 'given,' and as such, is often portrayed as static and universal across Hindu traditions and other traditions of South Asia.[2]

In my engagement with the transnational Gaudiya Vaishnava communities of the southeastern United States from 2010 to 2018, I interviewed and spoke with dozens of devotees spanning the diverse spectrum of backgrounds of this tradition. Through these conversations and my ethnographic observations, I noticed that devotees used the term *darshan* for more than simply seeing a deity within the context of temple worship. They used it also to describe being in the presence of the divine, during which they would dance and sing, play music and pray, eat and listen to lectures, dress the deities, and perform their personal practices of individual mantra meditation and community practices of worship, while also looking at the deity from time to time. *Darshan*, it seemed to me, was more than just seeing. Once I began speaking to devotees as part of my fieldwork for this project, I understood that the expansion of *darshan* beyond seeing was only the beginning of unsettling the term. *Darshan* is not a single practice; it is *more than that*. *Darshan* is 'seeing,' but it is also a category of practice. A time to be with the divine, which I refer to as *darshanic* moments, during which complex sensory experiences occur and relationships are created and sustained.

Elsewhere, I argue that *darshan* is an intersensorial performative experience that allows for creativity and agency in the creation of relationships with the divine, but which must be considered within theological and cultural contexts to determine the performative characteristics of the practice. Putting this broader concept of a *darshan* into use requires a move toward context, specifically, the aspects of daily, lived practice in a theological community. Without that context, we cannot determine how the community, its organizations, and individual devotees understand, describe, and perform practices they describe as *darshan*.

Here, I focus on the ways in which *darshan* is ideally imagined in conjunction with other bodily sensory practices, to create a specific sensory experience and expectation in the transnational Gaudiya Vaishnava community.[3] This tradition is an aesthetically based and emotionally driven form of Krishna worship founded by the saint Caitanya, which I refer to as Caitanya Vaishnavism as per Kenneth Valpey. This community includes, but is not limited to, the International Society of Krishna Consciousness (ISKCON) and its founder, A. C. Bhaktivedanta Srila Prabhupada (Valpey 2006:2). Founded in the sixteenth century by the saint Caitanya, the tradition reveres the god Krishna as the supreme being and provides devotees of Krishna with guidelines to reach the goal of living in eternal service to him. As such, the tradition provides the grounds for an exploration of the interplay between prescriptive traditions and lived practice, as Kenneth Valpey writes:

> Particular features of the Caitanya Vaiṣṇava tradition make it promising for study as an Indian theistic bhakti tradition featuring image worship. Some of these are (1) the richness of its textual (especially narrative, but also second-order) reflection on praxis, especially regarding the relation between rule-governed and emotion-driven worship ... (3) the particular ways the tradition blends this-worldly and otherworldly spirituality through devotional aesthetics; (4) its self-consciousness as a missionary community, negotiating, for example, between birthright-based class stratification and egalitarian inclusivism. (Valpey 2006:11)

Devotees across Caitanya Vaishnava communities are often well versed in a number of prescriptive texts and attend lectures or take courses on how to better themselves along their personal spiritual paths. Caitanya Vaishnavism has expanded to include distinctly transnational communities that follow the set of foundational texts of the tradition, but with additional commentaries in the vernacular by the gurus of the movement (e.g. A. C. Bhaktivedanta Srila Prabhupada's commentaries in English). In this contemporary transnational mode, these communities produce numerous resources to explain the intricacies of practice and theology to adopters of the tradition who may not be familiar with the grammar of religious practice or the nature of devotional intention of the tradition. By exploring *darshanic* moments in such a tradition, with its explicit and carefully laid out prescriptions and devotees' investment in practice to suit those norms, I am able to show how *darshan* can take shape in a specific theology and community, and how devotees navigate the structures of their tradition, to create their performances of *darshan*.[4]

To explore how this community imagines *darshan*, I first look to examples of how sources of authority create sensorial structures and prescriptions, specifically, how they conceive of the senses and the role of *darshan*, how they create sensorial hierarchies and prescribe specific experiences and 'fruits' of *darshan*, and how they teach people to 'see.' After a brief survey of how structures of 'seeing' are built, I turn to the ways in which devotees incorporate these sensorial structures into the way they conceive of and perform their *darshanic* moments. Finally, I propose that *darshan* is not so much about these structures or supporting them or fighting against them, nor is *darshan* something to learn and to strive *for* itself, as many times theories of practice may assume. Instead, it is a practice through which devotees strive *against* the structures of their 'material condition,' their very being in the world.[5]

A brief note on theology and practice in Caitanya Vaishnavism

To understand the possibilities of *darshan* in Caitanya Vaishnavism, it is necessary to look at the context of practice more broadly, and in doing so, to pay close attention to the theological structures in which *darshan* is performed. As David Haberman notes, the spiritual aim of Caitanya Vaishnavism is to share in the aspect of Krishna 'defined as love or infinite bliss.' The realization of this relationship to Krishna is found through embracing with mind and body the Krishna-*lila*, or the drama/play of Krishna, as reality.[6] Events in the physical location of Vrindavan in northern India in which an earthly young Krishna played with cowherd maidens and friends and delightfully played the trickster to his parents is both a historical event and an eternal, continuously occurring, divine play (Haberman 1988:32, 45). The characters of this divine play, both historical entities in this tradition and cosmic manifestations and loves of Krishna, are adored figures for devotees because of their perfected devotion toward him. The goal of devotee practice, and the system of theology upon which that practice is based, is to give the devotee the opportunity to grow spiritually closer to Krishna, so that their living existence is in a constant state of *lila* and service to him.

The theology of Caitanya Vaishnavism presents multiple stages of devotion to Krishna to reach this goal. With each stage, devotees realize that the illusion of their 'material existence' (that illusion of the material world as being a true reality) is slowly stripped away, revealing an increasing closeness to Krishna. Devotee progress through these stages requires an active cultivation of love toward Krishna through focusing on service to him in various forms. Service in early stages of spiritual development is regulated by rules that foster an embodied understanding of devotion to Krishna and act to purify the devotee from their 'material conditions,' so that they *can* proceed to further their devotion and love. Later stages of devotion build on this foundation toward a more spontaneous form of loving relationship with Krishna.

'Seeing' as created by the texts: creating structures for *darshan*

In this section, I explore the prescriptive landscape of *darshan* in Caitanya Vaishnavism through sources of authority that define the practice for devotees. Beginning with the Sanskrit and Bengali texts of the tradition that make up the foundations for devotee practice and which are a part of devotee initiation requirements, I look at how the tradition conceives of practice, the role of the senses in this practice, and finally the place of *darshan* in this complex system of spiritual developmental stages.[7] The textual narratives and prescriptions are not distant or elitist theories for only those with the education to study them; they are a foundational component of devotees' lives and their practices. Indeed, in his in-depth survey of deity worship in Caitanya Vaishnavism, Kenneth Valpey notes that the texts of the tradition are

> read, preached, recited, imbibed, and eventually expanded by Krishna devotees. These texts constitute a sophisticated discursive, narrative, and ritual-injunctive scriptural tradition that sustains and reflects on worship practice (*mūrti-sevā*) and the object(s) of worship. (Valpey 2006:2)

The texts detail the philosophy of the tradition, the forms of practice, and descriptions of the mindset needed to attain the goals of fostering relationships with Krishna: 'they also include the elements of grammar, syntax, and poetics upon which worship practice is built and sustained' (Valpey 2006:16). As such, text and practices are deeply connected: 'images are inseparable from texts; that practitioners understand and relate to each with the help of the other' (Valpey 2006:4). The texts inform image practice, underlining the importance of service to Krishna, and the image practice informs one's further devotional understanding of text and 'grounds reader-practitioners in sensory experience' (Valpey 2006:2).

Key texts of the tradition do not elaborate on how to perform *darshan* or what it means in daily life; as such, devotees learn more about the practice and how to perform it from priests, senior devotees, and from institutional online resources. For that reason, I go beyond the texts of the tradition and explore the roles of these resources, senior devotees, and priests as additional sources of prescriptive knowledge about *darshan*.

Levels of practice

The texts of the tradition outline the forms that devotee practices should take for different levels of devotional progress. The practices of early rules-based and later spontaneous love-based devotion, rather than being different forms, are often differentiated by degree of internal intention, as the following example from Srila Prabhupada's *Sri Caitanya-caritamrita* (CC) illustrates (Gosvami and Prabhupada 1975).

vaidhi

On the path of regulative devotional service, one must observe the following items: (1) One must accept a bona fide spiritual master. (2) One must accept initiation from him. (3) One must serve him. (4) One must receive instructions from the spiritual master and make inquiries in order to learn devotional service. (5) One must follow in the footsteps of the previous ācāryas and follow the directions given by the spiritual master ... (CC Madhya 22.115)

After one is established in devotional service, the positive actions are (1) hearing, (2) chanting, (3) remembering, (4) worshiping, (5) praying, (6) serving, (7) accepting servitorship, (8) becoming a friend and (9) surrendering fully. One should also (10) dance before the Deity, (11) sing before the Deity, (12) open one's mind to the Deity, (13) offer obeisances to the Deity, (14) stand up before the Deity and the spiritual master just to show them respect, (15) follow the Deity or the spiritual master, and (16) visit different places of pilgrimage or go see the Deity in the temple ... One should (23) attend ārati and festivals, (24) see the Deity, (25) present what is very dear to oneself to the Deity, (26) meditate on the Deity, and (27–30) serve those related to the Lord. (CC Madhya 22.121–124)

raga

There are two processes by which one may execute this rāgānugā bhakti – external and internal. When self-realized, the advanced devotee *externally remains like a neophyte and executes all the śāstric injunctions*, especially those concerning hearing and chanting. *But within his mind, in his original, purified, self-realized position, he serves Krishna in Vṛndāvana in his particular way.* He serves Krishna twenty-four hours a day, all day and night. The advanced devotee who is inclined to spontaneous loving service should follow the activities of a particular associate of Krishna's in Vṛndāvana. He should execute service externally as a regulative devotee as well as internally from his self-realized position. Thus he should perform devotional service both externally and internally... (CC Madhya 22.156–158, my emphasis)

If one engages in spontaneous loving service to the Lord, his affection for the lotus feet of Krishna gradually increases. (CC Madhya 22.164)

Once a devotee has progressed to spontaneous love-based devotion by adhering to rules-based practice, she may continue to do prescribed practices externally, but the mode, mood, intention, and effect of those practices are distinctively different than those of a novice devotee. Although not one of the most efficacious practices, this being hearing and chanting the names of Krishna, *darshan* is a part of both rules-based and love-based practices. As such, we can expect that the way devotees perform *darshan* and experience Krishna's presence will depend on the devotee's location on their spiritual path and the ways in which their particular community interprets textual prescription.

Role of the senses

A devotee's performance of *darshan* is highly influenced by the view of the senses from within the tradition. All the texts of Caitanya Vaishnavism agree that the senses should be restrained, harnessed, and directed toward Krishna alone.[8] Texts from across the tradition use the story of Maharaja Ambarisha as an example of an ideal devotee's focused restraint:[9]

> Mahārāja Ambarīṣa always engaged his *mind* in *meditating* upon the lotus feet of Krishna, his *words* in *describing* the glories of the Lord, his *hands* in *cleansing* the Lord's temple, and his *ears* in *hearing* the words spoken by Krishna or about Krishna. He engaged his *eyes* in *seeing* the Deity of Krishna, Krishna's temples and Krishna's places like Mathurā and Vṛndāvana, he engaged his sense of *touch* in *touching* the bodies of the Lord's devotees, he engaged his sense of *smell* in smelling the *fragrance of tulasī* [plant associated with Lakshmi or Radha] offered to the Lord, and he engaged his *tongue* in tasting the Lord's *prasāda* [blessed food]. He engaged his *legs* in *walking* to the holy places and temples of the Lord, his head in bowing down before the Lord, and all his desires in serving the Lord, twenty-four hours a day. Indeed, Mahārāja Ambarīṣa never desired anything for his own sense gratification. He engaged all his senses in devotional service, in various engagements related to the Lord. This is the way to increase attachment for the Lord and be completely free from all material desires. (BP 9.4.18–20, my emphasis)

By focusing all the senses on Krishna, as the description of Maharaja Ambarisha's practice illustrates, devotees should expect to find an 'increased attachment' to Krishna, which also means that they should expect eventually to be 'completely free from all material desires' if they follow this path. It is important to note that *seeing* is explicitly mentioned here *alongside* other sensory and bodily actions and intentions, not as a *separate* service to Krishna or a more efficacious or important practice.

Seeing and its fruits

In the texts of the tradition, there are few direct references to *darshan* as a practice separate from other forms of service. Either referred to by the Sanskrit roots *dṛś*, most commonly defined as 'to see, behold, look at, regard, consider' or *īkṣ*, 'to see, look, view, behold, look at, gaze at,'[10] the texts outline a practice that is explicitly woven into the performance of multiple forms of service and which engages multiple senses beyond seeing.

The influential *Bhaktirasāmṛtasindhu* (BRS) describes *darshan* as a part of a distinctive group of sensorial practices: 'seeing the deity [in a physical image]' (*śrī mūrter darshanam*) and 'seeing the ārati ceremony [in which Krishna is worshipped with lamp offerings]' (*ārātrika darshanam*), which further includes 'seeing the [deity in] festivals' (*utsava darshanam*) and 'seeing the worship [of Krishna]' (*pūjā darshanam*). In doing so, the text makes a specific statement about the connection between these forms of practice: that these visually related practices have certain fruits of action accorded to them.[11] For example, 'seeing the deity' and 'seeing the [deity in] festivals' indicate that the experience of seeing Krishna is transformative, causing a change in the liberative status of the devotee:

> [T]hose who see Govinda in Vṛndāvana [Krishna], O Earth, do not go to the abode of death, but rather to the goal of the virtuous. (BRS 1.2.166) (Haberman 2003:55)

The practice of 'seeing the ārati ceremony' indicates that seeing Krishna during *ārati* is especially effective for eliminating even the most egregious forms of negative *karma* (fruitive action):

> Just looking at the face of Viṣṇu [Krishna] illuminated with a lamp burns up the sin of killing a million *brāhmaṇas* [priests] or committing illicit intercourse millions of times. (BRS 1.2.167) (Haberman 2003:55)

Finally, tied directly to *ārati*, 'seeing the worship' not only negates bad *karma* but also instils all the positive *karma* of yoga in the devotee. This example also illustrates that it is not just seeing Krishna that is important, but one must do so with 'faith' and 'devotion':

> One who out of devotion witnesses with faith either Hari [Krishna] being worshipped or the worship itself becomes delighted and obtains the fruit of yoga. (BRS 1.2.169) (Haberman 2003:57)

These brief examples illustrate that *darshan* is directly tied to other bodily and sensory practices, and is transformative and purificatory for the devotee, all without requiring 'physical' contact or direct exchange of sight or blessings. The texts of the tradition are filled with examples like these and create an expectation that being in the presence of Krishna does something to the devotee.

Institutional structures: courses and resources

In addition to the traditional texts of Caitanya Vaishnavism, devotees have access to countless other authoritative sources of information about *darshan*. Senior devotees in ISKCON and other Caitanya Vaishnava communities have created courses and printed/online resources on various aspects of devotional life. Devotees may keep these works as a reference, use them to complete course credits at their home institution for initiation, or use them to take on additional responsibilities within their temple community, such as becoming a mentor or becoming more involved with deity worship at the temple.

Created by the ISKCON Chowpatty temple, *A Manual of Vaishnava Etiquette and Lifestyle* (2000), is an example of a novice devotee-oriented text that provides details about basic behavior, including *darshan*. While covering many introductory topics such as dress and behavior, the text provides a section entitled 'Meditating upon the Deity', which addresses basic principles of *darshan* (see Figure 9.1).

The *Manual* directly connects the terms 'meditation' and *darshan* in its prescriptions through an invocation of the oft-quoted *Srimad-Bhagavatam* 2.2.13, to which devotees and priests referred in my interviews:

a) After offering obeisances to the Deities one should take 'darsana' with great devotion and beg for Their mercy.

b) One should not, however, immediately look upon the Deities full in the face. The proper manner in which one should take 'darsana' of the Lord is described in Srimad Bhāgavatam 2.2.13 -

"The process of meditation should begin from lotus feet of the Lord and progress to His smiling face. The meditation should be concentrated upon the lotus feet then the calves, then the thighs and in this way higher and higher. The more the mind becomes fixed on different parts of the limbs one after another, the more the intelligence becomes purified."

c) Srila Prabhupāda explains in the purport that such meditation will help us get detached from sense gratification.

The mood of the devotee taking 'darsana' is "Sir, I am your eternal servant. Please let me know how can I serve You?." The functions of the big deities in the temple are for giving 'darsana' and usually are the istadevas of the sampradaya. So it is quite natural and respectful to see Them first.

There are also other considerations as :

If there are three altars Like the Krishna Balaram Mandir in Vrindavan (or Sri Sri Radha Rasbihari Mandir at Juhu), Srila Prabhupada would pay obeisances first at GaurNitai's Altar then go to Krishna Balaram's Altar and then to Sri Sri Radha Syamsunder .

Also the devotee may like to see his Guru first (but his Guru's Picture may not be present) then take 'darsana' in the assending order to Krishna.

While taking 'darsana' one may stand at the sides so that 'darsana' is not obstructed from the devotees who are sitting.

The 'darsana' should begin, as we face the Deities, from the left-hand corner and move progressively, Deity by Deity to the right-hand corner. In Radhā-Gopīnātha mandir this would mean beginning the darsana with Guru Parampara, then Lord Nityananda and ending with Sri Gopalji.

Figure 9.1: Meditating upon the Deity (Śrī Śrī Rādhā Gopīnātha Mandir 2000:4–5).

The process of meditation should begin from the lotus feet of the Lord and progress to His smiling face. The meditation should be concentrated upon the lotus feet, then the calves, then the thighs, and in this way higher and higher. The more the mind becomes fixed upon the different parts of the limbs, one after another, the more the intelligence becomes purified. (Prabhupada 1987a)

Not only does the guide direct devotees in the form of *darshan*, it also provides meaning to the practice by invoking a quotation from Srila Prabhupada that explains *darshan* as a form of service engagement.

Senior devotees and performing knowledge

Senior devotees in Caitanya Vaishnavism are exemplars and teachers of practice and theology.[12] They range from monastics and gurus to devotees who have years of experience and are recognized as having a deep sincerity in their service to Krishna. At the New Panihati Dham temple in Atlanta, I spoke with senior priests who could often be seen welcoming new faces to the temple. Ram, a priest from Nepal, told me that new devotees have to learn 'every step … like baby born [sic]' in the process of becoming a new devotee. Regarding *darshan*, Ram told me that devotees are taught to come to the images in the temple and look at them in a specific way, '*Darshan* mean [sic] that you see the deities properly,' meaning one should begin by looking at Krishna's feet and then 'slowly slowly' move up the body of Krishna, a description that stems from a prescription found in the *Srimad-Bhagavatam* 2.2.13, as I mentioned previously. The gaze of devotees should make its way to the face and the 'lotus eyes' and 'lotus mouth' of Krishna and then to the decorations and other forms of ornamentation around the deities – 'that is *darshan*.'[13] According to Ram, proper *darshan* also entails remembering and reliving the pastimes of Krishna, meaning that *darshan* actively requires multiple forms of 'seeing': physically seeing the deity Krishna in the temple and remembering Krishna and his pastimes in one's mind.

During fieldwork in Alachua, Florida I asked senior devotee David Wolf about the connection between spiritual progress and *darshan*. He readily responded that spiritual progress 'starts with the name [of Krishna] – form comes later.' He continued:

[T]he focus is on *sravanam-kirtanam*, hearing and chanting the name, and then gradually, the form, the qualities of Krishna, the pastimes of Krishna, they get revealed in the heart of the devotee through gradually purer and purer absorption in the name. So that's why the focus from Lord Caitanya, from Prabhupad, from

Krishna is in the name … So Prabhupad, he gave us deity worship but he emphasized the hearing and chanting.

Many devotees talk about this process of revelation as a gradual act of purification. The names of Krishna purify the devotee so that the devotee can chant Krishna's names with more of a focus on Krishna. Over the course of time, Krishna reveals more of himself to the devotee. In a sense, how one speaks and hears Krishna's names affects how one sees Krishna. In many cases, senior devotees and teachers minimize the importance of the visual components and weight of *darshan*, insisting that the practice does not carry the relational weight of hearing and speaking the names of Krishna.[14] A friend once told me that Srila Prabhupada said: 'You are hearing Krishna, why are you giving so much importance to seeing Krishna?' Or as Prabhupada's teacher Bhaktisiddhanta Sarasvati Thakura explains, you *listen* to the guru in order to learn to see Krishna:

[G]ive your ears to the Lord. In fact, this is how we take darshan. Taking darshan is not with the eyes; darshan is with the help of the ears. If you are interested in seeing or interested in darshan, you use the ears to hear … 'come near – sit here – do not fear – I am here.' (Swami 2015)

The sources of authority in this tradition, through these brief examples, create structures that promote a specific embodied sensorial experience of Krishna during times that devotees understand to be *darshanic* moments. The textual examples show that *darshan* can help liberate the devotee through a process of purification, that the practice affects devotees not through expected or physical exchanges but as something that resembles interactions or 'actions at a distance,' and finally that *darshan* is a *part* of a wider repertoire of sensorial services toward Krishna, not just seeing. The senior devotee stories expand on that understanding, to clarify that there are expectations about how *darshan* should be done and how intention matters in this practice. The senior devotees also explain something of the multisensorial nature of the practice, specifically how the visual components to *darshanic* moments are secondary to other practices like hearing and speaking the names of Krishna. They also indicate that seeing in *darshanic* moments is influenced by these other sensorial practices in a distinct hierarchy denoting a form of intersensoriality, 'the multi-directional interaction of the senses and of sensory ideologies' (Howes 2005).[15] These prescriptions provide a structure, a template of embodied sensorial experience for *darshan*.

Learning to see: transforming and recreating structures for *darshan*

Moving away from how *darshan* and its structures are created by sources of authority within the tradition, I now turn to excerpts from devotee stories of practice. Understanding how devotees learn to see is not about determining how well devotees know the rules of the tradition or how their bodies mirror idealized practices. Learning *darshan* is the embodiment of a mix of prescriptions for practices of the body and mind together with the expectations for service from texts and from the greater Caitanya Vaishnava community. The community and texts come together to form a structure for learning *darshan*, but what devotees do with that structure is unique to each individual. These brief stories illustrate some of the ways in which individuals grapple with these structures, to help them to purify themselves from their current material conditions and realize a closeness with Krishna – to truly see him.

Fighting sight

When I spoke to Vrinda in early 2018, she was a thirty-something Indian classical dancer with two young children who was both in and out of the ISKCON tradition. Vrinda was born to devout ISKCON devotees in Sweden, in a small farming community that she described as being very insular. She said that she didn't encounter the outside, non-ISKCON world until she was eighteen years old, when she came to the United States in her teens to attend an ISKCON boarding school in Alachua, Florida, the largest ISKCON community in North America. After high school, she went to a nearby public school outside of ISKCON where she found space for experimentation that she had not experienced before. She described this period of her life as being chiefly about 'partying hard,' so much so that by the end of her college years, she felt she needed to reset her lifestyle.

Vrinda then turned to a theme of our conversation: that the rules and regulations of the Caitanya tradition in the form of ISKCON were too much, too stifling, and that they somehow didn't line up with how she perceived her own service to Krishna. But if ISKCON and its rules had not been the answer to her spiritual seeking, neither was the partying. Being interested in dance, she decided that she could reset her life and mindset by attending a prestigious school of *bharatanatyam* in Tamil Nadu, India, to pursue a degree in dance. There, she was away from the partying urges of American college life, but she was also far from the ISKCON community in which she had grown up. After resetting herself and her devotional lifestyle, she returned to Alachua to start a family.

In Vrinda's description of the practices of her youth and as an adult, she argued for a personal and spontaneous form of devotion to Krishna, one that she felt aligned with Srila Prabhupada's teachings in general, but not with the institutional methods of executing them, and certainly not with the rigid attention to rules that she found in her youth. She tried to explain further that:

> [Krishna Consciousness] is supposed to be such a personal path: Krishna is a person and you are a person and you develop a personal relationship, but 'you can only do it in this way' and 'you have to walk this path' and 'you have to wear these kind of clothes' and 'you have to do it this way.' There's rules and regulations, and I feel like they've been really overemphasized to the detriment [of] the inner life and developing that personal relationship, not just to god, but to every person and your family.

Vrinda hinted at her personal forms of practice that have developed over the years as she struggled with the rules and regulations of ISKCON practice and service to Krishna. She said that in her college days she regularly went to the temple for *darshan* and sang *bhajans* (devotional songs) for the deities with other 'rebel' youth. The 'hardcore' devotees would wildly dance and play loud music as part of their *darshanic* moments, much to the chagrin of senior devotees and adults. Now, as an adult, Vrinda performs a calmer, yet no less enthusiastic, form of devotional music as part of her *darshan* practice. Although she may perform *kirtan* (communal devotional singing) during her *darshanic* moments, she also underlined many times that deity worship and *darshan*, specifically, are the forms of practice to which she feels the 'least connected.'

What would she like to do, I asked, if she had complete freedom to practice in her own way? Perhaps such practice would be closer to the practices of her youth in front of the deities: 'I like the idea of dancing for the deities. Wouldn't it be so cool if we did that? Had performances for the deities …' And she trailed off as she and I both noted silently that in *bharatanatyam* there was a long-standing tradition before its twentieth-century revival in which dancers did dance for the deities in the temple, a practice that now lies outside of what manuals and social standards may allow in the ISKCON community. But Vrinda never seemed to be one to follow those rules in the first place.

First sight

I first met Casey in 2013 on a chilly February at the Atlanta New Panihati Dham Temple. After speaking at length with another novice devotee, Casey joined us in the middle of our conversation but was reserved in telling me about her spiritual life. Intimidated by my recording of our conversation, she didn't feel as though she could speak on behalf of theological matters because she was so new to the tradition, having just joined months before. I explained to her that I wasn't looking for theological interpretations of advanced texts, but that I was more curious to learn about her experience in coming to ISKCON. She relaxed a bit as the three of us laughed at the awkward computer sitting in the middle of the room listening in on our conversation.

As we sat and talked about her experience as a new devotee in ISKCON and she started telling me about her experience in the temple, it was clear that Casey was very much still in an early phase of devotion, one that she described as a waxing and waning of closeness to Krishna as she tried to leave behind her attachment to material matters and come into her new spiritual life.

As we spoke about image worship in general, Casey began to tell me about how she understands *darshan*: 'you're not just seeing with your eyes, you're seeing with your body ... because our senses are so limited in our concepts ... it's much more than seeing. So *darshan* is much more *being in the presence of* to form this connection.' I asked her to clarify if *darshan*, as she understood it, was a single moment or if it was more than that and she replied, 'it's not a passive – it's not like here and then gone – it's not a passive thing, you have to be engaged.' Later, she told me about how she felt she was able to see beyond what was physically there in front of her when she was with the deities in the temple space, something akin to what Ram told me about being able to visualize the pastimes of Krishna during *darshan*:

> Sometimes you look and they're dancing [the deities], you know? You can see that their skirt is about to fall because [they're dancing] and sometimes [pause] we're like not there. And we are so fortunate that we live in the temple because every day we can strive to see and feel.

Her description aligns with what I'd heard mentioned previously from other devotees, that there is a form of *darshan* that is fleeting and, in this tradition, perhaps superficial. Priests and other devotees have told me that through *darshan* they 'see' more and find themselves purified in ways that non-Caitanya

Vaishnavas would not. When I asked Casey more directly what *darshan* is, she told me that

> it's not necessarily about what we get to see. We are engaging our eyes and we are engaging all of our senses in *darshan*. We engage all of our senses to purify them instead of using them for mundane purposes, we use them for spiritual purposes … We see the deity, we smell the incense, we smell the flowers, we sing and dance so we use our voices and our bodies, we hear the holy name, and we taste the *caranamrita* [water from the feet of the deity].

In her new understanding of the practice, she mentioned a familiar theme: that *darshan* is not only about what the devotee sees; it's about Krishna. Decentralizing the devotee's 'sight' is not only a way to privilege Krishna's experience in the *darshanic* moment, but, more specifically, it is an engagement of a holistic body experience centered on Krishna for his pleasure, a point that I discuss in my broader project.

During our visit together, I was able to see a snapshot in Casey's journey toward building her conception of *darshan* through the way she spoke about the practice, how she used terminology and concepts directly from the texts and theologically-specific ways of speaking in the community, and how she did all of this in her own personal way. She already understood the role of the senses in the tradition and the expectations that prescription creates for her *darshan* practice, that it should help her form a relationship to Krishna; yet she still struggled to find a consistent outcome to her practice. Being so new to the tradition, it wasn't clear to me then or on reflection years later what Casey's relationship to the structures of the ISKCON tradition was at the time. Whether in the end she accepted them or rebelled against them, in the beginning the structures of ISKCON seemed to act as foundations to help her create new structures for her practice.

Whether fighting rules and structures or accepting them, both women in these brief vignettes have Krishna as the goal of their *darshan* practices. If one devotee shrugs at some of the rules of a tradition while another embraces them, can they both reach Krishna? Does a devotee have to actively strive to master *darshan* to be successful, or do they have to adhere to the rules to cultivate love for Krishna? Perhaps the scholarly focus on rules and structures themselves, either perpetuating them or fighting them, keeps us from seeing the greater role of *darshan* practices in this context.

'The rules are here to free me': *darshan* as the creation of new structures

These structures of the tradition outline an ideal embodied sensorial experience – not necessarily the one that you actually find in the daily lives of devotees. When theorizing about how everyday practices are learned and embodied by individuals in light of structures and regulations, scholars often turn to Pierre Bourdieu's notion of the *habitus*, the 'structuring structures' in which we, theoretically, live our lives (Bourdieu 1980:53). The *habitus* concept describes how the structures of our lives affect us at the level of our daily practices, and how these practices perpetuate and reinforce the structures. In Bourdieu's theory, individuals are unaware of the 'internal logics' of their practice, in line with Foucault's observation that 'people know what they do; they frequently know why they do what they do; but what they don't know is what they do does' (Bourdieu 1980:18; Jones and Jones 2005:94). Individuals perform practices because 'they are "the done thing"', not because they are consciously trying to achieve a goal. Michel de Certeau's theory of practice seems to offer a remedy to the lack of agency in *habitus* models. In his theory of practice, institutions are assumed to have 'strategies' at their disposal to keep themselves in power, while the 'other' has 'tactics' that help them fight against institutional power and regulation. Though useful, the theory assumes that there is a relationship of violence and friction between individual and institution (Certeau 1984).

In the case of *darshan* in Caitanya Vaishnavism, devotees are aware consciously and through their bodies of the structures of the tradition and 'what their doing does'. Devotees recognize that these sensory structures assist them in striving for a certain level of devotional service that is embodied and spontaneous, but they are free to perform the practice in individual ways, as long as they do not commit any offense toward the deities. Devotees also recognize that *darshan* is one of many practices that act to purify them from their attachment to the 'material world,' but they also recognize that the goal of this process is not a mastery of *darshan* itself. Devotees do not master their forms of devotional service; they seek to master the quality of serving Krishna.

Although aware of the rules and structures, to focus on them too closely is counterproductive to the purpose of *darshan*. Malini Devi Dasi, a senior devotee in Alachua, explained to me once that: 'There is structure and guidelines [*sic*], but within that structure there is so much freedom because it's an individual process.' I realized that Malini's underscoring of 'individuality' meant something akin to creativity, specifically about emergent freedom in the *way* one does *darshan* and other practices. She went on to say that, 'we don't want to lose the forest for the tree[s], like "that's about the rules …"' The [rules and regulation of spiritual life] are here to free me to go where I want to go.' The practice of *darshan* in Caitanya Vaishnavism challenges the generalizability of traditional practice models and 'doing the done thing': focusing on rules and structures as inhibiting freedom and practice, or assuming that structures and regulations are meant to be either recreated, striven for, or fought against. As Malini notes, it's not really about these rules. Although Vrinda and Casey have different ways of approaching the learned structures and rules of *darshan*, they each have a meaningful practice that is, in the end, about their relationship with Krishna.

The structures that the founders of Caitanya Vaishnavism of the sixteenth century created, and which are continually recreated in different cultural contexts, are there to assist devotees in reaching the ultimate goal: the purification of the body–mind/heart from the material world, so that what is already there can be revealed; that is, a closeness to Krishna. In this context, learning to see means harnessing existing sensory predispositions in the service of the creative production of new ways of seeing. Devotees perpetuate old structures and create new ones purposefully and knowingly to reach this goal. *Darshan*, then, is not just a conscious way of striving *for* a goal (Krishna); it's an individualistic, embodied, and creative part of striving *against* as well – not against institutions or theological structures, but against the very 'material condition' in which we are born.

The structures of the material world that inform sensory practices of novice devotees (e.g. the impurities of material desire) could be described by the concept of *vasanas*. A Sanskrit term used widely across South Asian theologies, *vasanas* describe the predisposed tendencies of each individual. *Vasanas* are almost a 'residue,' a leftover predisposition to act a certain way or desire something based on *karma* (fruitive action) in this life or previous lives.[16] According to Srila Prabhupada, *vasana* is a 'desire' and is directly related to the state of the body as 'the cause of his material existence, constantly changing' as our bodies transform over the course of being reborn time and again in this material condition. These *vasanas* include not only the residues of the greater sociocultural powers that structure practices in the material world, but also those from previous births. According to Prabhupada, these residues cannot be destroyed, but they can be reoriented (Prabhupada 2018).

If we lift the concept of *vasanas* out of their specific usage in Caitanya Vaishnavism, we can say that *vasanas* are multi-layered residues of past *karmic* action that are known to the mind and body. Devotees seek to overcome these *vasanas* through purification practices. *Darshan*, then, is a tool that assists devotees in this greater goal. Devotees strive to overcome the structures of their *material existence*, their individual *vasanas* and specifically their attachment to the 'material world,' using the rules and regulations of their tradition *while they also seek to go beyond the rules themselves*. Instead of reinforcing certain attitudes of the 'material world,' the prescriptions of the tradition help devotees to break the bonds of this material world and create new ways of being toward Krishna.

About the author

Anandi Silva Knuppel is an Independent scholar. Her main research focuses on themes of lived religion, multisensory ethnography, and religious practices in transnational Hindu traditions. She has also published works on performance and classicality in Indian classical dance, and consults on digital humanities projects in South Asian Studies and related fields.

Acknowledgements

Grateful thanks to Joyce Flueckiger, James B. Hoesterey, and Ellen Gough for their support and guidance on the initial forms of the current work. Portions of this work were supported by the Emory University Religious Practices and Practical Theology fund.

Notes

1 These works often cite Diana L. Eck (1981) and/or Lawrence A. Babb (1981).
2 *Darshan*, from the Sanskrit root *dṛś*, is often simply translated as 'seeing.' For a review of the recent history of the term, with specific critiques from the Jain perspective, see John E. Cort (2012). For a review of the term and the field of *darshan* studies, see Anandi Silva Knuppel (2019).
3 For readers curious about the landscape of *darshan* studies within the Gaudiya/ Caitanya Vaishnava field, works by Margaret Case (2000) and Cynthia Packert (2010) provide important ethnographic examples that illustrate the context and aesthetics of image worship. Sukanya Sarbadhikary (2015) crafts an ethnography of space, affect, and the body in Bengali Vaishnavism. Ann Whitney Sanford (2008) argues that there exists a strong connection between sight and sound in Gaudiya Vaishnavism in the poems of the medieval Braj poet, Paramanand.

Kenneth Valpey (2006) describes image worship in Caitanya Vaishnava traditions from a distinctly transnational position. Julius Lipner (2017) attends to image worship in the Vaishnava context through a textual approach and is primarily concerned with iconography and theology in broader Vaishnavism. These studies do not question assumptions about *darshan* broadly across Hindu traditions or within the Gaudiya Vaishnava communities. Rather, they contextualize image worship within the unique environments – theological, textual, aesthetic – of the tradition.

4   Rather than attempt to provide a definition of *darshan* for the whole of a tradition with complex histories and contemporary transnational instantiations, this work seeks to investigate how the concept of *darshan* can be expanded beyond generalizations and static definitions. As such, the case studies highlighted in this project serve as examples that indicate the everyday possibilities of *darshan*, not as representative samples or generalizations.

5   A note on translation: in the transnational Gaudiya Vaishnava community, there is no standard transliteration scheme in use by institutions, websites, or devotees. I have chosen to use the most common spellings of terms as I have read them in the writings of devotees and from publishing institutions such as the Bhaktivedanta Book Trust.

6   Many studies describe the various components of Krishna's *lilas*. For more in-depth information on these pastimes, see Jayadeva (1977); David L. Haberman (1988, 1994); William Sax (2002); Edwin Bryant (2007); Graham M. Schweig (2005); and Barbara A. Holdrege (2015).

7   Citations from Srila Prabhupada's books come from VedaBase.com, the official Bhaktivedanta Book Trust (ISKCON) online library.

8   The *Bhagavad Gītā*, the earliest text of this tradition, advises devotees to restrain their senses, even abandon them, and instead focus entirely on Krishna. (e.g. BG 2.15, 2.58–64). At first glance, these prescriptions seem to be at odds with those in the later texts of Caitanya Vaishnavism that inspire emotional and complete sensory immersion in Krishna. I would argue that the texts are consistent, perhaps not in the description of practice forms, but in the degree and kind of restraint and focus. The *Bhagavad Gītā* and the later texts agree that devotees should restrain their senses from worldly attachments and focus them instead on Krishna.

9   Passage mentioned in both CC Madhya 22.137–139 and BRS (*Bhaktirasāmṛtasindhu*) 1.2.265. Select passage from A. C. Bhaktivedanta Prabhupada (1987b).

10 Definitions of *dṛś/īkṣ* from *Monier Williams Sanskrit-English Dictionary* (Monier-Williams 2008).

11 By grouping these forms of service together, this list suggests that the category of 'seeing the deity' is intimately associated with *doing* worship such as *ārati*

and *puja*, a common term for worship that includes a wide range of activities including offerings, which are themselves closely intertwined and often used as synonyms for each other in practice.

12 In the ISKCON organization, a number of levels of devotional progress have been outlined to support devotee care networks in communities. For example, there are designations for those who are at the stage of chanting one round of the *mahamantra* on their rosary beads and reading Srila Prabhupada's books (*Sraddhavan*), and at the other end of the spectrum there are designations for those with a high level of regular practice who are also initiated by a guru of the tradition (*Sri-Guru-Carana Asraya*). See 'Bhakti-Steps (Siksa Levels)', ISKCON Congregational Development Ministry, 31 July 2018 for a list of all levels created by the Congregation Development Ministry.

13 Some Caitanya Vaishnava resources such as Deitydarshan.com (Śrī Śrī Rādhā Gopīnātha Mandir 2006) maintain that this description is from the *Bhāgavata Purāṇa* 2.2.13: 'The process of meditation should begin from the lotus feet of the Lord and progress to His smiling face. The meditation should be concentrated upon the lotus feet, then the calves, then the thighs, and in this way higher and higher. The more the mind becomes fixed upon the different parts of the limbs, one after another, the more the intelligence becomes purified'. Both the official ISKCON translations and Srila Prabhupada's subsequent commentary use the term 'meditation', not '*darshan*' or *dṛś-/īkṣ-*based terms. This quotation in the text and how the prescription is used in daily life is another example of how the term *darshan* has multiple references, some referring to the sensory action of seeing and others referring to something more akin to meditation.

14 Another devotee pointed out to me that hearing and speaking the names of Krishna is even more efficacious when one associates with like-minded devotees, increasing the efficacy of the practice.

15 Note that this interaction is not that of *synesthesia*. Synesthesia refers to a type of sensory perception in which a sensory event triggers unexpected perception in multiple sensory modes, such as seeing colors through listening to music.

16 For a discussion of the role of *vasanas* in the *rasa* aesthetics of Abhinavagupta in comparison with Rupa Goswami, see Haberman (1988).

References

Babb, L. A. (1981) Glancing: visual interaction in Hinduism. *Journal of Anthropological Research* 37(4): 387–401. https://doi.org/10.1086/jar.37.4.3629835

Bourdieu, P. (1980) *The Logic of Practice*. Stanford: Stanford University Press.

Bryant, E. (2007) *Krishna: A Sourcebook*. Oxford: Oxford University Press.

Case, M. (2000) *Seeing Krishna: The Religious World of a Brahman Family in Vrindaban*. Oxford: Oxford University Press.

Certeau, M. de. (1984) *The Practice of Everyday Life*. Berkeley: University of California Press.

Cort, J. E. (2012) Situating *darśan*: seeing the Digambar Jina icon in eighteenth- and nineteenth-century north India. *International Journal of Hindu Studies* 16(1): 1–56. https://doi.org/10.1007/s11407-012-9110-6

Eck, D. L. (1981) *Darśan: Seeing the Divine Image in India*. Chambersburg, PA: Anima Books.

Gosvami, K. K. and Prabhupada, A. C. B. (1975) *Sri Caitanya-Caritamrta of Krsnadasa Kaviraja Gosvami Madhya-Lila, Volume 9*. Los Angeles: Bhaktivedanta Book Trust.

Haberman, D. L. (1988) *Acting as a Way of Salvation: A Study of Rāgānugā Bhakti Sādhana*. Delhi: Motilal Banarsidass.

Haberman, D. L. (1994) *Journey Through the Twelve Forests: An Encounter with Krishna*. New York: Oxford University Press.

Haberman, D. L. (2003) *The Bhaktirasamrtasindhu of Rupa Gosvamin*. New Delhi; Delhi: Indira Gandhi National Centre for the Arts; Motilal Banarsidass.

Holdrege, B. A. (2015) *Bhakti and Embodiment: Fashioning Divine Bodies and Devotional Bodies in Krsna Bhakti*. New York: Routledge. https://doi.org/10.4324/9781315769325

Howes, D. (2005) *Empire of the Senses: The Sensual Culture Reader*. Oxford: Berg.

ISKCON Congregational Development Ministry (2018) Bhakti-Steps (Sadhana Levels), 31 July. https://iskconcongregation.com/programs/bhakti-steps-sadhana-levels-2

Jayadeva (1977) *Love Song of the Dark Lord: Jayadeva's Gītagovinda* (trans. B. S. Miller). New York: Columbia University Press.

Jones, S.-M. and Jones, A. (2005) What the doing does: religious practice and the problem of meaning. *Journal for Religious and Cultural Theology* 6(1): 86–107.

Knuppel, A. S. (2019) Beyond seeing: embodied multisensory performance, experience, and practice in contemporary transnational Gaudiya Vaishnavism. PhD dissertation, Emory University, Atlanta, Georgia, USA.

Lipner, J. (2017) *Hindu Images and their Worship with Special Reference to Vaisnavism: A Philosophical-Theological Inquiry*. New York: Routledge.

McHugh, J. (2012) *Sandalwood and Carrion: Smell in Indian Religion and Culture*. New York: Oxford University Press. https://doi.org/10.1093/acprof:oso/9780199916306.001.0001

Monier-Williams, M. (2008) *Dṛś/īkṣ*. In M. Monier-Williams (ed.) *Monier Williams Sanskrit-English Dictionary*. Institute of Indology and Tamil Studies, Cologne University, Germany. https://www.sanskrit-lexicon.uni-koeln.de/monier

Packert, C. (2010) *The Art of Loving Krishna: Ornamentation and Devotion*. Indiana University Press: Bloomington.

Prabhupada, A. C. B. (1987a) *Srimad Bhagavatam: Second Canto*. Los Angeles: Bhaktivedanta Book Trust.

Prabhupada, A. C. B. (1987b) *Srimad Bhagavatam: Ninth Canto*. Los Angeles: Bhaktivedanta Book Trust.

Prabhupada, A. C. B. (n. d.) 680600 – Letter to Ved Prakash ji written from Montreal. Vaniquotes. Retrieved on 15 December 2018 from https://vanisource.org/w/index.php?title=680600_-_Letter_to_Ved_Prakash_ji_written_from_Montreal&t=hl#terms=human%20propensities.

Sanford, A. W. (2008) *Singing Krishna: Sound Becomes Sight in Paramanand's Poetry*. Albany: SUNY Press. https://doi.org/10.1111/j.1748-0922.2008.00331_2.x

Sarbadhikary, S. (2015) *The Place of Devotion*. Oakland: University of California Press. https://www.ucpress.edu/book/9780520287716/the-place-of-devotion

Sax, W. S. (2002) *Dancing the Self: Personhood and Performance in the Pāṇḍav Līlā of Garhwal*. New York: Oxford University Press. https://doi.org/10.1093/0195139151.003.0003

Schweig, G. M. (2005) *Dance of Divine Love: The Rasa Lila of Krishna from the 'Bhagavata Purana', India's Classic Sacred Love Story*. Princeton: Princeton University Press. https://doi.org/10.1515/9780691190174

Śrī Śrī Rādhā Gopīnātha Mandir (2000) *A Manual of Vaiṣṇava Etiquette and Lifestyle* (2nd edn). Chowpatty, Mumbai: Gopinath Books.

Swami, L. (2015) *Taking Darshan of Guru means to hear his Speech about Tattvas: Lokanath Swami Maharaj Transcripts*. http://lokanathswami.info/taking-darshan-of-guru-means-to-hear-his-speech-about-tattvas

Valpey, K. (2006) *Attending Kṛṣṇa's Image: Caitanya Vaiṣṇava Mūrti-Sevā as Devotional Truth*. New York: Routledge. https://doi.org/10.4324/9780203099896

10 'The body is a tool for remembrance': Healing, transformation, and the instrumentality of the body in a North American Sufi order

Megan Adamson Sijapati

Abstract

This article is a preliminary analysis of the role of the body in core rituals of a North American branch of the Shadhilyya Sufi order. It draws upon fieldwork conducted between 2016 and 2020 to consider how spiritual healing practices involve the human body sensorily and in experiential, imaginative realms, as conveyed through practitioners' verbal descriptions of what they feel in the body and how they understand their bodies and the bodies of others. I argue that, in these healing practices, the body is instrumentalized in three key modes – as barometer, controller, and ground of energy – that change the way it is experienced. I argue that the 'ordinary' – or, non-extraordinary – body is instrumentalized through these healing modalities to become the site of transformation from spirit to material and material to spirit, and that through this the body emerges as central to everyday, lived Sufi practice. The healings discussed incorporate traditional Muslim devotional practices and long-standing Islamic and Sufi rituals such as *dhikr* (remembrance, recollection of the divine), recitation of the 99 names of the divine, Qur'anic recitation, cupping, and less traditionally Islamic practices such as acupuncture.

Keywords: Sufi; Sufism; Islam; healing; ritual; embodiment

> [The] body is a tool for remembrance, remembrance that Allah is ever present, close to us. [When you are sick] so Allah, SWT,[1] is not sick, only yourself in that sense of separation becomes sick ... We usually do not pay much attention to what our body is, however in my perception it's like an interface. Because it is through the body where we manifest our life.
>
> (Sufi healer and *murshid*, Warfordsburg, Pennsylvania, 2017)

In rural Pennsylvania at the eastern edge of the Appalachian Mountain range lies Sufi Center East, the North American east coast center of a branch of the Shadhiliyya Sufi Muslim *tariqa* (Arabic, lit. 'path,' a religious order). This essay examines the role of the body in core rituals of this community, based on my fieldwork in the community from 2016 to 2020, primarily in the form of formal interviews I conducted with students and teachers of this Sufi order, participant observation in healings, seminars, and rituals, and study of the order's texts written by its leaders. In this Shadhiliyya community at Sufi Center East, ritual practice moves one along the adept's spiritual path, but in and through – and conceived as – practices of healing. This Sufi community's 'spiritual healing' practices involve the human body sensorily and in experiential, imaginative realms, as conveyed through practitioners' verbal descriptions of what they feel in the body and how they understand their bodies and the bodies of others.

Within Islamic tradition, Muslims have long located meaning in the human body as God's creation, and in particular its Sufi traditions, across cultures and time periods, have affirmed the immanence of the divine, and hence have rich traditions of locating religious meaning in the human body (Bashir 2010, 2013; Basu and Werbner 1998; Kugle 2007). Islamic conceptions of the body are rooted in the Abrahamic concept that human beings are created from dust and will return to dust and will be resurrected bodily on the day of judgment. Like many religious communities, Sufi Muslims use embodied rituals as a means of transforming their inner selves. This involves subduing the *nafs* (A., self, lower soul), or ego-self, in a journey of spiritual stages and states laid out by a Shaykh or Shaykha (A., Islamic, and particularly Sufi, religious leaders, either male or female, respectively) and practiced over generations in their particular order. These embodied rituals have the goal of bringing one closer to God, or, put more precisely, of invoking the reality of God's presence in the awareness of the religious adept.

This article is a preliminary analysis of the centrality of the body in the healing practices of this branch of the Shadhilyya Sufi order, and the Sufi Center East in particular. I will aim to demonstrate how in their healing practices the body is engaged in particular ways through practices that change the way it is experienced. These healing rituals bring the adept closer to the source of reality, which is understood to be the divine, Allah, and this is experienced as an essence not entirely separate from the adept. The practices create a proximity that is conceived as a continual movement: a movement from sickness to health, from separation to unity and/or proximity, from darkness to light. I will aim to demonstrate that among these Sufis the body is instrumentalized through healing techniques as the Sufi adept 'walks' on the path of the *tariqa* as led by their Shaykh or Shaykha. This is conceptualized teleologically, with the movement aimed at the Sufi adept's increasing access to the experience of divine presence. This is much like what we see in the history of Sufi healing, contemplation, and devotion (Kugle 2007) across orders, but I argue that here the body can be seen at work in three key modes, modes in which members of this Sufi community experience their body during their healing practices: as barometer, as controller, and as ground of energy.[2]

The healings that I will discuss here incorporate traditional Muslim devotional practices and long-standing Sufi rituals such as *dhikr* (A., remembrance, recollection of the divine), recitation of the 99 names of the divine, and even practices such as acupuncture and cupping.[3] As the 'ordinary' – or, non-extraordinary – body is instrumentalized through these healing modalities to become the site of transformation from spirit to material and material to spirit, we see how the body is central in everyday, lived Sufi practice. In fact, ritual engagement with the lived, embodied body is essential to this Sufi order's 'spiritual walking.' 'Walking' is a common way of Sufis, and these American Shadhiliyya *murid*s, to describe the individual's ongoing progress along the devotional[4] path to divine presence. This essay documents these practices, briefly situates them in the broader context of Islamic Sufi conceptions of the body, and offers a tripartite explanatory framework to argue for the centrality of body and embodiment in this religious order.

A Shadhiliyya *tariqa*, 'spiritual' healing, and North American Sufism

The Shadhiliyya Sufi order based at Sufi Center East, also called the Farm of Peace, was established by the community's recently deceased Shaykh, Muhammad Sa'id al-Jamal al-Rifa'i al-Shadhili (d. 2015). Al-Jamal was born in Jerusalem and taught at the al-Aqsa mosque. He traced his *silsila* (A., spiritual lineage) through Abu Hasan al-Shadhili (d. 1258) and Ibn Mashish (al-Shadhili's thirteenth-century teacher, d. 1227) all the way back to 'Ali and the Prophet Muhammad. According to oral histories I collected about the *tariqa* (A., path, or Sufi order), al-Jamal, affectionately called Sidi by his *murid*s (A., Sufi adepts, students), began giving lectures and spiritual teachings and healings in California in the 1990s. He developed a core of students who would eventually take a Sufi 'promise' (initiation into the order) with him, take a Sufi name,[5] and in many cases take the *shahada*[6] and begin to adopt the 'outer' practices of the normative rituals of Islam[7] in addition to the order's Sufi practices (some of which will be described below). Since al-Jamal's death in 2015, the *murid*s have developed a more diffuse leadership structure, remaining connected with one another and promoting the *tariqa* and Sidi's teachings in regional *dhikr* gatherings, annual conferences such as Sufi School East at the Pennsylvania site, healing workshops, webinars, and the networks of the order's degree granting the University of Sufism.[8]

One of the *tariqa*'s senior teachers tells of when she met Sidi in Jerusalem and became a student of Sufism with him there before the community was established in the United States. Among the practices she describes submersing herself in during those early years in Jerusalem studying Sufism with Sidi, the primary one was transcribing by hand Sidi's own books. She describes the ritual act of writing as connecting hand to heart, as a 'transmission of light' from Sidi to the student. When describing the founding of the Farm of Peace, she invokes the corporeal body of Sidi, describing him as an astral presence who consecrated the undeveloped farm land (in Pennsylvania, just north of the Maryland border) by appearing in an old barn on the land, even though he was living in Jerusalem at the time. She and others interpreted his physical presence as anchoring the space and consecrating it for the community. In the view of his students, Sidi did not teach many practices involving the body in an overt way, although he did emphasize nutrition and the healing power of organic, whole foods. As they describe it, he went from teaching few practices beyond *dhikr*, to later expressing a clear insistence on the need for community members to practice central normative Islamic rituals such as *salat* (ritual prayer) and fasting.

This Shadhiliyya *tariqa* has centers in Texas, Pennsylvania, California, Washington, Maryland, New York, Minnesota, Massachusetts, Rhode Island, Oregon, and Mexico. A number of the *murid*s earn their livings as healers, employing hybrid healing modalities ranging from acupuncture to hypnosis to allopathic medicine, all infused with Sufi principles and practices, as well as running businesses in their local communities. Many of the members of this *tariqa*, both those who have come to the path recently and those who started with Sidi in the 1990s, have been trained at its healing institute, the University of Sufism.[9] It offers a Master's degree in Spiritual Ministry with certificates in Spiritual Healing and Counseling for Physical and Emotional Well-Being (which is 'designed to produce high quality, professional healers who heal in the way of Allah'[10]), Spiritual Ministry and Healing, and Spiritual Peacemaking. At the Farm of Peace, healing workshops and wellness weekends, in addition to A., *dhikr*s (rituals for the remembrance of the divine), A., *zawiya*s (spiritual retreats), A., *khalwa*s (all-night vigils of prayer and remembrance), and the ongoing operations of the organic farm are held and promote these Sufi healing principles.

As I have already noted, this Shadhiliyya order thinks of itself as distinctive for its emphasis on healing: physical healing *and* spiritual healing, and the two are seen as interdependent. A senior member and past Imam of the Farm of Peace, one of Sidi's early students, explained what many others in the community also affirmed, and which I have observed in my fieldwork with this community in varying ways: 'the Shadhiliyya Sufi path is a path of healers, healing.' As another senior teacher explains it, healing is 'our primary *theme*.' At the Farm of Peace, the core teachers are long-standing members of the *tariqa* and play varying roles in and beyond the community as Sufi healers, teachers, and even corporate consultants. Of the people who reside at and around the Farm of Peace, take seminars there, or visit regularly from the surrounding area, many are graduates of the University of Sufism.

The majority of the Sufis in this order came to Sufism, and hence Islam, from other religious upbringings. Seekers come to this religious practice and community – which I will refer to in combination henceforth as 'path' – as a means for connecting with the ephemeral and seemingly distant (the divine) and something closer to them than anything else (i.e., one's own heart), yet from which they were estranged. Their entry into Sufism, and for many, their adoption of Islam (their taking the *shahada*) later, is inherently (as religious conversions are) a type of refashioning of the self made possible, and perhaps necessitated, by the conditions of modernity (Giddens 2013). The choice and move forward through the praxis of a new epistemological and somatic personhood, or, experience of being human, to put it more broadly, is the path the new Sufi embarks upon. It comes with a newcomers' manual and leads to enrollment at the University of Sufism. The choice is to transform through 'walking' this path: 'walking' is the emic term for spiritual work and progress. For members of the order who were raised in Islamic settings and identified as Muslim prior to joining the *tariqa*, the step into Islamic values, epistemologies, practices – the intellectual and embodied way of learning and knowing – and the tenets of faith and practice are not new. But the template of the 'walking' is the same for new Muslims as for Muslims by birth: a personal inward journey guided by the teachings of the Shaykh and the healing practices of the community. Although now deceased, al-Jamal is understood to be accessible through transmission in his books and videos and the teachings of the senior *murshid*s he designated to succeed him. The refashioning of the self is a personal journey undertaken within a community – the community of the order.

In *Living Sufism in North America*, Dickson shows how in North America Sufism has involved adaptations in the formulation of authority and practice. He suggests that in North America Sufism is 'being consciously adapted by Sufi teachers' (Dickson 2015:138). As he explains, 'Sufism itself is inherently adaptable … Sufi teachers have always altered teaching to suit the varieties of people and places, developing techniques that match the mentalities of those the techniques are intended for' (Dickson 2015:138). This is certainly not unique to North America. The sheer variety of expressions of Sufi practice and artistry globally across cultures testifies to this. Sufism's variations in North America are multitudinous, as my time doing fieldwork among North American Sufis attests, and as the rich and careful research of scholars of religion and Islam have documented in recent years affirms. Bazzano and Hermansen (2020), Dickson (2015), Dickson and Sharify-Funk (2017), Xavier (2018), and others have led the way in documenting and critically situating North American Sufi expressions in their North American cultural contexts and within Islam and Islamic studies.

The Shadhiliyya *tariqa* at the Farm of Peace evidences this adaptability in Sufi teachings and techniques through its healing modalities, which draw directly on Islamic and Sufi cosmology and metaphysics, sacred text (Qur'an and Sidi's books), and praxis (such as *salat*, *dhikr*, and *al-wird*[11]), and simultaneously exhibit elements of new age healing and contemplative work popular in North America today, such as meditation, acupuncture, and yoga. Such fluidity of praxis across healing modalities can appear to be 'new age' and thus deemed by critics 'less' Islamic or Sufi. The boundaries around what is Sufism or not go back to some of the core debates about Sufism's relationship to Islam that are particularly heated in twentieth- and twenty-first-century understandings of Islam. Dickson puts it succinctly: 'Sufism's place in Islam is one of the most contested topics in contemporary Islamic discourse' (Dickson 2015:19). And what qualifies as Sufi or not is also a question in studies of North American Sufism (Sedgwick 2017), with categories such as 'neo-Sufi' and 'Islamic Sufism' being marshalled to disentangle varying religious expressions from one another in order to generate a taxonomy that would facilitate their analysis. However, such categories have the potential to further complicate and obscure, and even limit the possibilities of what we can see and understand. My research shows that the Farm of Peace's Shadhiliyya *tariqa* rests on an Islamically centered Sufi metaphysics that speaks to the spiritual and somatic needs of its community, and that it resists definition. The earliest members of this Sufi community, who are now its senior leaders, came to this Sufi *tariqa* from new age movements. Several came from the Transcendental Meditation movement, others were exploring the edges of the Jewish, Christian, and Muslim faiths they were raised in and found that Sidi's path of Sufism and its focus on 'the heart' and 'unity' offered more of what they were looking for. When they met Sidi in the 1990s, they followed his spiritual teachings and took *bay'ah*, the ritual initiation into a *tariqa* and the guidance of its Shaykh. Many members also soon took the *shahada*, remarried in Sufi 'spiritual weddings,' and reoriented their professional lives to incorporate Sufism and Sufi healing into their businesses as corporate consultants, doctors, alternative medicine practitioners, and financial life coaches. Many now are *shari'a* practicing Muslims who pray *salat*, fast for Ramadan, and hope to complete the Hajj in their lifetimes. Like some other 'new age' hippies in North America, they made their way to Islam through overlapping religious groups along a spectrum of new age, Islamic, and Sufi groups and identities (Sedgwick 2017).

Healings take place in a variety of spaces at the Farm of Peace: in the mosque-barn, the International Peace Center (IPC), at the adjacent homes on the property, or even outdoors in the woods or on the gravel and dirt road lined with trees. The IPC has designated treatment rooms where healers can hold healing sessions. The dome room is the central space where teachings, *dhikr*, *al-wird*, ritual *salat*, and Jumah (Friday prayers) are held most months of the year. The front of the dome room is the wall facing Mecca, looking out on a grassy field and soft dip in the land that then rises to the dark green foothills. The center is built in adobe style with straw insulation and thermo-heated floors and ample natural light. The dome room, guest rooms, and healing rooms are adorned sparsely with posters of calligraphed Qur'anic verses and Sufi prayers, the names of Allah, and photographs of Mecca. Some have a small photo of Sidi on a shelf or on the wall. During the day and at night the rooms are dimly lit. One has comfortable pleather recliners, another has one chair and a massage table for healings, including the overtly body-oriented ones such as acupuncture, cupping, and lymphatic draining sessions. Women are usually veiled and men, too, dress modestly with legs, arms, and often heads covered. The space of these healings is not critical to their efficacy: the healing can take place anywhere. Members of the order flow quietly in and out of the healing spaces and the guest rooms and dome room, exchanging intimate '*assalamu alaikum* check-ins and questions about the state of one another's 'hearts' and the progress of their 'walking.'[12]

Healing as 'walking on the path'

This refashioning, this 'walking,' of these Shadhiliyya Sufis is a deeply bodily journey, involving somatic dimensions similar to those observed by Thomas Csordas, which he called 'somatic attention' (Csordas 1990). The person being healed is asked to enter into certain states of contemplation that engage the imagination to access subtle energies within the physical body. In the words of a senior teacher, an Iraqi-born Muslim scholar and Sidi's daughter-in-law, who studied closely with him in Jerusalem and is based in Vienna but gives teachings to members of the order in North America, 'We cannot develop without the body ... There is no spiritual development without the body, and the Sufis know this very well.'[13] This order's healing practices exemplify the central theme in Sufi piety and spiritual knowing of the body as both ephemeral and the very ground of spiritual being in the created world. This 'walking' is in fact healing, and the body is called upon as a tool to help affect transformation at both the subtle and gross levels. At times this is solely an imagined body, but often this is a body both felt and imagined, from the Sufi perspective, in one divinely infused somatic space.

The *tariqa*'s introductory literature provided to those who take 'the promise' or *bay'ah* (A., initiation), with Sidi or one of his senior teachers, describes the *tariqa* in this way:

> There are a number of Sufi paths out there. What makes the Shadhuliya (*sic*) path different is its emphasis on healing. Not just healing for our physical bodies, which you can find in most faiths, but healing our mind, heart, and spirit ... Our guide Sidi has given us numerous books on how to use natural remedies for all aspects of healing and many prophetic healing prayers combined with sacred energetic healing methods. Sidi founded our University of Spiritual Healing and Sufism where his students learn about spiritual healing that is based on the sacred knowledge of prophetic medicine, that has been handed down through the long lineage of this way. It is this combination of spiritual healing, gnosis, and sacred teachings that make this a complete path. A complete path that includes a guide, a map, a compass, practices, community support, and a *first-aid kit for body, mind and heart*.[14]

This conception of healing is to lift the veils that separate one from God: 'The Truth is Allah. And the Reality of Allah is perfection. Any sign of anxiety, agitation, fear, anger, sadness, or worry is a sign that we are veiled from the Truth. When the heart is witnessing the Truth, it is tranquil and at peace.' To get to this state the order provides a 'first-aid kit' of tools.

Healing has long been part of Sufism, although different Sufi orders have given it varying degrees of emphasis in their ritual repertoires. In general terms, all illness – the problem, the wound – is, in Sufi epistemology, a product of the individual's separation from the divine that is experienced at the bodily level. In this order's cosmology and epistemology, the body is secondary to the soul in the individual's relationship with the divine; the body must be engaged to allow energy to move and therefore 'spiritual' wounds to be healed. The body is, in Merleau-Ponty's sense, the very ground of being, and is the ground upon which an existential, spiritual healing occurs. Merleau-Ponty's view of the body as the ground of being is particularly helpful here, for the body 'escapes traditional conceptual divisions between subject and object' (Morris 2014:113). According to the lexicon of this particular branch of the Shadhiliyya Sufi order, energy blockages are in the body. All illnesses, all wounds, are 'spiritual' wounds of separation. In the Sufi lexicon, they are described as wounds in the heart, accumulated through experiences in life beginning at a very early age, and understood in the Sufi idiom of veils of separation. At the Farm of Peace, Sufis frequently reference two states of being: the state of unity (with the divine and its creation) and of separation (from the divine and its creation, always self-imposed); in this order, the goal is to 'be in the unity' and not to 'be in the separation.'

Allopathic medicine alters the body by introducing something foreign into it to make it 'do' things to combat the illness. But this Sufi healing harnesses the body's already existent resources, that is, the presence of the divine (which is veiled, or forgotten, or far away because of the *nafs*), the light or energy of God, as the means of healing the body. Spiritual healing, that is, healing that addresses dysfunctions of the spirit and soul, which are a matter of veils between the self and God, uses the body as the instrument for regaining *spiritual* health. Yet the degree of spiritual proximity is in fact gauged by one's physical health.[15] It is understood as an imbalance in one's relationship with God, one's false sense of separation from Allah. Healing, therefore, is an enactment of The Return (A., *ma'ad*, the Islamic principle of faith of the return to God at the end of time) over and over as necessary, and it is the primary template of religious praxis in this order. We learn from Merleau-Ponty to see how 'the body mediates meaning, is mediated by meaning, and is thus our opening to meaningful being' (Morris 2014:114). As the ground of being, the body then 'appears as neither a biological object nor as a mere vehicle of subjectivity,' and in the conception of the body as a lived body, 'meaning does not arise at a psychological level; it is born at an organic level that is pre-personal, which is thence modulated through one's bodily engagement with the intersubjective world, engendering a personal relation to the world' (Merleau-Ponty 2011

[1945]:82–5; Morris 2014:114). Might the body be salient in this Sufi *tariqa*, insofar as it is instrumentalized to escape such bifurcation of being 'in the unity' and being 'in the separation'? Bifurcation between the body and the spirit, between the individual and the divine? With this question and Merleau-Ponty's insights in mind, we can view the healing practices – the instrumentalization, the techniques – of the *murid*'s body as 'engagement with the intersubjective world,' leading to the experience of a shift of energy nearing proximity with the divine.

Modes of instrumentalization

Within Islam broadly, and within Sufism and this community more specifically, the body is the ground for movement of divine light, with the body being the densest emanation of the holy qualities of the divine. The healing practices in this Sufi order exhibit an understanding of the body as central to Sufi piety, but not because the practitioners inhabit 'extraordinary bodies' (Bashir 2010:85–90) such as those of saints. In this order, instead, it is the ordinary body that is central.

As the 'ordinary' – or, non-'extraordinary' – body is instrumentalized through these healing modalities to become the site of transformation from spirit to material and material to spirit, we see how the body is central in everyday, lived Sufi practice. This occurs in three primary modes. We may think of these modes as lenses, in a sense, for they are ways in which we can understand how the body is both embodied and imagined in this order as the tool for movement from material to spirit and from spirit to material. Each of these are modes of somatically experiencing the Sufi metaphysical concept of 'unity' in ways that resemble other new age practices, but which are fundamentally Sufi and Islamic. So how does this take place?

Body as barometer

The first mode in which the body is instrumentalized is as a barometer. In this view, the body is the tool to measure or assess the spiritual condition. This relates to the above discussion of the path of Sufism as a 'first-aid kit,' in that the body is the interface through which one determines what needs to be repaired by this 'kit.' The body is a barometer measuring the condition of the heart. In this conception, the heart is both the physical heart and the subtle heart. In the Shadhiliyya Sufism *Newcomers' Book*, this barometer function is explicated by statements I noted earlier, such as: 'The Truth is Allah. And the Reality of Allah is perfection. Any sign of anxiety, agitation, fear, anger, sadness, or worry is a sign that we are veiled from the Truth.' As one *murshid*, a male teacher originally from Australia and a retired professor in peace and conflict studies from an American research university, explains:

> So the body is a reflection of the heart, which is either showing balance or imbalance in its relation to its Lord, in any of those attributes. So the body will show you the places where you are really off. So you can be really mad for a moment, and return to Allah … [and not become sick] … but if you are in the sustained state [of distance from Allah], it will manifest in the body.

He explained to me as we sat in the dome room between prayers that any 'separation' one feels from others is an actual separation in one's heart from Allah. So one can measure their degree of separation from the divine through the degree of felt alienation from the world. This extends to one's felt separation from one's own interior spiritual, metaphysical landscape (a central component of Sufi metaphysics is the different levels, or types, of the *nafs*, or soul). And another *murshid* puts it like this: 'There's this place where the body becomes subtle and it's interconnected with the spirit and soul and this place, it's constantly receiving and sending information from the body into the body, like the breath, in and out.'

Body as controller

The second of the three modes of instrumentality is the body as a controller. In this mode, the body is instrumentalized to control the self, the *nafs*[16] or the ego-self, and by extension, the condition of the heart. The struggle against the *nafs*, or the lower soul, is a focus of Sufi practice generally, and in this order the *nafs* is referred to regularly. The heart is conceived as the central site of vitality and as the source of connection to the divine – the place where separation ends and unity with the divine creation begins. The body is the tool to direct the heart's state and the Sufi's 'walking,' which, again, is referred to as a 'path of the heart.' For example, a student explained to me: 'Using your limbs and senses so that you are in alignment with good things, this is what the first part of the spiritual walking is about.' So the body's own aspects that are potential tools – body limbs, which conduct tasks, effect change, touch others, open books and hold prayer beads, care for animals as they are raised halal – are ways of 'using' the body to 'align' with the things seen as good, which are those modes of living that Sidi advocated as pleasing to God.

In the ritual use of divine names and somatic imagery, the body is neither the source of the meaning nor its ending point. In these practices, the body is where meaning is experienced, where being is rendered meaningful. The Sufi use of the 'quality' of *al-Fatah* (the divine name, The Opener) is to invoke a feeling of being open, but as a quality of being, of divine essence, that can be experienced in a mirrored version within the corporeal confines of the created human body, and as a dimension of reality. The body is the place that opens to this meaning and gives it a seat.

One Sufi in the order, in her late thirties, joined the *tariqa* in Mexico City and resided and worked at the Farm of Peace for almost a year as she finished her master's program at the University of Sufism. She put it this way: 'How you use your body has an effect on and an impact on your heart.' In other words, how you *use* it, she said. In this rendering, the subjective, individual self is the agent, directing the body in which it is situated, in ways to align it with a subtler aspect of the same body, that is, the heart. Similarly, the controlling is achieved through a redirecting back after the 'forgetting,' through the paradigmatic Sufi practice of remembrance: as a senior healer/teacher in the *tariqa* stated it, '[The] body [is] a tool for remembrance, remembrance that Allah is ever present, close to us. [When you are sick] so Allah, SWT, is not sick, only yourself in that sense of separation becomes sick.' The body is instrumentalized to induce a state of remembrance, which brings physical healing, balance. The body is the instrument through which remembrance is enforced, even if in a gentle sense. Another female healer explains: 'Sometimes I put people in *sajda* during a healing [because] it bridges the mind to the spirit.' She does this regardless of whether or not the healee[17] is Muslim. Physical prostration (A., *sajda*), part of Islamic ritual prayer (A., *salat*), is a ritual technology in which the physical body is thought to facilitate a connection between the intellectual part of the self and the material part. It connects the body and the mind, in which the neural networks of one's unproductive or spiritually detrimental habits are lodged, with the spirit.

This invocation of 'the outer and the inner' (A., *zahir* and *batin*)[18] is a core Sufi concept, and the particular focus here is *not* that the 'outer' reality (*zahir*) is superficial and the 'inner, esoteric' reality (*batin*) is more real, but instead that the outer harnesses the inner. The outer is the human body in which the inner is contained, and in which the inner is accessed. But the outer, the body, is to be subjected to disciplinary practices necessary to access the inner spirit, or truth. Each Sufi order has its own taxonomy of stations and states (A., *maqam* and *hal*), usually elaborated by the Shaykh of an order. In this Sufi community, the stations and states are elaborated in Sidi's writings, particularly in his key text *Music of the Soul*, which *murids* at the Farm of Peace use almost as a canonical text: writing and rewriting it, studying the stations and states codified in it, and engaging with it as a source of direct spiritual transmission from Sidi beyond his death. For example, a central practice on Sufi retreats (A., *zawiya*) is the writing of Sidi's books by those in retreat. At retreats, participants sit with lap desks or at tables, or lying on couches by the windows overlooking the foothills, with spiral notebooks and prayer beads – reading and writing portions of Sidi's books. These portions are assigned individually by the Sufi teacher leading the session, and the adept is encouraged to feel the transmission from pen to arm to heart, from Sidi to them, into their bodies to their hearts. The lead healer and spiritual director of the order, who studied under the guidance of Sidi in Jerusalem for years, explained that the hand that is conducting the physical act of writing connects the guide's (i.e., the Shaykh's) words to the beloved's (i.e., the student's) heart. Sidi's book *Music of the Soul*, one of the lead *murshid*s explains, 'is a transmission of light.' She teaches students that 'writing engages the senses. You're working your heart and your mind. There is a nerve connecting the hand and the heart.' The transmission of the Shaykh's light, and his teaching, transpires through the physical apparatus of the hand and the nerves in the hand and arm. The hand and nerves in this case could be seen as the transmitters, but as the parts of the corporeal self they are more accurately conceived as controllers. Why? Because the act of writing is all consuming for the student: the hand and the eyes, and the lap upon which the book and notebook are laid, the legs crossed on the seat or stretched out on the floor, etc., are all engaged for the sensorial experience of writing, and the limbs, the senses, are controlling the direction of the mind, which controls the disposition of the self (the individual human, discrete, embodied self).

Body as ground

A third way the body is instrumentalized is as the ground for the movement of energy, wherein practices create a physical resonance that vibrates spiritual shifts into place. This movement is sometimes described as a light, sometimes as 'energy,' and is always attributed to God. This is achieved in a variety of practices, one of which is group *dhikr*, or remembrance of the divine. Remembrance as a solitary activity can achieve it too, but the energy levels are understood to be higher when the *dhikr* is performed in a collective: *murid*s sway back and forth together, rhythmically, to the verbal repetition of the word '*Allah*' or the phrase '*la illaha il-llaha*,' and move their heads to the right and left together rhythmically. In this community, these body techniques are understood to cause vibrations that unsettle energetic blockages, which start with the physical vibrating of the sternum that occurs when chanting out loud. The sick liver receives light through the remembrance (*dhikr*); it is 'shaken' up, just as when a kidney stone is shaken out by allopathic doctors at a hospital, the name of Allah and the vibrations of the chants 'shake up' the blockage that is the illness in an organ and disintegrate it. When it comes to energy, the template is of the opposing poles of 'constriction' (A., *al-jalal*) and 'ease' (A., *al-jamal*). A senior female teacher in the order explains:

> We usually work with a place that we call the subtle heart, which is not necessarily where the physical heart is, but somewhere in the center of the chest, and from there I would say the most subtle [levels of energy] goes to the vibrations and then interconnects with the most subtle of the systems which might be the lymphatic system and from there to the glands, and from the glands slowly interconnected with the rest of the body.

So, too, it is understood that the vibration of Qur'anic recitation heals, for '[reciting] the Qur'an ... when it's pronounced, the sound has a vibration that our cells can recognize and even the DNA in the most subtle particles react to it in a way that they bring harmony and healing.' By referencing DNA, this senior teacher and healer anchors the healings in biology in general terms, using it as verification that these spiritual healings are fundamentally physical and material. Similarly, in cupping sessions, allopathic-medical explanations are given for the benefits of draining 'toxic' blood out of the body and out of specific organ systems. This blood is described as dark and heavy, thereby preventing light from residing in and circulating through the body. In cupping sessions, prayers for healing are read from the Qur'an and other liturgy, and Prophetic prayers are read aloud in the direction of the patient's body as they lie supine, face down, with cups on the back and blood trickling out.

One healer said that healing experiences can feel like 'an electric current going through my joints.' We sat together in a healing room in the large reclining chairs under dim evening light, and she spoke softly about the power of the divine in the healings. She explained that the energy has a source beyond the body, although the body is used to manipulate it:

> the interconnection the healer has to the Creator, and the way it comes out [it] requires [a] certain orientation of movement to give direction to the, I won't say light, I want to call it energy, that is coming through the healer to the healee. It is very common to see that a healer swipes [his] hand in front of the healee, and that's to establish the intention of removing something or letting something move through,

but it's also not a movement that I decide to do, but it's like, as a healer I may kind of receive the instruction, by guidance, to behave this way.

So the energy is a resource within the container of the body, and without intentional use of the body to let it flow, one is living in separation, which is seen as a condition, or state in need of healing (this may be likened to the notion of *hal*, or spiritual state, which can align with a spiritual station, *maqam*, discussed earlier). These states are paired with stations, both fundamental concepts in Sufi piety. As the ground of being, in Merleau-Ponty's sense, the binary of subject and object (self/body and self/divine) is transcended; here, through the manipulation of the object both by the self and by the divine, for, note how she explains that 'it's like, as a healer I may kind of receive the instruction, by guidance, to behave this way.' There is a dialectical relationship between the healer and the divine, both working with the 'ground' of the body of the one being healed.

The body is the ground of energy, and the healer seeks to move the energy and allow divine light to infuse it, thereby activating a physical body part into an energetic mode that is aligned with the person and the divine. A senior teacher cited earlier says the task is to

> work with energy ... bring it into the areas that are in pain ... it can be an energy center or it can be a physical body part ... let's bring that energy, let's bring the name of Allah, which brings into being, evokes, this energy of love. Bring that name into the liver... It's already there, but we've forgotten so what we're doing is using remembrance to remember that that light is present in the liver, then it starts to release all the negative energies.

This is practiced by some of the healers with acupuncture by placing needles in specific parts of the body associated with physical disorders and by reciting one of the 'qualities,' or divine names.

We may think of the body in this view as a material conduit to what is understood to be the subtle heart, and hence, to the divine because, in the words of a senior teacher, 'the heart is the opening to divine truth.' Another healer is a former psychologist, who discussed with me how she had once struggled with feeling connected to the divine when she was in the outside world (i.e., outside the Sufi center), but since her 40-day retreat (called a *zawiya*) she reached a new spiritual state. She discussed the body in the sense of a ground of energy, explaining that 'we are beings of light, we are all energy, who are having an experience of density. In order to have a spiritual experience of this density we have to have a vehicle of some sort.' The vehicle here is, paradoxically, the body itself, which gets the physical body into a mode more aligned with the energetic forces of the divine. Others explain the same sense of the body as conduit, and of embodiment, in similar language: 'we usually do not pay much attention to what our body is, however in my perception it's like an interface. Because it is through the body where we manifest our life.' In this view, the life of the individual is infused with divine light and is manifest both physically and spiritually through this energy; when it is unlocked, and this is a continual process, life in material terms is a spiritual experience. This is not the body as an instrument extrinsic to itself. It is the body akin to Merleau-Ponty's ground of being, but here the being is energy – divine energy – and the body is the recipient of it, the conduit of it, and the home for it. Much as the ground, or soil, is to the life of a seed. Another way we can think of the ground is through the Sufi concept of dying before you die; the body as we know it, the 'ordinary' body, may metaphorically go into the ground, into the grave, to become then the new ground for the Sufi Muslim spiritual rebirth.

Conclusion

In a senior teacher's lecture at Sufi School East, he exclaimed enthusiastically: 'This is full body Sufism! God's *rahmah* [A., mercy] is flowing, don't shut the valve off. We don't say "this hand is separate from God or this body," we say, "*la illaha ill-lalah*".' One of the most senior teachers explained at another teaching during Sufi School East at the Farm of Peace: 'Your fingers are not separate from Allah. Are your toes separate from your existence? An *illah*? [a god] ... our bodies are not independent entities but also are not outside of Allah. Every single being is filled with Allah's *rahmah*. He is giving us this moment to feel that light.' The tool has been 'given' by the divine and should be used to reach a more whole, healthy state, which is ultimately a 'spiritual' condition.

I hope to have demonstrated how the centrality of the body in the 'walking' of the Sufis in this American Shadhiliyya order illustrates a focus on the body as a tool for healing that is ultimately not just physically corporeal. It is material, but also, more dynamically, 'spiritual' in the ways described by the Sufis themselves. As the 'ground of being,' the body's instrumentalization – seen in three different ways as barometer, controller, ground of energy – facilitates transcendence of the division between the 'ordinary' body and the spirit.

Observing the body in these three modes of instrumentalization, which bring together core Islamic and Sufi concepts with practices observed in broader social cultural contexts, should prompt us to approach the study of embodied practices in North American Sufism as deeply situated in their Islamic traditions. All three modes of instrumentalization centralize the body as Sufis work to imagine and experience the body in new ways that uplift and minimize it simultaneously. The body is deployed, or engaged, to bring the adept closer to the source of reality, which is understood to be the divine, and this is not an essence entirely separate from the adept. This closeness is a continual movement – a movement from sickness to health, from separation to unity and/or proximity, from darkness to light. The body is the ground for movement of divine light, with the body as the densest emanation of the qualities of the divine, and the power of the 'ordinary body' of a Sufi adept as a site of transformation from spirit to material and material to spirit.

About the author

Megan Adamson Sijapati is Professor of Religious Studies at Gettysburg College in Gettysburg, Pennsylvania. She received her PhD from the University of California Santa Barbara. Her interests are in modernity and religion, the body, contemplative traditions, digital religion, contemporary Islam and Sufism. She is the author of the book *Islamic Revival in Nepal: Religion and a New Nation* (2011) and co-editor of the books *Religion and Modernity in the Himalaya* (2016) and *Muslim Communities and Cultures of the Himalaya: Conceptualizing the Global Ummah* (2021), all published with Routledge Press. Her most recent publications examine connections between Islamic piety, the body, and contemplative practices in digital contexts: 'Sufi Remembrance Practices in a Meditation Marketplace of Mobile Apps' in *Anthropological Perspectives on the Religious Uses of Mobile Apps* (Palgrave 2019) and 'Islamic Meditation: Mindfulness Apps for Muslims in the Digital Spiritual Marketplace' in *Cyber Muslims: Mapping Islamic Networks in the Digital Age* (OneWorld 2022).

Acknowledgments

Many thanks to the journal editor Katherine Zubko, Brian Pennington, Pamela Winfield, and Elon University for hosting the sympoisum for which this paper was first written, and the two anonymous reviewers for valuable feedback. I am also grateful to members of the *tariqa* for graciously welcoming me and my research inquiries and for sharing their experiences and knowledge.

Portions of this work were supported by a Gettysburg College research and professional development grant.

Notes

1. *Subhanahu wa ta'ala* – Arabic for 'the most glorified, the most high'.
2. Methodologically, this essay's discussion is based on ongoing fieldwork engagement with the *tariqa* at its Pennsylvania center since 2016. I draw upon discussions of the body among Sufi healers, observations of the community's healings, informal conversations and formal interviews with healers and those being healed, and a print publication of the *tariqa*.
3. Cupping (*al-hijama* in Arabic) has long been a modality in Islamic medicine, or Unani medicine, and is reported in *hadith* to have been recommended by the Prophet Muhammad. For an overview of cupping, see Qureshi and co-authors (2017).
4. In some cases I use the words 'devotional' and 'spiritual' interchangeably in this essay, in an attempt to avoid the pitfalls of using the term 'spiritual' uncritically, since this is the common word used in this *tariqa*; however, this essay is not the place to attempt a suitable working definition for it beyond its emic meaning. The practices are not strictly devotional, per se, but are in devotion to the divine, and so I use this an alternative to the *tariqa*'s emic term 'spiritual.'
5. These are Arabic names. There is nothing distinctly Sufi about them, but members of the order refer to them as 'Sufi' names.
6. The testament of Islamic faith that makes one officially Muslim. The Shaykh would typically give adepts a certificate after they had taken *shahada*, which could be used later to prove their identities as Muslims. This is needed for the Hajj, for example.
7. As Bazzano puts it, 'al-Jamal's students have struggled to find the balance between how they experience Sufism both as a universal message of love and as framed within a context of Islamic rules, rituals, and hierarchies' (Bazzano 2020:3). In my fieldwork, I heard this theme arise frequently in casual conversations and in formal teachings.
8. The structure of the university has evolved and transformed several times since 2015. It is currently undergoing a name and location change.
9. This institute was not started by Sidi. This senior member of the *tariqa* was one of Sidi's early students. Upon a radically transformative experience (according to his description of it) at the hands of Sidi, he committed to Sidi's path of Sufism and became a devoted student. He adopted the healing techniques and the Islamic and Sufi aspects that Sidi taught, and his own healing institute took on

Islamic and Sufi qualities such as working with the Qur'an and Muslim prayer. Many of Sidi's first students came to him through this particular healer, with whom they had been studying other healing modalities. Some were deeply involved in Transcendental Meditation. The senior *murshid* at the Farm of Peace was also a healer before meeting Sidi and taking the Sufi initiation and *shahada*. Both are senior teachers in the order's university, the University of Sufism, which was previously called the University of Spiritual Healing and Sufism.

10 See http://www.sufiuniversity.org
11 *Al-wird* is any litany for recitation; Sufi orders often have their own specific ones. Since 2020, this order has held a group practice of its *al-wird* (that was taught by Sidi) in person and on Zoom twice a day. The larger national Shadhiliyya organization holds online *al-wird*, *dhikr*, and prayer circles on Zoom.
12 The formal interviews I conducted took place in these rooms, and most of my participant observations of healing practices took place in the healing rooms, the dome room, the guest rooms, and the barn (which is the larger mosque). One interview was off-site with a healer who at that time was not directly involved with the Farm of Peace but remains a highly respected senior healer in the order.
13 Sufi Center East, August 2019.
14 *Newcomers' Book*, p. 31, Sidi Muhammad Press. No date. Emphasis mine.
15 Al-Jamal elaborates upon this in his book, *Music of the Soul*. Even chronic illnesses are thought to be caused by separation from God understood as a spiritual imbalance. Head teachers of this order hold healing sessions for cancer patients that aim to restore the patients' relationship with God and within the body, in order to cure the cancer.
16 The Arabic term *nafs* translates most simply as the 'self,' and in Sufi thought the term takes on the sense of 'ego' or 'lower soul' (in contrast to the spirit, *ruh*).
17 This neologism is used by one of the healers.
18 A core concept in Islamic religious thought, rooted in the Qur'an and expanded upon in Shia and Sufi traditions.

References

Al-Jamal, S. A R. (1994) *Music of the Soul*. California: Sidi Muhammad Press.
Al-Rawi, R. F. (2015) *Divine Names: The 99 Healing Names of the One Love*. North Hampton: Interlink Books.
Bashir, S. (2010) Body. In J. Elias (ed.) *Key Themes for the Study of Islam* 72–92. Oxford: One World.

Bashir, S. (2013) *Sufi Bodies: Religion and Society in Medieval Islam*. New York: Columbia University Press. https://doi.org/10.7312/columbia/9780231144919.001.0001

Basu, H., and Werbner, P. (eds) (1998) *Embodying Charisma: Modernity, Locality, and Performance of Emotion in Sufi Cults*. London, New York: Routledge.

Bazzano, E. (2020) A Shadhiliyya Sufi order in America: traditional Islam meets American hippies. In Bazzano, E. and Hermansen, M. (eds) *Varieties of American Sufism: Islam, Sufi Ordes, and Authority in a Time of Transition*. Albany: SUNY Press.

Bazzano, E., and Hermansen, M. (eds) (2020) *Varieties of American Sufism: Islam, Sufi Orders, and Authority in a Time of Transition*. Albany: SUNY Press.

Coakley, S. (2000) Introduction: religion and the body. In S. Coakley (ed.) *Religion and the Body* 1–14. Cambridge: Cambridge University Press.

Csordas, T. (1990) Embodiment as a paradigm for anthropology. *Ethos* 18(1): 5–47. https://doi.org/10.1525/eth.1990.18.1.02a00010

Culianu, I. P. (1995) Introduction: the body reexamined. In J. M. Law (ed.) *Religious Reflections on the Human Body* 1–20. Bloomington: Indiana University Press.

Dickson, W. R. (2015) *Living Sufism in North America: Between Tradition and Transformation*. Albany: SUNY Press.

Dickson, W. R., and Sharify-Funk, M. (2017) *Unveiling Sufism: From Manhattan to Mecca*. New York: Equinox.

Genn, C. A. (2007) The development of a modern Western Sufism. In M. van Bruinessen and J. D. Howell (eds) *Sufism and the 'Modern' in Islam* 257–78. London: I. B. Taurus. https://doi.org/10.5040/9780755607983.ch-014

Giddens, A. (2013) *Modernity and Self-Identity: Self and Society in the Late Modern Age*. Cambridge: Polity Press.

Hazard, S. (2013) The material turn in the study of religion. *Religion and Society* 4(1): 58–78. https://doi.org/10.3167/arrs.2013.040104

Kugle, S. A. (2007) *Sufis and Saints' Bodies: Mysticism, Corporeality and Sacred Power in Islam*. Chapel Hill: University of North Carolina Press. https://doi.org/10.5149/9780807872772_kugle

Mauss, M. (1973) Techniques of the body. *Economy and Society* 2(1): 70–88. https://doi.org/10.1080/03085147300000003

McGuire, M. B. (1990) Religion and the body: rematerializing the human body in the social sciences of religion. *Journal for the Scientific Study of Religion* 29(3): 283–96. https://doi.org/10.2307/1386459

Merleau-Ponty, M. (2011 [1945]) *Phenomenology of Perception*. London: Routledge. https://doi.org/10.4324/9780203720714

Morgan, D. (2010) The material culture of lived religion: visuality and embodiment. In J. Vakkari (ed.) *Mind and matter: selected papers of Nordik 2009 conference for art historians. Studies in Art History* vol. 41, 14–31. Helsinki: Society of Art History.

Morris, D. (2014) Body. In R. Diprose and J. Reynolds (eds) *Merleau-Ponty: Key Concepts*. Durham: Routledge.

Qureshi, N. A., Ali, G. I., Abushanab, T. S., El-Olemy, A. T., Alqaed, M. S., El-Subai, I. S., and Al-Bedah, A. M. N. (2017) History of cupping (*Hijama*): a narrative review of literature. *Journal of Integrative Medicine* (15)3: 172–81. https://doi.org/10.1016/S2095-4964(17)60339-X

Sedgwick, M. (2017) *Western Sufism: From the Abbasids to the New Age*. New York: Oxford University Press. https://doi.org/10.1093/acprof:oso/9780199977642.001.0001

Sijapati, M. A. (2019) Sufi remembrance practices in the meditation marketplace of a mobile app. In J. H. Fewkes (ed.) *Anthropological Perspectives on the Religious Uses of Mobile Apps* 19–41. London: Palgrave Macmillan. https://doi.org/10.1007/978-3-030-26376-8_2

Xavier, M. S. (2018) *Sacred Spaces and Transnational Networks in American Sufism: Bawa Muhaiyaddeen and Contemporary Shrine Cultures*. New York: Bloomsbury Academic. https://doi.org/10.5040/9781350026681

Index

9/11 65, 106
99 names of the divine *see* recitation

abhinaya 133, 137
abortion 23, 26
Abraham 224
acupuncture 223, 225–226, 228, 237
adhān 91
aesthetics 6, 9, 123–132, 136–145, 202–203
Africa 107, 113, 117, 119
agnosticism 59–60, 183–184
AIDS 71, 73, 129
ʿĀʾishah 83
Aizawa Seishisai 157
al-Fathah 234
al-wird 228–229
al-ʿajūz 84
alchemy 155, 179, 195
alcohol 180, 188
Allah 224–239
Alma Viva Teatro 5, 105–106, 113–114, 119
Alpujarras, War of the 107
altar 131, 166–167, 169
Amaterasu 154, 157–161, 170, 172
Ambarisha, Maharaja 207
American Academy of Religion 8, 30, 173
amrita 134–135
animal 113, 117–119, 129, 233
Annals of Japan see Nihon Shoki
anorexia 43–44
anthropomorphizing 134, 185, 187–188, 191
Anti-Nautch Movement 134
apocalypse 187
apocryphal 6, 178–179, 181, 195
Appalachian Mountains 7, 224
Apsaras Arts 5, 123–124, 133, 138
Arab, Arabic 117–118, 224

ārati 206, 208
Ark 25
arm 63, 132, 155, 166, 229, 235
asceticism 3–4, 35, 37, 39, 42–47, 135
Asia 8, 129, 160, 173
   Central 179
   East 6, 162, 180, 196
   South 9, 123–128, 131, 145, 202, 217–218
astapadi 147
asura 134–135, 143
atman 134
Augustine 40–42
auto-da-fé 5, 118–119
ʿawrah see modesty
axis mundi 156

B'Sha'ah Tovah: Madrich Refu'i Hilchati L'herayon v'Leida 21–22
Baḥrī Mamlūk Sultanate 81
baptism 109, 118–119
Barló, César 119–121
baroque 120
Basic Questions 182–187, 191, 194–195
batin 234
bayah 229
bayat 230
Benevolent Kings 166, 168
   ceremony 155
   Sūtra 165–166, 172
Bengal, Bengali 126, 204, 218
Bernard of Clairvaux 36, 45
bhajan 213
bhakti 203 *see also* rasa
   rāgānugā 206
Bhaktirasāmṛtasindhu 208
Bhaktivedanta Srila Prabhupada, A. C. 202–203, 205, 210–213, 217
bharatanatyam 5, 123–134, 136, 141, 144, 212–213

Bharatiya Vidya Bhavan 130–131
bhava 137–139
  sanchari 135, 144
  sattvika 137
bhayanaka see *rasa*
biànwén 195
Bible, Hebrew 21
binary, sexual 5, 35, 80–82, 94, 97, 237
birth control 21, 23
Birushana 153, 162, 136f7.3, 172
blood 22–23, 38, 46–47, 66, 108, 155, 161, 189, 236
bodhisattva 166
body politic, imperial 6, 8, 153–157, 163–164, 167–172
body-state 7, 153, 155
Bolz-Weber, Nadia 69
Book of Han 155
Book of the Master Who Embraces Simplicity 155
Book of the Way and its Power see *Dàodéjīng* 185
Borgia or Borja, Francis 38, 40–41, 47, 49
Bourdieu, Pierre 216
Brahma 135
Brahman 144
Brahminical Vedic tradition 180
Bright Hall *see* Ming Tang
Buddha 153–154, 162, 164–166, 169, 172, 180, 182, 194
  Birushana 163f7.3
  Great Buddha of Light 162
  Lochana 163, 163f7.3
  Mahāvairocana 168
  Śākyamuni 179
bullfighting 113, 120
bureaucracy 97, 178, 182, 185–194
Byzantine
  Christianity 63, 67
  icon, image 60–61, 69

Caitanya, saint 202
cakravartin 164, 172
caliphate, Abbasid 81
Candalika 129
Candralekha 129
canonization 59–60, 65, 71, 73

Castro Street neighborhood 62
Catholicism 1, 3–5, 8, 35–39, 47–9, 63, 65, 69, 72 *see also* family
caturmahārāja see Four Heavenly Kings
Celestial Masters 185–188, 195
Central Scripture of Laozi see *Lǎozi Zhōngjīng*
Ceparius, Virgilius 41–47
Certeau, Michel 86–87, 216
chanting 7, 91, 164, 169, 180, 206–207, 210–211, 236
Charles V, King of Spain 38
Chennai 125, 130–131, 136, 140
Chikafusa, Kitabatake 159
Chin, Marilyn 127
China, Chinese 1, 6, 8, 127, 154–157, 162–166, 172–173, 178–182, 185–196
Christ 4, 35, 38–39, 68–69, 109
Chronicles of the Authentic Lineages of the Divine Emperors see *Jinnō Shōtoki*
cisgender 5
clothing 17–20, 65–68, 126, 153, 166, 169, 171, 213
Collected Records of the Tripitaka 180
communion 38–39, 42, 48, 73
confession 36, 48, 72, 180
Confucianism 155–156, 163, 178, 181, 184, 188, 191, 193, 195
congregation 5, 25, 69, 72–73, 81–88, 92–96, 131
consecration 162, 166, 168, 226
contemplation 47, 225, 228, 230, 239
contraception 19, 26
convent 4, 36, 40–41, 164
conversion, convert 5, 105, 112, 227
converso 5, 9
cosmology 94, 126, 181–187, 190–191, 194–195, 228, 231
Council of Milan 42
counter-reformation 5
country-body 6, 155–158, 161, 163
Country-Body's Fundamental Principles see *Kokutai no hongi*
Cross, John of the 37, 40
cuatro libros de la confitería, Los 40
cultural studies 1, 17, 106

cúnsī 186
cupping 223, 225, 229, 236
cycle
  karmic 181
  natural 6, 178, 183–184, 187–188, 190–191, 194

dafu 155
Dainichi nyorai 166, 172
Daitya 135
Dalit 128–129,
dào 185
Dàodéjīng 185
Daoism 1, 6, 8, 155, 178–181, 185–195
Darpana Performing Arts Academy 128
Darwinism 170
de Ávila, Juan 48
de Baeza, Miguel 40
de Covarrubias, Sebastián 116
de Granada, Luis 39
demon 18, 134, 188–189, 192–193
demonologist 112
de Rivadeneira, Pedro 40–41, 43, 45
de Rojas, Simón 47–48
Deva 135, 143
devadasi 128, 133–134
Devi Dasi, Malini 216–217
Devi, Rukmini 134
de Yepes, Francisco 38
dharma 166, 193
dharmakāya 153–154, 162, 163f7.3, 164–165, 167–172
Dharmakṣema 181
dhikr 223–229, 235–236
disease 43, 116, 183–184, 189, 193, 195
  see also illness and sickness

earth 119, 132, 156, 182, 186–189, 192, 194, 204
Egypt 1, 8
El cocinero religioso 40
El recetario de Marcilla 40
emotion 6, 37–39, 44, 67–68, 116, 124–131, 134, 137–144, 186, 189, 202–203, 227
empathy 5–6, 123, 125, 136, 139, 141–145
empire 6, 182, 186, 190–192

Han 156, 184–5
British 127, 134, 180
Spanish 9, 38, 120
energy 129, 139, 155–156, 168, 182, 223, 225, 230–232, 235–238
English 21, 130, 157–158, 203
Episcopalian 59, 63
esoterism 153–154, 164–166, 169, 172, 234
ethics, ethical 124–125, 141, 143, 145, 170, 178–181, 184, 189–192
ethnography 3–4, 7, 13–19, 123–126, 130, 202
Eucharist 4, 35–39, 42, 44, 48
Europe 5, 35–38, 41, 117, 129, 141–142, 168, 170, 172, 190
eye 1, 67, 82, 116, 131–132, 139, 161–162, 182, 184, 189, 192, 207, 210–211, 214–15, 235

Facebook 62–63
Fag Nun Assunta Femia 73
fāḥishah 95
Falungong 195
family 14, 30–31, 38, 77, 126–127, 140, 147, 188, 213
  avrech 24
  Catholic 75
  country-family 154, 163, 171
  Haredi 24
  -state 153, 164–165, 171
Farm of Peace 225–231, 234, 238 *see also* Sufi Center East
fasting 43–47, 180, 226, 229
feminism 36, 68
Fenellosa, Ernest 170
fetus 15, 19, 21–27
fever 41, 44
Finkelstein, Michal 21
Finkelstein, Rabbi Baruch 21
First part of the Life of the Reverend Father Master F. Simón de Rojas 48
Five Aggregates 182
Five Confucian virtues 184
Five Depots 182–191
Five Great Wisdom Kings *see godai myōō*
Five Mythical Emperors 182

Five Precepts 180–182, 189–193
Five Sacred Peaks 182, 186
flagellation 45, 47
food 3–4, 35–45, 115, 126, 130, 183, 207, 226
foot 18, 62, 69, 132, 162, 206–207, 210, 215
Forest of Gems in the Garden of the Dharma see *Fǎyuàn Zhūlín* 196
Foucault, Michel 189–190, 216
Four Heavenly Kings 164, 194
Four Seas 183, 186
Francis of Assisi 36
fǔ 183
Fudō myōō 166–167, 167f7.4

Ge Hong 155
gender 5, 17, 35, 37, 40–41, 43, 49, 80–81, 129 see also pan-gender *and* transgender
GLBT (Gay, Lesbian, Bisexual, and Transgender) 60, 65–66
al-Ghaffār, Ibn ʿAbd 84
gluttony 188
Go-Daigo, Emperor 159
godai myōō 166, 169
goddess 134, 157–159
Golden Hall 166
Golden Light Sūtra 164–165, 172
Gonzaga, Aloysius 40, 43–46
Gopal, Ram 129
goshichinichi mishuhō see Latter Seven Day Rite
goshintai 158, 159f7.2
Great Abyss 186
Great Granary 186
greed 111, 188
Guliang zhuan 155
guoti 154–157, 163, 172, *see also* body politic *and* country-body

habitus 216
Hachana Ruchanit L'Leida 21–22, 29
hadith 84
hagiography 44
Hajj 229
hal 237

halo 60
Han dynasty 155–156, 183–188, 191–194 *see also* empire
Western Han 182
Ḥanbalī school 84–85
Handscroll of Annual Ceremonies *see* Nenjū gyōji emaki
Hapsburg dynasty 38
Hasidism 17
Hayashi Fumiko 160
head covering 18
healthcare 15, 164, 180
heart 39, 68, 73 131, 133, 137–138, 160–163, 170, 182–189, 210, 217, 226–237
heaven 22, 69, 156–157, 160, 164, 186–189, 192, 194
Heaven, Temple of 156
Hebrew 19, 21–22, 26
Heian period 154, 164–165, 168, 172
hell 191, 194
heresy 38, 49
hermit 38–41
Héshànggōng 185
Hinduism 1, 6–8, 123–125, 128–136, 144–145, 201–202, 218
Hirohito, Emperor 160
HIV *see* AIDS
Hokkekyō see *Lotus Sūtra*
Holocaust 67
Honjo Shigeru 160
Host 37–39, 42–43
House of All Sinners and Saints 69
Hozumi Yatsuka 160
Huángdì Nèijīng Sùwèn 182
Huángdì Nèijīng Sùwèn see *Basic Questions*
hún 185
hypnosis 226

Ibāḍī 85
Ibn Mashish 225
iconoclasm 68
Īḍāḥ al-Mushkil fī Aḥkām al-Khunthā al-Mushkil 80
Ignatius of Loyola 38, 45–47
illness 18, 44, 129, 186–188, 231, 236 *see also* disease *and* sickness

imām 93–94
imāmah 93–94
immigration *see* migration
Imperial Rescript on Education 169
imperial *see* empire *see also* body politic
Impious I, Pope 72–73
infidel 5, 46, 105, 111
inner alchemy *see nèidān*
Inner Canon of the Yellow Emperor–Basic Questions see *Basic Questions*
International Peace Center 229
International Society of Krishna Consciousness 7, 202
iqāmah 91
Isaiah 47
al-Isnawī, Abd al-Raḥīm 5, 80, 84–85, 91, 94
isolation, isolationism 5, 80, 82, 8–97, 159
Israel 1, 8, 13–14, 19–20, 27
Iwai Masuko 161
Izālat al-Ghishā ' 84

al-Jamal al-Rifa'i al-Shadhili, Muhammad Sa'id 7, 224–228, 236
jati 140
Jerusalem 4, 7, 13, 15, 19–21, 225–226, 230, 235
Jesuit 40–47
Jesus 129
jiāo 187, 195
Jimmu 157
jīng 179, 181–182, 185–188
Jinnō Shōtoki 159
John Paul II, Pope 71–72
John the Baptist, Saint 107, 109, 119
Jones, Cleve 62–71, 74
Judge, Father Mychal 65
Judson Memorial Church 69

al-Kalbī, Abū Thawr 85
kaji 154, 165, 168–169
Kalakshetra 134
Kaliya 136
kami 157–160, 166
Kamsa 136
Kapaleeshwarar Temple 131
karma 181, 191, 208, 217 *see also* cycle

Karuna Sakti: The Power of Compassion 129
karuna see *rasa*
kathakali 128
kalarippayattu, Keralan martial art 132
khalwa 227
khaṭīb 93
khunūthah 90
King Yama *see yánluówang*
kirtan 210, 213
Kiyozawa Manshi 153, 155, 169–172
Kojiki 157
kokka 54, 164, 171 *see also* body politic
kokubun-niji 154
kokubunji 164, 172
kokugaku see School of National Learning
kokutai 6, 153–154, 157, 160–162, 172 *see* country-body
Kokutai no hongi 160
Kōmyō, Empress 164
Konkōmyōkyō see Golden Light Sūtra
Korea 164–165
Kronenberg, Anne 61
Kūkai, patriarch 165
Kunlun, Mount 186
Kumarasamy, Aravinth 131, 137, 140, 142
Kurdi, Aylan 124
Kurma 134
Kyūshū 162

lamb, sacrificial 4
Lao, Most Venerable Lord *see* Tàishàng Lǎojūn
Laozi 185–186
Lǎozi Zhōngjīng 186
Latter Seven Day Rite 155, 166
Latin America 9, 120
leg 155, 207, 229, 235
Lentz, Robert 60, 63, 68–70
Lepanto, Battle of 107
LGBTQ+ 1, 3–4, 63–66, 75
lila 204
limb 139, 171, 210, 233, 235
Lira, Jack 71
liturgy 71–72, 95, 168, 178, 193–194, 236
Lochana 162–163
London 125, 131, 136, 139, 141, 180

López, Cristóbal 40
López, Gregorio 38, 41, 49
Lord of the Dance 134
Losa, Francisco 38
lotus 206–207, 210
Lotus Sūtra 164–165, 172
Lotze, Hermann 170
lymphatic draining 229, 236

macrocosm *see* cosmology
Mahābhārata 134
Mahāvairocana 166, 168
Mahāvairocana Sūtra 165
makrūh 88
Mamlūk 5, 80–81, 97
manas 137
mandala 154–155, 165–169
mantra 154, 165, 168, 195, 202
Manual of Vaishnava Etiquette and Lifestyle, A 209
Manyōshū 161
maqam 234, 237
Mary, Virgin 48
Mass 38, 71
Master of the Riverbank *see Héshànggōng*
maurofilia 110
Mayor of Castro Street, The 70, 72
Mecca 83–84, 229
medicine 18–23, 27–28, 30, 41, 44, 156, 178–183, 189
  allopathic 226, 231, 236
  alternative 229
  Chinese 182
  prophetic 230
Medina 83
meditation 2, 39, 47, 65, 165, 168, 186–187, 195, 202, 206–210, 228–229, 239
Meiji 169–171
  emperor 159
  Restoration 168
mercy 109, 238
Merleau-Ponty, Maurice 231–232, 237–238
Meru, Mount 134
miào 187
microcosm *see* cosmology

migration, immigration 3, 5, 6, 8, 105–106, 119, 123–125, 127, 130, 132, 145, 187
Milk, Stuart 62
Ming Tang 156
Minobe Tatsukichi 153, 155, 170–171
modesty 18, 20, 23, 27, 37, 47, 88–92, 129, 229
monk 4, 180–181
monogamy 70, 74
morality 18, 27, 115, 135–136, 144, 169–170, 180, 184–194
Morisco 5, 105–107, 111
mortification 41, 45–47
Moscone, George 59, 62, 65
Motoori Norinaga 157
mudrā 154, 165, 168
Muhammad, Prophet 7, 226
murid 225–226, 232, 234–235
murti 133
Murugan 134
Music of the Soul 234–235
Mylapore 131
myth, mythology 6, 123, 125, 128–129, 144, 154, 157–158, 182

naf 224, 231, 233
Nanboku-chō period 159
Nara period 154, 162, 165, 172
Nataraja 134
Natya 130–131
Natyasastra 128, 135, 137–141, 144
Natyaveda 135
nayika 134, 144
nectar of immortality *see amrita*
nèidān 195
Nenjū gyōji emaki 166
neuroscience 141–142
new age 228–229, 232
New Panihati Dham temple 210, 214
New Year 166, 171–172
New York 21, 63, 65, 69, 71, 97, 226
Newcomers' Book 232
Nicoletta, Daniel 62, 69, 72
Nihon Shoki 157–158
nimbus *see* halo
Ninigi 157

Ninnōkyō 165–166
Nippon Kaigi 161
non-binary, *see* binary
Northern Wei dynasty 180
nrtta 133
nrtya 133
nun 4, 65, 71, 73, 181

obedience 37, 46, 189, 192
Off Our Backs 78
Offering Rite *see jiāo*
ōhō 155, 170
Ōmotokyō 161
Onfroy, Francisco 47

Pabich, Dick 71
pan-gender 39
pañca-skandhaka see Five Aggregates
pañcaśīla see Five Precepts
Panopticism 190–192
pater familias 171
Peace Preservation Laws 161
Peaceful Nation Shrine 161
penance 45–47
penis 18, 90
penitence 41, 43, 45
Pennsylvania 7, 224, 226, 239
Philip II, King of Spain 5, 107, 112
Philip III, King of Spain 105–106
physical prostration *see sajda*
physician 183–184 *see also* doctor
plague 43–44
Plato 1
Plaza de Zocodover 119
pleasure 20, 43 74, 116, 215
pò 185
poison 115, 121
poṣadha see Purification Rite
postcolonial theory 1
Prabhupada, Srila 202–205, 210–213, 217
prayer 5, 20, 24, 36–38, 45–47, 63, 73, 82, 85, 91, 93–96, 227, 233–235
  book 21
  congregation 84, 88
  female leader *see imāmah*
  Islamic ritual 89 *see also salat*
  male leader *see imām*

noon 93
preacher, preaching 38–39, 93, 205
prenatal 18–22, 26
priest 35, 38, 47, 165, 168, 205, 208–210, 214
procession 156, 169
Prophet *see* Muhammad
Protestantism 38
psalm 28
psychology 116, 142, 231, 237
Purification Rite 180, 193–195

qi 155–156, 182–183, 185, 187, 189–191, 194–195
qigong 195
Qin dynasty 190
qiyās 85
Qurʾan 99, 107, 127, 223, 228–229, 231, 236 *see also* recitation

rabbi, rabbinic 4, 13–15, 18–30
rahmah 238
Ramadan 229
Ramayana 129, 134
rasa
  bhakti 128
  bhayanaka 138, 144
  karuna 123, 125, 139–140, 144
  srngara 137, 140
  vatsalya 136, 139, 144
Ratzinger, Cardinal 72
raʾy 85
rebirth 181, 191, 217, 238
recitation 73, 91, 172
  mantra 165, 195
  of the 99 names of the divine 223, 225
  Qurʾanic 223, 236
  tajwīd-style 91
Record of Ancient Matters, The see Kojiki
Refu'i Hilchati L'herayon v'Leida 21
refugee 5, 120, 123–124, 129–144
relic 4, 65–68, 167–168
Renjith 138
Rennyō, patriarch 169
revelation 47–48, 185, 211
Robinson, Frank 61
Rome 40, 43

Russian River Sisters 65
Russo-Japanese War 160

sacrament 37–39, 48
sacrifice 4, 61, 105, 113, 119–120, 183, 187, 192
saint 4, 38, 42, 44–45, 47, 59–75, 107, 202, 232
sajda 234
sakti 129
ṣalāh 80–82
salvation 39, 105, 119, 187, 193
saṃsāra 181
San Francisco 4, 59–60, 66, 68–73
  City Hall 59, 62, 69
Sisters of Perpetual Indulgence 64–65, 71, 73–74
sanchari bhavas 135, 144
sangha 155, 174
Sanskrit 128, 133, 137, 154, 180–182, 191, 194, 204, 217
Sarabhai, Mallika 128–129
Sarabhai, Mrnalini 128–129
al-Sarakhsī 84, 86
Sarasvati Thakura, Bhaktisiddhanta 211
sattvika 137
Saviour Applause, Sister 65
School of National Learning 154, 157, 160, 172
Scripture of the Precepts and Codes Taught by the Celestial Master 168, 192
Sea Prayer 124
secularism 1, 23, 61, 69, 125, 134, 171, 195
seforim 24
segulot 25
sermon 93
shābbah 84, 88
al-Shadhili, Abu Hasan 225
Shāfi'ī school of Sunnī Islamic law 80
shahada 226, 229Shang dynasty 183
shari'a or *Sharia* 4, 229
Shaykh 7, 224–225, 228–229, 234–235
Shaykha 224–225
shén 185
Shilts, Randy 70, 72
Shingon'in 166, 168

shintennō see Four Heavenly Kings
Shintō 153, 157–162, 168, 170, 172
shǐzhě 191
Shī'ī 84–85
shōgun 159
Shōmu, Emperor 153–154, 162–164, 163f7.3, 171–172
Shūkyō tetsugaku gaikotsu 170
sickness 224, 236 *see also* disease *and* illness
Sidi *see* Muhammad Sa'id al-Jamal al-Rifa'i al-Shadhili
silence 48
Silla period 164
silsila 225
Sino-Japanese War 160
sìshí see Four Seas
Sita's Daughters 129
sìtiānwáng see Four Heavenly Kings
Siva 131, 134
Six Corrupters 182
Six Palaces *see fǔ*
Skeleton for the Philosophy of Other Power, A see Tarikimon tetsugaku gaikotsu shikō
Skeleton for The Philosophy of Religion see Shūkyō tetsugaku gaikotsu
slavery 5, 48, 107–108, 110–113, 117
Smith, Scott 60, 71, 73
social justice 1, 105
Socrates 1
Soil and Grain, Temple of 156
śoka see sthayibhava
sokushin jōbutsu 153, 165
soul 1, 5, 17, 37, 39, 47, 64, 112, 119, 185, 194, 224, 227, 231–235
Southern and Northern Courts *see* Nanboku-chō
Spanish Armada 107
Sparks of the Love of God and His Mother which, Being Unable to Contain Them, the Ignited and Enflamed Heart of the Very Venerable and Most Reverend Master Fray Simon de Rojas Emitted 48
Spencer, Herbert 170
Spiritual Preparation for Labor see Hachana Ruchanit L'Leida

Spring and Autumn Annals 155
Sr Species of Crow *see* Fag Nun Assunta
    Femia
sravanam-kirtanam 210
Sri Lanka 1, 5, 8
    civil war 130
Srimad-Bhagavatam 209–210
srngara see rasa
starvation 42–45
sthayibhava 137–139
storytelling 128, 133
Stretching Book, The see *Yǐnshū*
Sufi 7, 223–239
    American 7–8
    Shadhiliyya 7, 223, 231–232, 238
    University of Sufism 226–227, 234
Sunnī 80–81, 84–85, 89
superstition 25, 109, 112, 120
sura 107
Susanoo 158
Suso, Henry 36
sutra 164–166
Sūtra on Lay Precepts 181–182
Sūtra of Trapuṣa and Bhallika 6, 178–182, 194

Tagore, Rabindranath 128–129
Tàishàng Lǎojūn 185
Taishō Tripiṭaka 180
Taiwu, Emperor 180
takbīr 91
Tamura Toshiko 160
Tang dynasty 164, 181, 195
Tanjing 180
taqlīd 85
Tarikimon tetsugaku gaikotsu shikō 170
tariqah 7, 224- 234, 239
tasbīḥ 91
Teresa of Ávila 48
theater 121, 124, 128
    Spanish 105
    Tagorean 128
tiān 185, 187–188, 194
Tiānshī Dào 185
titan 134
Tíwèi Bōlì Jīng see *The Sūtra of Trapuṣa and Bhallika*

Tōdaiji 154, 163f7.3, 164, 172
    temple 154, 162
Tōji temple 155, 165–166, 167f7.4, 168
Torah 14, 25
torture 5, 8, 68, 105, 113, 118, 190
Transcendental Meditation movement 229
Transformation Texts see *biànwén*
transgender 4, 66 *see also* GLBT, LGBTQ+
transubstantiation 38
Trump, Donald 5, 106, 120
Turkey 118, 124
TWBLJ see *The Sūtra of Trapuṣa and Bhallika*

Uesugi Shinkichi 160
ultrasound 18–20, 24, 26
ʿUmar, Caliph 83
United States 7, 20, 106, 202, 212, 226
universe 6, 136, 166, 178, 182 185, 191
Upāsaka-śīla Sūtra see *Sūtra on Lay Precepts*

Vairocana 162
Vaishnavism
    Caitanya 202–204, 207, 210, 217
    Gaudiya 7, 201–202
vasana 217–218
Vasuki the snake 134
vatsalya see *rasa*
Vázquez, Dionisio 40, 46, 49
veil 230–231, 233
Vicious Power Hungry Bitch, Sister *see* Vish-Knew
violence 1, 35, 47, 62, 73, 106–120, 189, 216
    anti-gay or homophobic 66, 68
    political 132
    towards women 128
virtue 37, 42, 46, 48, 135, 157–160, 172, 184, 191
Vish-Knew, Grand Mother 64–65, 72
Vishnu 144
visualization 154, 165, 186, 187
Vrindavan 204

Wang Mang 156

Waraqah, Umm 85
Warring States period 185, 190
Way of the Celestial Masters *see* Tiānshī Dào
wellness 3, 227
White Night Riot 62
White, Daniel 60, 62, 68
will, divine 26, 170
Wisdom Kings 167f7.4 *see also* Five Wisdom Kings
World War II 154, 160–162, 171
wǔjiè see Five Precepts
Wutai, Mount 180
Wǔyīn see Five Aggregates

yánluówang 194
Yashoda 136, 143–144
Yasukuni Jinja 161

Yeshiva 14–16, 20
yin and *yang* 183, 188
Yĭnshū 184
yoga 3, 208, 228
Yosano Akiko 160
Yōupó Sāijiè Jīng see *Sūtra on Lay Precepts*

zahir 234
al-Ẓāhirī, Abū Sulaymān Dāwūd 85
zawiya 235
zhāi see Purification Rite
Zhang Daoling 185
Zhéngyī Fǎwén Tiānshī Jiàojiè Kējīng see *Scripture of the Precepts and Codes Taught by the Celestial Master*
zhi 156, 164
zhì 184, 186

www.ingramcontent.com/pod-product-compliance
Lightning Source LLC
Chambersburg PA
CBHW062011220426

43662CB00010B/1287